W9-AUG-986

RUNAWAY STAR

+++

AN APPRECIATION
OF HENRY ADAMS

+++

By Robert A. Hume

CORNELL UNIVERSITY PRESS

Ithaca, New York

Copyright 1951 by Cornell University

CORNELL UNIVERSITY PRESS

LONDON: GEOFFREY CUMBERLEGE

OXFORD UNIVERSITY PRESS

PRINTED IN THE UNITED STATES OF AMERICA BY THE

VAIL-BALLOU PRESS, INC., BINGHAMTON, NEW YORK

928.1
A13h

E
175
.5
A175
1951

recat /ms 3/e87   fy 23054

4Oct51   SUS 3.00 (Eng)

424360

For A. N. H. and R. T. H.

EVERY MAN with self-respect enough to become effective, if only as a machine, has had to account to himself for himself somehow, and to invent a formula of his own for his universe, if the standard formulas failed. There, whether finished or not, education stopped. The formula, once made, could be but verified.

The effort must begin at once, for time pressed. The old formulas had failed, and a new one had to be made, but, after all, the object was not extravagant or eccentric. One sought no absolute truth. One sought only a spool on which to wind the thread of history without breaking it. Among indefinite possible orbits, one sought the orbit which would best satisfy the observed movement of the runaway star Groombridge, 1838, commonly called Henry Adams.—*The Education of Henry Adams*

Preface

NO ONE means all he says," wrote Henry Adams, "and
yet very few say all they mean, for words are slippery
and thought is viscous. . . ." With such counsel before him,
one might wisely decide to write nothing. Silence not being,
however, unmistakably a human attribute, one usually deter-
mines that on matters that deeply concern him some sort of
statement must be made. I have written this book to explain
to myself, and to any others interested, why Henry Adams is
one of the most meaningful persons to have lived in the
present century.

From Adams's own attempts at biography, one may infer
two ways of considering the meaningful person. First is that
of the critic and scholar, who regards his subject in causal
terms. Through attention to qualities and actions, he relates
his man to his time and to times before and after, by noting
either agreement or opposition. The scholar-critic says, in
effect: To whatever extent this man may be regarded as being
the product of antecedents, and as affecting other people and
us, let us examine him. We shall define him as a social consequence and agent, and so appraise him.

The other way is that of the artist and philosopher, who
contemplates the man and his work as a terminal experience.
The question under this method is not so much, What forces

produced him and what results did he effect? as, Exactly what was he and what was the temper of his days? Every human being and every outcome of human endeavor deserves in the name of philosophic truth to be thus considered, though doing so is seldom easy.

As I have worked, I have tried to achieve the twofold emphasis indicated by this distinction. My book is meant somewhat less for the learned specialist than for the serious general reader whom I like to imagine as sharing many of my own convictions and tastes; yet I hope that I have been able to point out certain matters that the scholar has overlooked and to report others, already known to him, in accents he will appreciate. With the less specializing reader in mind, I have not hesitated to provide summaries of most of Adams's works, nor to quote from them rather frequently. One result of this procedure may be to stimulate a greater curiosity and excitement than now exist concerning Adams's writings and to bring him a growing number of understanding readers. In this harassing mid-century, Americans need, probably more urgently than ever before, to assess and utilize the worthier elements in their diverse heritage. Increasingly dedicated to money, loveless sex, and mass killing, they especially need to think and feel, and it is not their habit to do so. Thinking and feeling were, however, habitual with Henry Adams, and a comprehensive awareness of him can only be salutary.

Granted the unlikelihood of reasserting accurately all the elements in a human uniqueness, now physically dead, that one never knew, there is still much that can be rescued. It may be said of Adams's biography, as Emerson said of Plato's, that it is mostly interior, to be discerned in his writings. Thus, though only my first chapter is devoted strictly to delineating Adams as a person, I have sought to make each of the following chapters contribute additional touches to an authentic portrait, well knowing any biographer's risk of qualifying, in Adams's words, as "the promiscuous unutterable fool, male or female, who . . . always assumes that you never knew anything of life, and have no feelings. . . ."

Where I have directly borrowed from other students of the life and thought of Henry Adams, I have usually indicated so in my text, without subjecting the reader to copious annotations. Doubtless there are points, however, where unaware I have drawn on the work of others, and for such instances the Bibliography must serve as general acknowledgment. The editor of *The Pacific Spectator* has kindly permitted me to utilize portions of an article that appeared under my name in that periodical. For permission to quote from copyrighted material authored by Henry Adams, the following acknowledgments are due: to Houghton Mifflin Company for passages from *The Education of Henry Adams, Mont-Saint-Michel and Chartres, Letters to a Niece and Prayer to the Virgin of Chartres* edited by Mabel H. La Farge, *Letters of Henry Adams, 1858–1918* edited by Worthington C. Ford, and *Henry Adams and His Friends* edited by Harold Dean Cater; to The Macmillan Company for passages from *The Degradation of the Democratic Dogma, with an Introduction by Brooks Adams;* to Scholars' Facsimiles and Reprints for passages from *Tahiti* edited by Robert E. Spiller; to G. P. Putnam's Sons for the passage from Adams's address, "King," in the *Clarence King Memoirs;* and to *The American Historical Review* for the passage on Garibaldi reprinted from Adams's letters to the Boston *Daily Courier.* Acknowledgment is also made to the University of Chicago Press for permission to quote from *The Outlook for American Prose* by Joseph Warren Beach, to the Harvard University Press for permission to quote from *The Young Henry Adams* by Ernest Samuels, and to the Duke University Press for the use of certain material that I wrote for *American Literature.*

In other respects, too, I am conscious of a manifold indebtedness. I owe thanks to the Research Committee of the University of Nevada, of which W. Dwight Billings is chairman, for grants-in-aid, and to Lorry Miller and Mrs. Effie McQueen for secretarial help beyond the call of duty. I am especially grateful to Mrs. Edith J. Holmes, in the sympathetic quiet of whose home most of these pages were written, and to Dr. and Mrs. Samuel T. Clarke for substantial encouragement. Many friends—among them Charlton G. Laird, Robert M. Gorrell, Henry Bugbee, Milton Miller, and George D. Bennett—stimulated me with discussion. Robert E. Spiller read the manuscript in rough draft and generously pointed out certain blemishes, which, I hope, have been removed. It is particularly satisfying to record that this work is in many respects a belated consequence of impulses set in motion in me about a decade ago by Frederick C. Prescott of Cornell University, a wise and humane teacher. Finally, what I owe to my parents, to whom I have dedicated this volume, and to my wife, Laurabel Neville Hume, I must ask the understanding reader to infer.

R. A. H.

Reno, Nevada
October, 1950

Contents

RUNAWAY STAR

HIC JACET

HOMUNCULUS SCRIPTOR

DOCTOR BARBARICUS

HENRICUS ADAMS

ADAE FILIUS ET EVAE

PRIMO EXPLICUIT

SOCNAM

—*The Education of Henry Adams*

I

Of Adam and Eve the Son

A MAN'S birth is indispensable to his physical existence but is intellectually unimportant, belonging on the same level with his conception about nine months earlier, or with his taking successive breaths and imbibing maternal milk. It is difficult, therefore, to identify the author of *The Education of Henry Adams* with a certain helpless, presumably intractable male brat that appeared on February 18, 1838, in Boston, Massachusetts, to be promptly designated the fourth child and third son of Charles Francis Adams, who was the son of John Quincy Adams, who was the son of John Adams. That complicated entity Henry Brooks Adams—diffident, contemptuous; energetic, indolent; rebellious, tradition-conscious; eye-twinkling, dour—did not indubitably emerge for a number of years, just how many it is hard to say.

Probably he did not come fully into being until about 1907, when *The Education* first appeared in a private printing. Before that time there existed a person who bore his name and who often thought, felt, and acted in a manner unmistakably his. Yet in a fundamental sense this earlier person was not quite Henry Adams. If you doubt this, total up the writings under his name that came before *The Education*, read all the surviving letters from that period, collect all the anecdotes (Ernest Samuels has done an admirable job of compilation and summary in *The Young Henry Adams*), and then ask what or whom you have. You have someone very learned, very interesting, someone who often seems to be Henry Adams and yet somehow is not; for the astounding function of an effective work of art, such as *The Education,* is that it can reach back into the past and transform it in a fashion that even the then present chief actor could not have foreseen. It is the immemorial triumph of literature over nature, and this triumph was achieved—though not as fully as the author wished—in *The Education.* So the story of Henry Adams is best told in terms of the pattern and meaning of his life as he himself defined it. This does not mean that one should ignore information from sources other than *The Education.* It does mean that such information should be used strategically, tested always for its contribution to the essential portrait.

The male infant who sat on the kitchen floor in yellow sunlight solemnly learning a lesson in color was Henry Adams. The child not in the least aware of having scarlet fever and almost dying of it, but fully aware of his aunt entering the sickroom with a baked apple, was Henry Adams. Later, the ten-year-old boy seated in the Quincy church contemplating the mortal remains of his grandfather was Henry Adams. The man who wrote *The Education* looked back on this last-named experience as particularly impressive, and one may justifiably pause to reflect for an instant on a few of the elements that gave it depth.

By 1848 the Adams family had been in America more than two hundred years, an earlier Henry Adams having brought his wife and nine children from Somersetshire to Massachusetts at about the time Harvard University was being founded, 1636. Except for one Adams who became a village pastor in New Hampshire, the patriarchal Henry and his descendants for three generations lived as farmers, without distinction beyond their chosen town of Braintree (now Quincy). In 1735, however, to the subsequent discomfiture of George III and other prominent Englishmen, John Adams was born.

Most Americans are aware in a general way of the story of the Adams line from this point on and may review it conveniently in dozens if not scores of books, one of the more readable being *The Adams Family* (1930) by James Truslow Adams. The importance of John Adams to this narrative is not so much that he helped draft and adopt the Declaration of Independence and the Constitution of the United States, that he determined the appointment of Washington as Commander-in-Chief during the Revolution, started the American Navy, became the second President of his country, averted war with France in the opening lustrum of the century, and in numerous other ways qualified as one of the true founding fathers, as that he always exhibited an unexampled boldness of character and mind. Against the wishes of his family he became a lawyer rather than a clergyman, yet a lawyer who read Voltaire, Milton, Addison, Bolingbroke, Virgil, Homer, Horace, and Ovid, as well as Coke, Harrington, Hobbes, and Locke. Unwittingly furnishing a model for his descendants, he was rather impatient of detail and had a penchant for formulating sweeping, general principles. Outwardly he was almost impervious to criticism, of which he had to endure an unjustly large amount. "I have never sacrificed my judgment to kings, ministers, nor people, and I never will," he wrote, and so became—except for his son—the only American President over a period of more than forty years to be rejected for a second term. Cherishing a republican ideal of government by the best for the less enlightened, he refused to be in any respect a politician and, again like his descendants, abhorred the very thought of asking for an office, though he always served to the utmost when called. Beneath his usually controlled surface,

3

he was highly emotional and could be easily hurt; and he had a curiously exaggerated way (which his great-grandson was to show still more than he) of denouncing himself for failures. Always a writer more than a speaker, he produced some of his most vigorous and charming letters at the age of ninety, addressing them to his sometime rival who had become the friend of his old age, Thomas Jefferson.

The forthrightness, brilliance, and political ill fortune of the second President descended unimpaired to his son. The American people have never had sufficient appreciation for the services of John Quincy Adams on his numerous foreign missions, for his initiative that led to the acquisition of Florida, for conceiving the Monroe Doctrine, for defining a coherent system of weights and measures, for fathering the Smithsonian Institution, and for rescuing the right of citizens to petition their government; but they have had even less appreciation for the qualities of his intellect and character. He was born in 1767 and spent many years of his first three decades in Europe, a fact which may help to account for the strongly eighteenth-century quality of his outlook. Combining a robust curiosity with an endless capacity for work, he learned most of the classic and modern languages and qualified himself in mathematics and astronomy. He became even more widely read and better educated than his father and developed a more sensitive imagination, with an awareness of esthetics. He loved the theatre, wrote competent sonnets, and translated European poetry. As a young man his particular wish was to devote himself to literature, but, discerning the needs of his country, he turned unflinchingly to law and statesmanship. One may observe in parentheses that numerous Americans in the middle years of the twentieth century can disport themselves parasitically in Reno, Brookings, and Palm Beach because, unknown to them, a very few intense and able men like John Quincy Adams once chose to lead dedicated lives. The introspective,

4

self-tormenting quality of his spirit found its record in the most impressive diary of our literature. More consciously than his father, because the opposition was more blatant, he tested his actions by a code of a priori morality, by that "Law of Nature" formulated by reference to Cicero, the Stoics, and the founder of the Christian religion. Far more deeply devoted to the nation's welfare than most of his critics put together, he could dismiss Decatur's famous right-or-wrong toast with the simple statement: "I disdain all patriotism incompatible with the principles of eternal justice," and he knew what he meant. He wanted his country to be great not so much in material power as in mind and ethics. Perhaps no statesman ever worked harder, and with less reward, to promote the sciences and the arts and to transmit a civilized heritage to those who could deserve it.

This was the man whom the citizens of Quincy, early in 1848, had gathered to honor. A few days before, he had collapsed in Washington on the floor of the House of Representatives, where by seventeen years' service he had won post-Presidential distinction as Old Man Eloquent, fighting always as a nonparty man for the rights of the humblest against odds nearly overwhelming. His son, Charles Francis Adams, whose career will be referred to later, was already attracting notice; but probably most of the citizens were scarcely aware of the grandson who was destined, in his own mode, to win particular attention.

What did it mean, in 1848, to be, by way of anticipation, Henry Adams? The mood of the boy at this ceremonial moment was probably more one of precocious contemplation than of sorrow. This old man, who had seemed to be immortal, now lay dead. Henry had spent hundreds of hours in the same home with him, had experienced his silence and austerity, but also his tolerance for children that, for Henry at least, had grown into a version of that intimacy possible

between old men and small boys. The boy had soon discovered that there were established duties to perform, such
as that of going to school. When he had protested, his grandfather had taken him wordlessly by the hand and had led
him there every step of the way. The conventional process of
becoming educated was but one of many traditional restraints
in life to which one was expected to submit as a matter of
course. But education was not to be achieved exclusively in
a formal mode. The grandfather had habitually admitted
Henry to his study, permitting him to become familiar first
of all with the sight and feeling of books, a familiarity that
was to intensify with the years. In the present century, books
seem often to be regarded by the male as alien if not unfriendly objects; most American boys and men grasp them,
if at all, only to hand them to their mothers or wives; but
the grandfather and grandson had basis for knowing that books
were more than friends—they were sources of life. Day in
and day out, they were probably the most fascinating tangi-
bles in the study, though there were other fascinations, too.
The old man had imprisoned caterpillars under inverted
tumblers on his closet shelf and had imbedded peach stones
and acorns in rich dirt within glass bowls. The caterpillars,
the boy observed, never became butterflies, and the peach
stones and acorns seldom became saplings; but any one of
them was nevertheless a productive symbol of a restless, perpetually inquiring human mind. The grandfather and the
grandson, without being particularly aware of it, each possessed such a mind. To be Henry Adams, then, was as a matter
of course to have such a mind and to use it. It was to assume
automatically an attitude of intellectual and moral *noblesse
oblige*, in opposition to the inertia through which most people
remain the animals they were born. One approached the status
of a human being only through dint of an artificial and labori-
ous process called education.

More than a half-century after this dramatic funeral of the sixth President over the ashes of the second, the grandson wrote of the basic conflict between the ideals of the family and those of State Street, Boston; between thinkers and bankers. This conflict was real, and young Henry sensed how it was summed up in the contrast between his grandfathers —scholarly, rebellious Adams of the White House and wealthy, satisfied Brooks of the Suffolk Bank. Here again it is surely the small boy on whom the old man looked back who was confronted by the indicated dilemma: the choice between "failure" and "success." Of the two old men the former had been the more exciting and understanding; the boy and this grandfather had enjoyed things in common; now the grandfather was gone. Until his own death seventy years later, in a different century and a far different human atmosphere, Henry Adams was to experience repeatedly that poignant isolation reserved for those who can realize their survivorship.

Not that one should make out the boy, or later the man, to have been incessantly a victim of pathos. Though most of the specific proof is tenuous or lost, enough is suggested in *The Education* to convince one that Henry Adams was a wiry, vital specimen most of his days, even though through much of his maturity he was annoyed by dyspepsia, the frequent curse of intense people. Perhaps because of his infant bout with scarlet fever, perhaps just because he was meant to be so, he was smaller than his brothers; but he evidently did most of the things habitual to New England boys of the period. There is allusion to rolling in the grass, wading in the brook, and swimming in the ocean; to fishing for smelts in the creeks and netting minnows in the salt marshes; and to chasing muskrats and hunting snapping turtles in the swamps. Presumably he could skate and play "a rudimentary game of baseball, football, and hockey." He seldom had occa-

sion to think of himself as other than normal, and he was
accepted by his companions. Whether in his early teens he
joined them in the barroom and the billiard room, better
known to young Boston males than their parents suspected,
is now hardly to be ascertained; but certainly he shared with
them the petty violence of battles, with snowballs and rocks
for weapons, waged between the students of the Latin School
and all comers. More genteelly, at his parents' bidding, he
received instruction in dancing.

There was always a vigorous, fun-loving element in Henry
Adams that one does well to recognize; it is revealed, though
not stressed, in his own account of his years. The healthy,
companionable child of Quincy and Boston was essentially
the same person who later as a Harvard student was repeatedly
disciplined, though for deportment no more baleful than "calling up to a college window under aggravating circumstances"
and for smoking in the yard (one's official ranking in his class
was a matter not of scholarship but of conduct acceptable to
the authorities); who, again as a student, was often a leading
bon vivant at select convivial gatherings, consuming his portion of cheese and crackers, and brandy and gin; who, according to a companion's diary, one night in Hildesheim,
Germany, after an evening with friends in Dom Tavern, "wandered off mistily into the night, walked into a strange house
and insisted on making his bed on a convenient trunk, over
the protests of a bevy of young women"; who, as an unofficial
member of the American legation in London during our Civil
War, once, so avers his account to his brother Charles, improvised "a double-shuffle in the shape of a Scotch reel, with
the daughter of an unbelieving Turk for a partner" and drew
the acclaim of a Dowager Duchess and her guests; who in
middle age climbed mountains with Clarence King; who past
the age of fifty started riding a bicycle; and who at sixty-five
tried out a roller coaster at the St. Louis Exposition, so en-

joying the sport that seven years later in Paris he urged friends there to join him in it.

Yet he was always serious-minded, too. Another glimpse of the growing child shows him at a writing table in his father's library, studying enough Latin to satisfy his teachers on the morrow and listening with boyishly mature sympathy to the antislavery discussions held in the same room by his father and three distinguished friends: Dr. John G. Palfrey, Richard Henry Dana, and Charles Sumner. One result of these discussions was that in 1848 Charles Francis Adams ran for Vice-President on the ticket of the Free-Soil party. Even a boy of ten could sense how distinctly these four men stood out in opposition to the political majority, as represented by Daniel Webster with his policy of compromise; could understand that they led a minority and might be accepted as proof that a minority could be not only respectable but exalted. These men were statesmen rather than politicians, somewhat self-consciously dedicated—as they had to be, in the New England tradition of John Quincy Adams—to the Platonic and Ciceronian ideal of government not by the many but by the best, though the government would act scrupulously in the ultimate interest of the many. On other occasions these same gentlemen were present at the Adams dinner table and contributed to some of the best conversation Henry was ever to hear.

Always, books remained the source of life. Charles Francis Adams pursued the mild patriarchal habit of reading to his children aloud, often choosing political satire, such as the speeches of Horace Mann or *The Biglow Papers* of James Russell Lowell; or he gave them Longfellow and Tennyson. With his brothers and sisters, Henry "took possession" of Dickens and Thackeray. As time went on he read to himself almost constantly, turning especially to the eighteenth-century historians, whose works rested in great number on his father's

9

SIU Libraries

shelves. He delighted in Pope and Gray but had difficulty, at this early stage, with Wordsworth. Bulwer, Macaulay, and Carlyle—all of their books were devoured as they came out, and, lying "on a musty heap of Congressional Documents in the old farmhouse at Quincy," Henry absorbed the novels of Sir Walter Scott. Books were a lifelong habit. Even aside from the deliberate scholarship of his mature years, Henry Adams could hardly help becoming one of the most widely read Americans of his time. The intellectual stamp was placed upon him early, to be at once a mark of distinction and of penalty. He was to be a person of extraordinary knowledge, with a poise and detachment especially useful to one inclined to observe and analyze human affairs. He was to be a thinker and a scholar almost without rival, nor was he to refine his emotions so far as not to show noteworthy devotion and tenderness toward members of his family and those friends who could share his attitudes and interests. On the other hand, he was never to display that uncritical warmth of feeling for the precarious cause of mankind so strongly present in a poet like Walt Whitman or in a reformer like Matthew Arnold. Nor was he ever, like his forebears, to be inclined to give himself fully to a career of political action.

The main external events of his life can be briefly submitted. As already indicated, he first attended the public Latin School. From the age of twelve to sixteen, however, he was enrolled in Epes Dixwell's school in Boylston Place, Boston, and for the following four years duly went to Harvard College, graduating in 1858. Then he crossed to Europe, ostensibly to study civil law at the University of Berlin, but actually to turn instead to the sufficient task of studying the language and becoming acquainted with various parts of the Continent, especially Italy. Two years later he was back in America, casually looking toward a quiet legal career in Boston, but the mounting violence of national affairs compelled a change in his plans. He became private secretary to his father, who in 1860–1861 represented Massachusetts in the memorable Congressional session just before the Civil War, and who, when the war broke, went to London as American Minister to England. As private secretary to the Minister, Henry remained in England, except for a six-month stay in Italy and numerous trips to Paris, until 1868, when he returned to the United States and engaged in free-lance journalism for two years. From 1870 to 1877, he taught medieval history at Harvard and edited the *North American Review*, then the country's leading quarterly. In 1872 he married Marian Hooper of Boston. Resigning his professorship and editorship, he went to live in Washington, where he devoted himself to the writing of history and satirical fiction and shared with his wife an unusually brilliant social life until her death by suicide in 1885. Thereafter, until his own death on March 28, 1918, he spent much time in travel, leaving few regions of the world untouched. As a general pattern of life, however, he spent his summers in Paris and his winters in Washington. To this final period belong his most original reflections and writings, and it was then that his artistic sensibilities reached their fullest growth and that the man who is the subject of this appreciation fully emerged.

So prosaic an outline cannot be filled in with spectacular details. Yet many specific moments in the life of Henry Adams merit attention for what they tell of a richly endowed human being, worth appreciation for his own sake. Both from Adams's letters and from *The Education* one learns that the final aspect of his mind and character may be regarded as an artistic near-masterpiece, wrought by deliberation and chance, touched by deeply ironic shadowings, and occasionally flawed by irruptions of experience with which the sensitive artist could never be quite prepared to deal. The average human being reaches the height of his physical maturity in his early twenties and his mental maturity, such as it is, not much later. Thereafter he submits passively to time's attrition; each day, each hour, is a subtle loss, appalling in its ultimate accumulation. Not to many are given the ability and will, as they were to Henry Adams, to compensate the irremediable corporeal damage with a steady intellectual increment.

From the first, he had not only a sensitive, restless mind, like that of his grandfather, but also a generous endowment of humor and irony and a distinct liking for leisure, which often left him disinclined to follow a rigid plan. He was well capable, as his grandfather had never been, of turning aside from experiences he did not relish. As Harold Dean Cater points out, however, Henry early indicated a general direction for his career from which he never seriously deviated; and in this respect he was in the long run more fortunate than his grandfather, who, as already noted, was prevented by the press of affairs from leading the distinctly literary life he would have chosen. On July 21, 1858, Henry wrote in his Harvard Class Book: "My immediate object is to become a scholar, and master of more languages than I pretend to know now. Ultimately it is most probable that I shall study and practice law, but where and to what extent is as yet undecided. My wishes are for a quiet literary life, as I believe that to be the happiest and in this country not the least useful." Along with his classmates in school and college, he had studied the classical languages. His father had thoroughly taught him French, so that he did not have to depend on the smattering he received at Dixwell's. His meager knowledge of German, however, threatened to be a handicap. He would go to Germany, then, to study the language and law.

Both *The Education* and his letters dealing with this European episode show that, however serious he initially thought his purpose to be, he went essentially as a tourist—though not with the gawking self-abasement that American travelers were to reveal after the Civil War. The English midlands, seen as he journeyed from Liverpool to London, already cringed beneath the coal-grimy touch of the nineteenth century: the mills and factories, pride of the industrial age, created a dense, smoky darkness lurid with flames, and the young man—so the old one averred—felt a sense of unknown horror. London, however, still belonged in many ways to the eighteenth century. "History muttered down Fleet Street, like Dr. Johnson, in Adams's ear. . . ." He hated it and could not know that with the passing years he was to like it best when he hated it most. Across the Channel, he found the sixteenth century. As Henry and his party sailed up the Scheldt, peasants in the fields dropped their tools to dance to the music of a band playing on the deck. At Antwerp, with its cathedral, he suddenly entered the Middle Ages. "The taste of the town was thick, rich, ripe, like a sweet wine. . . ." He could not understand it, as he would fifty years later, but he got drunk on it.

At the University of Berlin he attended one lecture in civil law and never went again. His excuse was that, not knowing the language well, he could not understand the lecturer. Such rationale had only a dwindling validity, of course; with the passing months he gained competence in German; nevertheless he stayed away from the university. Those paragraphs in *The Education* dealing with his German sojourn are characteristically apologetic with a sense of time ill spent, though droll exception is made for the fact that he learned to follow the movement of a Beethoven sinfonie. He became aware of this new faculty one day, much to his astonishment, while drinking beer in a music hall. It was curious and perplexing, he concluded years later, "that the student's only clear gain —his single step to a higher life—came from time wasted;

studies neglected; vices indulged; education reversed;—it came from the despised beer-garden and music-hall; and it was accidental, unintended, unforeseen."

The irony of the older man is probably not unlike that in which the younger man, unaware of future impacts, might have clothed his comment to himself or others at the time. It is interesting to watch him, in retrospect, sitting at the age of twenty in a German music hall. More than three thousand miles away from home, he savors the genteel indolence of being his own master. The tobacco may be coarse and the beer poor, but he enjoys them both. Too deeply read, too genuinely thoughtful, too sedulously controlled in emotion to become a mere esthete, he is nonetheless a confident dabbler in life, with a late-adolescent smugness in need of startling; and the startling comes, most admirably, from Beethoven. The instant is premonitory of the final period of his life, when he would be taken in a sense unawares by the wonder and medieval naïveté of the French cathedrals and, in partial solace of his despair, would kneel in secular Mariolatry at the feet of the Virgin.

Another moment, somewhat differently revealing, taken from these early European years, shows Adams sitting in a schoolroom among German boys twelve or thirteen years old, reciting their lessons with them and catching their phrases. Seven or eight years their senior, and a foreigner as well, he is doubly an object of irreverent curiosity. Further, he is innately shy of large groups and has an antipathy, according to his later recollections as set forth in *The Education,* to "high schools." But he is in earnest about wishing to learn the language, and after three months of this performance he has the satisfaction of finding himself near the fulfillment of his wishes. One half of his avowed purpose in coming to Germany has been carried out with resolution. The other, that of discovering some of the principles of civil law, has been pushed aside. More than one word would seem to be required to characterize such a young man—relinquishing part of his design with apparent ease but pursuing another part with fortitude and industry; a young man at once faithless and faithful to the Puritan habit of thoroughly doing what one dislikes to do. If he is disinclined, however, to carry out a plan as originally formed, he is at least in no danger of becoming a loafer.

With the arrival of spring, 1859, Adams left Berlin for a tour of Bavaria, Switzerland, and the Rhine country. Here again, as *The Education* hints and the letters reveal, the young man was greatly at his ease and could thumb his nose at the narrower aspects of the Puritan tradition. "Bier," he wrote to his brother Charles, "is a first rate thing to walk on. . . . The next morning we set off [from Oberhof] again at eight o'clock in a snow-storm. . . . You may think this wasn't much fun, and indeed I believe I was the only one who really enjoyed it, but the glow, the feeling of adventure and the novelty; above all, the freedom and some wildness after six months in Berlin, made it really delightful to me. I haven't felt so well and fresh for ever-so-long. After two hours we reached the Schmücke, a couple of houses on the other side of the hills, and here, sir, we indulged ourselves in a real American tipple. We procured the materials and under Ben Crowninshield's skilled direction, we brewed ourselves a real ten-horsepower Tom and Jerry, which had a perfectly miraculous effect on our spirits. . . ."

One sees him again about three years later, in London, when the Civil War was at its worst from the standpoint of Northern fortunes and the prestige of the American Minister and his staff was at its lowest. Concomitant with Henry Adams's outward control and modesty there was always a vast if less securely poised self-assurance. In these circumstances the control and the modesty were apparent in a perfect equilibrium of manner before the most absurd accusations made by Englishmen friendly to the Rebel cause. With only a noncommittal smile he could listen, for example, to statements from someone like Thackeray that made out Abraham Lincoln to be a coarse, ferocious brute deliberately engaged in harrowing the emotions of Southern women. At the same time, Henry was showing less control in writing letters about the English to his friend H. J. Raymond, editor of the New York *Times,* who printed them in his paper, fortunately without signature. Had Henry's father known of this journalistic activity, he might have remonstrated, for certain passages in the letters urged the conclusion that the English wanted war with the North and would shortly have it. Matters came to a head when the Boston *Daily Courier* in December, 1861, printed "extracts from a private diary" describing the Manchester cotton famine, occasioned by the North's blockade of the South, and made plain in its editorial column that their author was young Henry Adams. Shortly, the London *Times,* to the embarrassment of the secretary, called sarcastic attention to them. No catastrophe, however, ensued. The father took the minor incident with the same wonderful calm with which he took major incidents, and Henry belatedly played the part of good sense and desisted from political journalism. As the days advanced, however, he grew restive. He knew that under the leadership of McClellan many of his contemporaries were dying in the swamps about Richmond. After a sleepless night, during which he kept his father and mother awake by pacing the floor in the room above, Henry announced his decision to return to America and join the army. The parents demurred; so did Charles, when he was informed; and young Henry Adams continued in London.

It would be easy to accord this abortive decision quick contempt; at least one critic, James Truslow Adams, refuses to treat it seriously. It was, nevertheless, a resolve reached after much thought and in good faith, as Henry's letters to his brother survive to prove. Here is an instance of the reflective personality not quite content with its habits, working itself up therefore to the point of action, and then being turned back from that point by superior arguments. Studying the record, one accepts the assertions of the father and the brother that Henry Adams was more useful copying diplomatic documents in London than he could possibly have been fighting rebels in America; there was, further, much force at the time in the father's argument that the entire Adams family would shortly have to return home, since the British government seemed increasingly to be throwing its weight to the Southern cause. But one should value, too, the portrait here depicted: that of a thoughtful, conscientious young man, slightly humiliated in his own eyes by the prosaic quality of necessity, and conceding, as he often would, that the less spectacular course was the wiser. Again and again, Henry Adams was sardonically to acknowledge that the human will seems to find itself at the mercy of motives, and that the sensitive individual must repeatedly feel oppressed at his own submissions to good sense.

Somewhat in contrast, one sees Adams in late December, 1869, strolling by himself along an unpopulous street in the suburbs of Washington. The Civil War, of course, was done. Lincoln was dead, and the efforts of Andrew Johnson to safeguard the great leader's generous policies toward the defeated had failed. Ulysses S. Grant was stolidly launched upon that Presidentiad which, splendid in anticipation, was showing signs of becoming a national calamity. One need not romanticize to the extent of deciding whether Henry Adams's mood, as he took his constitutional that December afternoon, was one of quiet despair at the state of national politics or of quiet elation at his own successes in recent months as a free-lance journalist, or whether perhaps his emotion was quite different from either of these. It can be asserted, however—from information obtainable in his letters—that at thirty-one he was beginning to appear middle-aged, with a beard to compensate for increasing, congenital baldness: a small, well-dressed, thoughtful-looking figure. Whatever the train of his reflections, it was broken by a swift, rushing noise behind him. Before he could turn, a soft but heavy substance struck him on the back of the head and flung him to the ground. Half-stunned he struggled to his feet and, aware of lost dignity and a lost hat, retrieved them both. The cause? There on the ground half a rod in front, flapping painfully and gazing at him with eyes as bewildered as his own, was a huge, white, tame goose.

Examining himself, Henry found that he was covered with sand from beard to boots. His gloves were torn. One of his fingers was flayed, and two others were nearly dislocated. Over one knee burgeoned a painful swelling; the joint stiffened, not to become fully flexible again for a week. "Daedalus [Icarus] was nothing by comparison," he wrote to an English friend. "He melted at the rays of the sun. But I was floored by the stupidest, dirtiest and coarsest of domestic dung-hill fowl." He went on to wonder ironically whether the bird were a portent.

One need not join him in this speculation except to suggest that the incident, which would otherwise not be resurrected, somehow shows Henry Adams feeling what he so often felt—that life holds as much of the absurd as of the heroic, and that human poise is constantly subject to sudden, humiliating attack, though usually by a means less laughable than a fate-blown goose.

One observes him again, about 1871, grown still balder and more heavily bearded, sitting in a Harvard classroom

18

disgustedly counting the large number of students enrolled for his instruction. Henry Osborn Taylor recalls that the teacher "took a look around at the students, and then delivered a screed on the difficulty of his proposed course, which frightened away a good half—as he intended." Those who remained discovered that he was a teacher of great force and originality who expected them to disclose the same qualities. He used no textbooks but compelled the students to go whenever possible to the primary documents; in effect, he introduced the seminar method of study at Harvard, eventually adopted by other American universities. To urge the young men on he would pretend, Socratically, utter ignorance in himself. "Just what does *transubstantiation* mean?" one of them asked one day. "Good Heavens!" was the reply. "How should I know! Look it up!"

He was always an "original," prone to say or do the unexpected thing. He shocked many a Bostonian and pleased himself in doing so. After seven years of teaching, he was content to forsake Harvard and its community because, he wrote, "I care a great deal to prevent myself from becoming what of all things I despise, a Boston prig. . . ." At the same time there was evidently much about his appearance, his manner, and his way of life that betrayed his origins. He knew this and playfully lamented it while knowing nothing could be done. "If I stood on Fifth Avenue in front of the Brunswick Hotel," he subsequently growled, "and in a state of obvious inebriety hugged and kissed every pretty woman that passed, they would only say that I was a cold Beacon St. aristocrat. . . ."

Probably his happiest years were those of the half-decade or so between his resignation from Harvard and the loss of his wife. Having conceived the plan for his *History,* he sailed for Europe with Mrs. Adams in May, 1879, there to spend a year and a half gathering documents among the Foreign

Office records in London, Paris, and Madrid. Temporarily balked at the last-named capital, the couple "fled southward."

Andalusia [he wrote to his friend Gaskell] received us with open arms. The sun came out. Cordova was fascinating. The great mosque was glorious. The little houses, and especially their hammered iron gates, were adorable. We reached Granada Tuesday evening and stayed there a week with more amusement than I ever supposed my effete existence was now capable of feeling. . . . While there I made acquaintance with one of the best of the Granadans, Don Leopoldo Equilaz, the local antiquarian, a charming fellow, who took us about, told us stories and showed us curiosities, had us at his house, and led us into temptation, for he inflamed our minds with a wild fancy for following up the Granada fugitives to their final refuge at Tetuan. You would have been delighted if you had seen us at an evening tea in Don Leopoldo's renaissance palace, talking fluid Spanish with the Senora, two padres of the holy inquisition, and two pure Moors of the race of Boabdil; it was life of the fifteenth century with full local color.

The dark day in his life was Sunday, December 6, 1885. For more than a year—as a result, first, of her father's illness and, later, of his death—Mrs. Henry Adams had been nervously depressed. Like her husband she evidently was a person who felt the need of a central interest or faith to give purpose to living and was less able than he to find it, or to survive without it. Unfortunately, too, she had no children to help give meaning to her emotional tensions. She ceased seeing anyone except Henry and a few most intimate friends and lost her wonted cheerfulness. With complete loyalty he spent most of his time with her, encouraging her in diversions, such as amateur photography, in which she developed considerable proficiency. On that fatal Sunday they breakfasted at noon. Then she retired to her room while he went for his habitual walk. He never saw her alive again. The coroner pronounced that she had died from drinking potassium cyanide, which, by bitter irony, was part of the photographic equipment secured for her by her husband.

One might know much of Henry Adams that is now scarcely to be guessed were it possible to study a minute record of his thoughts and feelings at that instant when, returning from his walk, he became aware of what Marian Adams had done. But the moment is substantially lost and to fictionize it would be presumptuous. This much, however, can be inferred: though the shock staggered him—and he was never to be quite the same again—he did not lose control. Probably no earthly circumstances could make Henry Adams really lose control, though they might, and did, exact a punishing emotional payment. The messages of condolence that poured in upon him were promptly, if briefly, answered. To George Bancroft, the venerable historian: "Your note goes to my heart. You must forgive me for being silent. I can endure, but I cannot talk, unless I must." To Edwin L. Godkin, editor of the *Nation:* "Never fear for me. I have had happiness enough to carry me over some years of misery; and even in my worst prostration I have found myself strengthened by two thoughts. One was that life could have no other experience so crushing. The other was that at least I had got out of life all the pleasure it had to give." To Oliver Wendell Holmes, the elder:

Your kind letter touches me so closely that I hasten to thank you for it; fearing that if I lay it aside I shall never have courage to open it again. You will not expect me to say anything. All my energy is now turned to the task of endurance; and you, as physician and as poet, know that the effort to endure, if not as exhausting as the effort to express, is at least as painful. I can only thank you, and I do it with all my heart.

He seldom wrote or spoke of his wife again. He was not to mention her name in *The Education*. His life with her, he indicated several months after her death in a letter to Henry

Holt, the publisher, was the only chapter of his existence for which he could care, and it was "closed forever, locked up, and put away, to be kept, as a sort of open secret, between oneself and eternity."

Years later he was conversing one day in Washington with two young ladies, daughters of Francis G. Newlands, then residing with their father in the old house where Adams and his wife had lived. With awed excitement they related a mysterious occurrence of a night or so before. One of them, sleeping in her bedroom in the old Adams house, had been awakened by the guttering of a candle on the dresser. Knowing that she herself had not lighted it, she called to her sister, the only other person in the house, who came and was as startled as she. Who or what had lighted the candle? What deepened the mystery for them was that they could find no burnt match, either by the candlestick or anywhere else in the house.

Listening to the remarkable narration, Adams at first was silent. Then he leaned forward and asked intensely: "Just which room in the house was it?" They told him: it was the room off the stairway landing—the room in which Marian Adams had died. He straightened back in his chair and then relaxed in it, as though dismissing the whole matter. "Of course," he said simply.[1] No one was ever to know just what he made of the girls' story.

Only an expert in the nuances of silence can measure the tribute Adams paid his wife in seldom mentioning her again. References to her in his letters are few, and the narrative in *The Education* is remarkable for having a twenty-year gap, 1871–1891. A few phrases hint at the central sorrow. "For reasons that had nothing to do with education," he says, alluding to his circumstances in 1891, "he was tired; his nervous

[1] This unusual anecdote was related to me in May, 1945, by one of the sisters concerned, Mrs. W. B. Johnston of Reno, Nevada.

energy ran low; and, like a horse that wears out, he quitted the race-course, left the stable, and sought pastures as far as possible from the old."

The Adamses had spent part of their honeymoon in Egypt. In 1898 he took a trip up the Nile with friends and found some of the memories overpowering. "I knew it would be a risky thing," he wrote to Elizabeth Cameron, "but it came so suddenly that before I could catch myself, I was unconsciously wringing my hands and the tears rolled down in the old way, and I had to get off by myself for a few minutes."

When Henry James died, in 1916, the effect on Adams was not so much one of grief at the loss of an old acquaintance as a sudden intensification of those memories clustering about that person whom James had also known. The decade of the 1870's, especially, belonged ineffaceably to Marian Adams. "We really were happy then." An old man waiting for death, though never resigned to it, he spent many hours by his wife's grave in Rock Creek Cemetery, seeming to merge himself in the time-free contemplation symbolized there by the seated memorial figure sculptured at his direction by Saint-Gaudens. Some conventional observers, feeling the need for a recognizable label, have called this statue "Grief"; but in the profundities of its aspect there dwells no sorrow. It was not intended, said Adams, to answer a question but to ask one; and he might have added that anyone mature enough to pose the problem would know better than to expect a solution. It remains a triumph of philosophic art: a bronze-wrought, perpetual assertion of the inexplicable universal innateness felt by the creative few in each human generation. Perhaps the best commentary is the closing of Adams's poem, "Buddha and Brahma":

> Life, Time, Space, Thought, the World, the Universe
> End where they first begin, in one sole thought
> Of Purity in Silence.

The mind and personality of the woman who evoked the memorial can be discovered to some extent through her letters, edited in 1946 by Ward Thoron. Possessing an ample supply of satiric wit, good sense, and artistic awareness, Marian Adams was at once a person in her own right and a worthy companion to one with the complicated temperament of a scholar-artist. Unfortunately for the curiosity of many readers, the letters, addressed to her father, seldom refer explicitly to her married relationship, although there sounds throughout an undertone of affectionate rapport with her husband. Mainly, the letters fall within the period 1872–1883 and deal with the Adamses' travels and with their social life in Washington.

Like Henry she was adept at summing up people, sometimes not too kindly. Mrs. Alma-Tadema "looked like a lymphatic tigress"; James McNeill Whistler was "even more mad away from his paint pots than near them"; a Mrs. Mackintosh was "fat, rosy, placid, torpid, like a nerveless featherbed"; Senator John Sherman "swallows his sentences, perhaps fearing no one else will"; Nelly Grant Sartoris "has taken to frescoing her face till, as Henry James says (he knew her in England), she looks like a ceiling of Michael Angelo"; and E. A. Freeman, the English historian, "was simply and inexpensively attired in a rusty brown beard of unusual length." Such phrasings are almost typical.

Yet the letters show her also to have been sympathetic and generous, cheerfully intent on making her husband's days untroubled and zestful. She instantly accepted all of his chosen friends, like the Gaskells, the Hays, Clarence King, Aristarchi Bey, and Henry James. The last-named adored her above all other American women he knew, and she accepted his tribute gracefully, though of his literary art she had to comment: "It's not that he 'bites off more than he can chaw,' . . . he chaws more than he bites off." She was fond of her servants, a fair number of whom were needed to assist her in making the Adams home the distinguished social center that it was. She also had a particular liking for horses and dogs. Freudians must make what they will of her pronounced tenderness toward pets and of the fact that she loved children but was childless.

In addition to her seldom failing wit, which her husband must have appreciated ("Tell that story again," she reports his saying, in effect), she had an easy grasp of ideas, a copious store of miscellaneous, nonscientific knowledge, and a quick appreciation of beauty in art and nature that must have made her companionship of special value. Beyond everything else she had, one discerns, a sense of how life should be lived, rendered more poignant for the reader by his foreknowledge that she was to prove unequal to the incessant ordeal of remaining alive.

As the letters advance, one surmises from them that she had not quite enough physical strength to play the arduous role her Washington life demanded: reports of colds, headaches, and fatigue are frequent, and the quietude for which she occasionally expresses a longing was only intermittently hers. She did not, however, actively complain. Not until some months after her father's death in April, 1885, did her broken health become alarmingly apparent. Cater quotes the journal of Nicholas Longworth Anderson for November 4: "Mrs. Adams is suffering from nervous prostration," and also cites a confidential source to the effect that at the time of the honeymoon trip up the Nile in 1872 she had undergone a kind of nervous collapse accompanied by depression, and that her husband feared a repetition. His devotion to her is pathetically emphasized in one of the recollections of Mrs. Charles W. Rae, also reported by Cater: "Mrs. Rae called daily and told stories or brought in the latest humorous gossip about the antics of Washington politicos. Once after a visit early that fall, Henry accompanied her to the door and said, 'I shall never forget what you've done.' 'Done?' asked Mrs. Rae. 'What have I done?' 'You made Clover smile.' "

Such testimony enables the conjecture that when Marian Adams abruptly concluded her life in December, 1885, she was seriously ill; but the letters suggest that her condition was brought on not alone by strain at her father's illness and death, but also by a long accumulation of impatience with triviality. Lacking her husband's capacity to deal with life as an abstract intellectual challenge, she fronted the impossible task of finding meaning in a limitless series of teas and dinners. She needed a central reason for living (a careful reading of Henry's novel *Esther* may here be instructive), but she found only pretexts and realized too readily that they were not enough. Beyond this one has small right to guess.

Without reference to her tragedy, her letters echo a mode of life now seldom found, in which taste and intelligence are invariably honored and touch the least moment with vividness and grace. "Is it any consolation," wrote John Hay to Henry, "to remember her as she was? that bright, intrepid spirit, that keen, fine intellect, that lofty scorn of all that was mean, that social charm which made your house such a one as Washington never knew before, and made hundreds of people love her as much as they admired her. No, that makes it all so much harder to bear."

If Marian Hooper Adams had not died when she did, one might not know the Henry Adams who wrote *The Education*. One probably would know only the Henry Adams who bore a distinguished American name and proved his title to it by historical scholarship rather than statesmanship, and who enjoyed a reputation in his day as a droll and provoking conversationalist. He probably would not have written his two most thoughtful books, *Mont-Saint-Michel and Chartres* and *The Education*, or, if he had, would not have given evidence in them of a preoccupation with man's deepest dilemma. Borrowing a hint from Arnold J. Toynbee, one can detect in the career of Henry Adams the motif of Withdrawal-and-Return, by which the heroic personality assesses itself in a period of quietude and escape and then turns back to fulfill its destiny. The loss of his wife brought Adams, in effect, to a state of spiritual exile; it caused him literally and figuratively, in his own plain words, to seek "pastures as far as possible from the old." Had his character been less vital, he would never have come back to the arena of other minds. But he did come back, if not as a prophet returning from self-discipline in the wilderness to lead his disciples to salvation, certainly as a man whose emotions had been deepened and redirected and whose mind was thereafter prepared to range daringly over problems that the uninitiated ignore.

His journey into the South Seas, 1890–1891, with the artist John La Farge, formed one of the most diverting chapters in his interlude of escape. Hawaii, Samoa, Tahiti, the Fiji Islands—all of them, though Samoa more than the others, offered experiences in tropical languor and color that his nerves badly needed. Influenced by his talented companion he started to sketch and paint, though by the time they reached Tahiti he was content only to appraise the efforts of his friend. Even after several months in Samoa, with infrequent word from the world left behind, he was not bored. "I go to bed soon after nine o'clock," he wrote, "and sleep well till half past five. I eat bananas, mangoes, oranges, pineapples and mummy-apples by the peck. I smoke like a lobster. I write, or study watercolor drawing all day. . . . I ought to take more exercise, but I don't, and time slides as though it were Fang-alo on the Sliding Rock."

He especially admired the Samoan natives, their physical handsomeness, and their simplicities. Never a son of the

Puritans in Brahminical fashion, he loafed and invited his soul to consort avuncularly with old-gold girls dancing the Siva in the red light of burning palm leaves. "The sensation of seeing extremely fine women, with superb forms, perfectly unconscious of undress, and yet evidently aware of their beauty and dignity, is worth a week's seasickness to experience." In his letters one catches a glimpse of the grief-ravaged, 62-year-old man, not quite losing his self-awareness (he was never able to lose that) as he sits in a large native hut with his back against an outer post in the midst of perfect, muscular bodies glistening with cocoanut oil. Outside, the moon shines dazzlingly, the night air is soft, and the palms barely stir. His legs ache from long sitting cross-legged and his eyes droop —for the dance before him, presented mainly in his honor, goes on almost interminably, and it would be an unthinkable breach of manners to retire. Suddenly one of the girls, perfectly modeled on a six-foot scale and wearing only an ornamented strip of black cloth, stands out against the russet background like an ivory image. With movements large and free and strong, she dances with breath-catching, spontaneous art—splashing imitation water over companions in bathing, or, in an ecstasy of agility, swinging on the crossbeam; and by way of climax she rushes upon Adams and encircles him in her arms and kisses him. Later, one of the girls innocently announces her desire to run off with him. It is a Samoan custom that might be worth trying, he writes John Hay, if only for economic reasons; for Adams, for almost the only time in his life, is temporarily short of funds. Nevertheless, he chuckles, "as yet, their raiment of cocoanut oil has proved an impassable barrier between them and me; for I cannot take a bath every time my beloved touches me; but bankruptcy is a powerful motive for a marriage of inconvenience, and I know not what number of pigs and fine mats might save me from starvation. Everyone has his price."

This is the same Henry Adams as the one to be seen several years later in Europe, immersed in medieval art and engaged in a half-mystical adoration of the Virgin, for both enthusiasms were a part of his apparent transformation from mere scholar to artist and scholar together. It was not a fundamental transformation, because, far more than his contemporaries, Adams had always been a sensitive admirer of the talented and beautiful women in his circle; and his tribute to the Virgin, like his delight in the old-gold girls, was the twilight flowering of a devotion he had always known: to the delicacy, the mystery, and the vital power of the female. The artist in him sensed her exquisiteness and strength as weapons to be invoked against chaos.

In France at about the turn of the century, in the nave of Chartres Cathedral, he trained a pair of binoculars on the minutiae of carvings too high above the ground to have been meant for the appreciation of merely mortal eyes. He asked himself not only how but why such exquisiteness resulted and began to understand the authority with which a once valid ideal had compelled the human mind. The Virgin was the response to men's weariness with their own mortality. She was the emblem of men's impatience with their own rigidly logical concept of justice, applied both to this life and their notions of the life hereafter. She was the protest of motherly gentleness against things as they usually are. Chartres Cathedral was her house, her palace, fashioned to her divinely exalted taste. As her cult amplified, she imposed a loving tyranny that brought men closer than they had ever been, and perhaps would ever be again, to a unified concept of their society.

Van Wyck Brooks points out that Adams's characterizations of the Virgin, in *Mont-Saint-Michel and Chartres,* are in many ways applicable to the nineteenth-century woman. One might go further and suspect that Marian Hooper Adams served as the original for many sentences of delineation, as, for example, the following:

The Queen Mother was as majestic as you like; she was absolute; she could be stern; she was not above being angry; but she was still a woman, who loved grace, beauty, ornament,—her toilette, robes, jewels;—who considered the arrangements of her palace with attention, and liked both light and colour. . . . She was extremely sensitive to neglect, to disagreeable impressions, to want of intelligence in her surroundings.

Unquestionably he found some of that solace that the Virgin, as a symbol of compassionate force, was able to provide, and it requires no wrenching of the fancy to see him in a mood of profound dedication penning his "Prayer to the Virgin," one copy of which was found in his wallet after his death:

> Help me to see! not with my mimic sight—
> With yours! which carried radiance, like the sun,
> Giving the rays you saw with—light in light—
> Tying all suns and stars and worlds in one.

To employ George Herbert's metaphor, cited in *The Education,* weariness was the pulley that tossed Henry Adams to the breast of infinite mercy. He had known beauty, wisdom, honor, and pleasure, but he suffered increasingly the intellectual's curse of ennui. The weight of loneliness that had lain on him even as a small boy, at the loss of his grandfather, had by now increased. Death, having taken his wife, took also his friends—the old and tested, like Clarence King and John Hay, and the young and auspicious, like William Hallett Phillips and George Cabot Lodge. In *The Education* Adams makes clear the strength of his attachment to the two older men and also, particularly in his remarks on King, the high price at which he reckoned friendship: "One friend in a lifetime is much; two are many; three are hardly possible." For friendship, he explains, requires a certain parallelism of life and a community of thought.

According to his account in *The Education* Adams recognized Hay as a friend when he first met him early in 1861 in Washington, where Hay had just arrived to serve Abraham Lincoln as private secretary; and Adams "never lost sight of him at the future crossing of their paths." In her appreciative essay, *A Niece's Memories,* Mabel Hooper La Farge tells how on one occasion, when the two friends had known many years of association, Hay sought to symbolize Adams's particular combination of brusqueness and tenderness. He commissioned Saint-Gaudens to cast three copies of a small medallion of Adams's head attached to the body of a porcupine with an angel's wings. The inscription was "Henricus Adams Porcupinus Angelicus." "No one who loved him really feared him," comments Mrs. La Farge, "though his manner might at times be alarming to a stranger."

Adams and King met during the summer of 1871 in the Uintah Mountains, where the latter was helping conduct the Fortieth Parallel Survey. Having written a long and careful article on Sir Charles Lyell, Adams knew something of geology, on which subject King was probably the leading American authority; but their close friendship over the years touched at innumerable points. In a memorial address on King published in 1904, two years after King's death, Adams recalls vacationing with him in 1894 near Santiago, Cuba. It was Adams's part to keep his friend, who had recently suffered a nervous breakdown, constantly occupied. One means to this end consisted, as often in the past, in disputing points of geology with him. "Unfortunately," reports Adams, "he knew only too well that I could not tell the difference between a trilobite and a land-crab and we disagreed entirely in regard to a favorite theory of mine that if we could get deep enough down into the archaean rocks, we should find President Eliot and the whole Faculty of Harvard College, besides all the geologists there. . . ." He also quotes the last letter he ever got from King, written in the spring of 1897, urging Adams to come to Mexico. The writer was by then a very sick man, but he could still reveal the quality that drew Adams's devotion:

I grieve that you cannot go to Mexico with me; all I lack is a pessimist addicted to water-colors and capable of a humorous view of the infinite. . . . Come along, and I will, in the secrecy of the primeval woods admit the truth of all your geological criticisms of me; and I will even execute in advance an assignment of half the brown girls we meet. Moreover I will be a second La Farge, and never tell. Dear me! I will do anything you like. I will read your complete works. . . .

"He remained," says Adams, "the best companion in the world to the end."

Looking strictly to Adams's definition of friendship, perhaps King and Hay were his only friends, though one has difficulty in not also counting John La Farge and possibly Charles Milnes Gaskell. The letters, however, testify to the pleasure he derived from associating with many people, of whichever sex and whatever age, who necessarily had less in common with him than did the pair of his contemporaries for whom he reserved highest tribute. William Hallett Phillips was a young lawyer in Washington, beloved for his warmheartedness and wit, who more than once accompanied Adams on sailing and camping expeditions. Devoted to Adams, he could jest with him and about him in a way that the latter relished. (Commenting on a letter received one day from Adams, then in Europe, Phillips remarked: "He seems to be well and unhappy." [2] Phillips's death came abruptly in May, 1897, from a boating mishap on the Potomac. Adams, who

[2] Unpublished letter from W. Hallett Phillips to (Bancel?) La Farge, July 13, 1896, on file in the Huntington Library, San Marino, California.

was in Paris at the time, was deeply distressed at his loss; he quietly arranged to buy some of Phillips's effects in order that his affairs might be settled. Young Lodge, nicknamed Bay, was often Adams's companion in Paris and was prized not only for his literary promise but for his conversational gifts, often employed to pour contempt over the conventional ideals of the Boston Brahmins, in whose ranks he was entitled by birth to move. With him Adams formed the party of Conservative Christian Anarchists—logically limited to a total membership of two, each constantly denouncing the principles of the other. When Lodge suddenly died on Nantucket Island in the summer of 1909, Adams was in Europe trying to maintain the morale of a group of acquaintances, all of them seriously ill, and the death of the young poet was but one calamity in a series. "My own formula that I always expect the worse, and always find it worse than I expected," wrote Adams to Bay's father, Henry Cabot Lodge, "comes into play now with awful application. When life suddenly becomes a dream, and one seems to go on with it mechanically, without touching an actuality on any side, one can only drift until something touches us that we can again fasten on. . . ." Friendship, too, was one of the defenses set up against the irruptions of chaos; and friendship, like feminine beauty, had to submit to mortality's chances.

The cult of the Virgin and the unitive faith that built the cathedrals were perhaps an actuality that Adams, as an imaginative historian, could feel himself touched by and thus regain, after many losses, the semblance of a workable belief in life. Readers vary, no doubt, in being relieved or regretful that he did not adopt the solution achieved by certain sensitive spirits in each generation and fully embrace the consolations of religion; but the simple fact is that he did not, notwithstanding the later assertion of his niece, Mabel Hooper La Farge, that he had perceived "the true light." His

Mariolatry, though at moments showing the emotion found in his "Prayer to the Virgin," usually was accompanied by the skeptical reservations of the scholar, and was in the end esthetic and secular rather than traditionally religious. "I am in near peril," he confessed to Henry Osborn Taylor in 1915, "of turning Christian, and rolling in the mud in an agony of human mortification"; but he never did. He had seen too much and read too much of the world not to discern the word Failure written over the door to the religious labyrinth. Christian faith was a "supernatural or hypothetical supplement" to Stoicism, nailed to it by violence. "Father Fay is no bore—far from it," he confided to a correspondent concerning the friendly visitations of a Catholic priest at the time of the first World War, "but I think he has an idea that I want conversion. . . . Bless the congenial sinner! He had best look out that I don't convert him, for his old church is really too childish for a hell like this year of grace."

To what purpose, he asked, had the Virgin existed if, after nineteen hundred years, the world was bloodier than when she was born?

At the time of his wife's death he had accepted the counsel of an admired Harvard teacher, E. W. Gurney, and invoked the Stoic philosophy but found it less of a practical than a theoretical aid. As he assured Taylor, he respected Marcus Aurelius as the type of highest human attainment in the ancient world; but the respect was not unqualified, since he added: "I need badly to find one man in history to admire." Neither in the past nor in the present could he establish a companionship sufficiently sympathetic to efface the loneliness of his old age and to convince himself fully that harmony rather than disorder prevailed in his private universe.

One of the more melancholy glimpses of Henry Adams shows him in his sixty-third year standing on the deck of a small steamer that bore northward along the Norwegian coast toward Hammerfest. The spectacle of the fiords was appropriate to his own sense of desolation, which he expresses in a letter to Elizabeth Cameron. He speaks of the impact of "this show" as being like that of the Götterdämmerung. "It takes hold of an elderly person with unfair brutality and suddenness. At first one gets off one's balance. One cries." Not because of its beauty, he urges somewhat ambiguously, but because of its sadness:

These long mountains stretching their legs out into the sea never knew what it was like to be a volcano. They lie, one after another, like corpses, with their toes up, and you pass by them, and look five or ten miles up the fiords between them, and see their noses, tipped by cloud or snow, high in behind, with one corpse occasionally lying on another, and a skull or a thigh-bone chucked about, and hundreds of glaciers and snow-patches hanging to them, as though it was a winter battle-field; and a weird after-glow light; and a silent, oily gleaming sea just lapping them all around as though it were as tired as they are. . . .

It is dangerously easy to overstress the near-tragic quality of the aging scholar, caught as never before in the impingement of beauty but knowing, too, the final ineffectuality of its comfort for one whose mind insisted on discovering monstrosity and chaos on every side. He still was one to relish good food and drink, to enjoy the company of handsome women and vigorous men and stimulate them by questions and banter. He was by no means the bitter, broken prophet that many critics, gullibly misreading his own account, have pronounced him to be. He had asserted in *The Education,* with rather ponderous irony, that he had failed in various specific efforts—to be a teacher, an editor, a historian—but he never attached the term failure to his total being. The distinction here is important, constituting, as S. I. Hayakawa has urged, the difference between sanity and self-destruction.

35

Nevertheless, one comprehends Adams most clearly as a man who to the last felt and not quite successfully defied the personal and universal disorder encroaching upon a sensitive dweller in the nineteenth and twentieth centuries. His dilemma was at once individual and typical.

Probably every period in history has seemed inharmonious and oppressive to the acute minority living in it, though in writing *Mont-Saint-Michel and Chartres* Adams purported to find that the twelfth century had offered a congenial milieu to the most demanding sensibility. The twelfth century, however, is not to be recovered or repeated, and the twentieth century proves to be particularly trying to that person innately unable to adjust his ideals to those of men at large. To the inevitable isolations of space and time, which each human being earns at birth, are added the isolations wrought by the corporate aspects of society. Both government and business—at times battling each other, at times co-operating, for the control of people's lives—operate in terms of millions and billions, while the vital human integer is ignored. Much of the impelling literature of contemporary time has risen from the protest of individual men and women against being thus forgotten. In their denunciation of things as they are, many writers have been misled into espousing a fascistic or communistic ideal that in its realization would betray the same contempt for the human unit as the present scheme, only with greater vengeance. The mark of poise, and of a real if unlauded heroism, in Henry Adams is that though he explored the pseudosolutions of *la recherche du temps perdu,* of mystical religion, and of political and economic revolution, he discovered the flaws in each that made full acceptance of it egregious in a rational, humane world, and turned to the obvious course remaining: that of describing and explaining, though not of justifying, present and impending events. It is possible to suppose that, were he alive today, he might furnish the dispassionate comment so sorely needed concerning the antagonism between East and West, wherein both sides are engaged in eager idolatry of the same shabby, mammonistic gods, though each side mutters its own ritual while it worships.

His dynamic theory of history was, as will be seen, a logical failure in its violent (and deliberate) misapplication of the rules of physics to human affairs; but artistically it was a metaphorical triumph comparable, as Robert E. Spiller has said, to Milton's utilization in *Paradise Lost* of the outmoded Ptolemaic system of astronomy. The fitness of the result poetically redeems the daring illogic of the method. In formulating the theory, Adams must have achieved that satisfaction which comes to an intellectually restless person only when his mind is worthily at work; but he did not save himself from disillusion.

Every fabulist [he had written in *The Education*] has told how the human mind has always struggled like a frightened bird to escape the chaos which caged it; how—appearing suddenly and inexplicably out of some unknown and unimaginable void; passing half its known life in the mental chaos of sleep; victim even when awake, to its own ill-adjustment, to disease, to age, to external suggestion, to nature's compulsion; doubting its sensations, and, in the last resort, trusting only to instruments and averages—after sixty or seventy years of growing astonishment, the mind wakes to find itself looking blankly into the void of death. That it should profess itself pleased by this performance was all that the highest rules of good breeding could ask; but that it should actually be satisfied would prove that it existed only as idiocy.[3]

Death's imminence, however, did not take from him his spirit's lightness, his blended humility and defiance, and his marvelous curiosity. Among his very last letters was one

[3] This passage by Adams may be interestingly compared with T. S. Eliot's poem "Animula."

dictated to Charles F. Thwing, president of Western Reserve University, who had been one of Adams's scholars years ago at Harvard:

> For myself, I have no longer time to run far—but I would still do the best I could if you could tell me how. . . .
>
> It is astonishing how very little good advice I can get from you old scholars, who should have learned so much from me—in your better days, so that now I am left without a clue to guide me. . . . Literally I do not know where to turn. . . . I fear I shall have to begin again in that garret in University Hall where the venerable Evangelinus Apostolides Sophocles once tried to teach me the Greek tongue, and I believe I shall have to begin again and labor in the pages of Plato for more light than you are willing to bestow upon me. Never mind! I forgive you—I will not bear you a grudge and I will trust that time may still endow you with that wisdom which I tried in vain to shed—forgive *me* too and believe me—
>
> Ever yours. . . .

The date was February 17, 1918; the next day was his eightieth birthday; and he had less than six weeks to live. As the Germans, furnishing one more instance of human energy without civilized direction, prepared their abortive drive on Paris, he sat in Washington trying vainly to forget humanity's debacle in listening to twelfth-century French chansons. They were sung to him by one of his many "nieces in wishes," Miss Aileen Tone, his almost constant companion during the last five years of his life. Together they would take morning walks or afternoon carriage drives beside the river. Often they would visit Marian Hooper Adams's grave, soon to be the site of his own, with its Saint-Gaudens memorial. One day she asked her aged companion to break his silence concerning his wife; after a long pause he complied, and thereafter he referred frequently, with evident pleasure, to "your Aunt Clover." Until the end, his company was prized by all who were near him, including small children.

"Dear child," he said to Miss Tone on his last afternoon, "keep me alive." When they found him in the morning, his face did not suggest death, nor that he had yielded to that mystery which, more audaciously than most men, he had undertaken to define.

I AM no better than a procrastinating cuss and since being married I do less than ever before. Here is another winter gone and I am again nursing nasturtiums and feeding mosquitoes. I am going on to thirty-eight years old, the yawning gulf of middle-age. Another, the fifth, year of professordom is expiring this week. I am balder, duller, more pedantic, and more lazy than ever. I have lost my love of travel. My fits of wrath and rebellion against the weaknesses and shortcomings of mankind are less violent than they were, though grumbling has become my favorite occupation. I have ceased to grow rapidly either in public esteem or in mental development. One year resembles another and if it weren't for occasional disturbing dreams of decay, disaster or collapse, I should consider myself as having attained as much of Nirwana as a man of my race and temperament can expect to do.—To Charles Milnes Gaskell, May 24, 1875

II

Fits of Wrath and Rebellion

A LITTLE reading, a little study, a little smoking, a glass of wine occasionally, a select acquaintance which frowns gently on vice, and various homeopathic doses of negative virtues." So wrote Henry Adams at the age of eighteen, offering a sketch of a "respectable" Harvard student, which to all appearances he was. Already one detects the note of ambivalent irony that was to become, especially when he referred in any way to himself, a stylistic trademark. His essay "My Old Room," from which these phrases are quoted, was published in the *Harvard Magazine* in September, 1856. In the files of this periodical from 1855 to 1858 one finds about a dozen pieces of writing,[1] constituting his earliest preserved literary efforts. Furnishing no evidence of remarkable precocity, and concerned mainly with the transient issues of student life, they call for only brief attention. Summarizing them in *The Young Henry Adams*, Ernest Samuels notes that their author already showed a penchant for "the depiction of character and concern with the fortunes of his ancestors." Like his father before him he was opposed to secret societies ("College Politics," published in May, 1857, delivered a blast

[1] See the bibliography submitted by Ernest Samuels, *The Young Henry Adams*, pp. 313–314. For a brief summary and discussion of these student essays, see *ibid.*, pp. 42–47.

against Greek-letter organizations), and, although he could indicate that he relished many of the active pleasures known to normal youth, he could foreshadow the curse of his declining years by asserting at one point: "Ennui is fearful." One discovers also an early instance of self-depreciation: in "My Old Room" he duly acknowledges some of his own imperfections and mildly repents his failure, along with that of most of his classmates, to take full advantage of his educational chances. Some years were to pass before he would start making sarcastic remarks about the curriculum.

The particular composition of these student days that might draw closest interest is Adams's senior class oration (June 25, 1858), extant but still unpublished. In *The Education* the older author avers to remember nothing of what he said in this piece of eloquence, though he concedes the probable pertinence of comments offered at the time by two of his listeners: first, that, "as the work of so young a man, the oration was singularly wanting in enthusiasm"; and, second, that the orator showed " 'perfect self-possession.' " The summary and the excerpts submitted by Samuels furnish little obvious basis for the first of these comments, though a certain caution in the phrasing may have been accompanied by a matter-of-factness in speaking, so that the total effect became the reverse of ardor. The main theme—which the author of *The Young Henry Adams* summarizes as "the dangers of materialism and the commercial spirit"—was to be a permanent favorite with Henry Adams, though in his maturer writings he was not to express his opposition in the same accents of almost unqualified confidence: "Some of us still persist in believing that there are prizes to be sought in life which will not disgust us in the event of success. . . . There are some who believe that this long education of ours, the best that the land can give, was not meant to be thrown away and forgotten; that this nation of ours furnishes the grandest theatre in the world

42

for the exercise of that refinement of mind and those high principles which it is a disgrace to us if we have not acquired." He concluded that the students so minded "will still put their whole faith in those great truths, to the advancement of which Omnipotence itself has not refused its aid." It was perhaps inevitable that a commencement-day flavor should have attached itself to his remarks; but here, nevertheless, can be found a creed of sincere high-mindedness, a plain repudiation of most of the values ordinarily prized by his countrymen, that remained implicit in the writings and conduct of Henry Adams to the end of his days.

One moves forward two years beyond the Harvard graduation in order to discover some of the more interesting writing, still surviving, of the maturing Henry Adams. After a winter each in Berlin and Dresden, only to become, according to his self-condemnatory account in *The Education,* a "mere tourist," he journeyed down into Italy, writing to his brother Charles a series of reportorial epistles which appeared in the Boston *Daily Courier.* The final pair of these letters, dated respectively June 9 and June 15, 1860, are now fairly accessible, since they were reprinted in the *American Historical Review* for January, 1920. Recording a visit to Palermo shortly after the triumphant investment of that city by Garibaldi and his red-shirts, they possess undoubted historical value; but they are especially worth attention for what they reveal of their author.

Unmistakably touristlike in his fastidiousness, though a bit bolder in his curiosity than tourists are wont to be, the sedate young sport from Boston and Berlin strolled unattended around Palermo a little more than a week after Garibaldi had made his dramatic entry.

It was now comparatively respectable [he records] to what it had been, and the dead bodies and disgusting sights had all been

43

cleared away. After a long detour and [with] a very indefinite idea of my whereabouts, I made my way through all the particularly nasty lanes and alleys I could find, back to the Toledo. For dirt, Palermo is a city equalled by few. I do not know whether I ran any danger of being robbed; indeed it hardly occurred to me that it was possible. I never dreamed of going armed, was all alone, and looked I suppose as if I had just stepped out of the Strand in London, so far as dress went, but no one spoke to me or interfered with me in any way. Possibly Garibaldi may have exercised some influence on the robbers and rascals, for he has them shot as they are taken, and the people occasionally amuse themselves by kicking and stoning them to death. I believe about a dozen have kicked their heels at heaven already by the Dictator's orders.

In the grisly, sophomoric gaiety of the last two sentences, the writer betrays his immaturity; but one finds too, and somewhat more significantly, a perhaps innate disinclination to sympathize in any close way with the enthusiasms of unwashed humanity. With some distaste he speaks of the "armed and howling mob" and records that "the Sicilian common people are famous . . . for being the most brutal and savage crowd known in modern Europe."

More Bostonian than he might have liked to confess, he could not avoid patronizing even the leader whose exploit in capturing a force ten times larger than his own had evoked world-wide astonishment: "Europeans are fond of calling him [Garibaldi] the Washington of Italy, principally because they know nothing about Washington. Catch Washington invading a foreign kingdom on his own hook, in a fireman's shirt! You might as well call Tom Sayers, Sir Charles Grandison." [2]

2 Most readers will readily identify Sir Charles as the perfect-gentleman hero of Samuel Richardson's last novel, *Sir Charles Grandison*. They may wish to be reminded, however, that Tom Sayers was a party to the Sayers-Heenan prize fight, fought to a draw in England, April 17, 1860. Quoting Adams's apt antithesis, Ernest Samuels in *The Young Henry Adams* (p. 71) writes *Jones* for *Sayers*. Though I do not have the file of the Boston *Daily Courier* at hand—

Nevertheless, face to face Adams found Garibaldi impressive for his quiet command of the situation and for his simplicity, which present-day readers may contrast to the obnoxiously infantile bearing of twentieth-century dictators: "He talked with each of us, and talked perfectly naturally; no stump oratory and no sham." There seems to be a touch of juvenile pride in the relation of the climactic personal incident: "I was seated next him, and as the head of our party remarked that I had come all the way from Naples in order to see him, he turned round and took my hand, thanking me as if I had done him a favor. . . ."

On the way to the interview Adams had observed that the square before the Palazzo Municipale was "even rowdier than usual," with a ragamuffin band of musicians playing in it. "Of course the louder they played, the louder the people howled *viva Italia,* and the more chaotic the crowd became. The effect was quite striking, except that it was rather laughable." Always, somewhat in spite of himself, the slightly supercilious observer; always the intellectual. The amazing triumph of Garibaldi was, the writer implies, as much the reward of luck as of genius. When he had entered the heart of Palermo on May 27, 1860, and with 1,500 men had strategically isolated the 23,000 royal troops in several separate positions, "This was a real Garibaldian move, which ought to have cost him his life and the Sicilians their cause; but as it did not, it put the whole game in his hands." Not many youths, one might add, write in accents suggesting so strongly a certain distrust in the principle of free will.

Yet it is mistaken to conclude that Adams, in his early twenties or later, was invariably fatalistic, or that here he was unfriendly to the political change then becoming manifest in Italy. He approved, in general, of this movement that

working instead from the reprint in the *American Historical Review*—I infer that this is simply the kind of slip that a literary scholar can easily make.

seemed to him to be taking place in a definitely "American" direction: "All these Italian troubles reduce themselves simply to a single process, by which one more of the civilized races is forming itself on the ground that we have always declared to be the heart and soul of modern civilization." He could afford to pity the losers, he said, because as an American he was sure of the result. True, after observing "as a traveller, not as an insurgent" the excesses of the Sicilian mob, he expressed misgivings over a proposed popular vote to settle the question of annexation to Piedmont: "These European popular elections have a little too much demonstration in them. . . . If I were a conservative I should wish nothing better than these elections for an argument against and a sarcasm on popular governments in their whole length and breadth." There is almost too much caution in such a remark, but it is the caution of an Adams, believing by inheritance in representative government by an elite; and it is a hint of the insistence, to appear explicitly in the *History of the United States,* that people are to be revered not because biologically they are people but because of an achieved enlightenment which may evoke for them a government and a culture appropriate to their wisdom and virtue.

The events of the next two years in Henry Adams's own country made the Palermo spectacle look like an episode from light opera. Again with the encouragement of his brother Charles, he wrote a series of letters for the press. The first of these issued from Washington during the "Great Secession Winter" of 1860–1861, when Charles Francis Adams spoke for Massachusetts in Congress and strove, with William H. Seward, to avert the break between North and South. As private secretary and social companion to his father, Henry was in a position to be informed. His effort in the letters— which appeared in the Boston *Daily Advertiser* through agreement with the editor, Charles Hale—was to encourage support of the mediatory steps taken by Seward and the elder Adams. In view of the situation, at once delicate and tumultuous, this was far from easy; but he showed unmistakable adroitness. "What impresses the present-day reader," observes Ernest Samuels, "is the aplomb with which Henry at twenty-three skillfully sailed the course plotted by Seward and his father, contriving somehow to tack and run before the wind almost simultaneously." Necessarily, the identity of the author of the letters had to be kept secret, lest the more militant element in the Republican party should make capital of them. At least two influences besides young Henry's sometimes fallible judgment helped to counteract the advice of his brother Charles that the letters should be boldly written: first, the guiding voice of the father ("It was but this morning," wrote Henry on one occasion to Charles, "that C. F. A. cautioned me against writing too freely") and, secondly, the blue pencil and shears of the editor. Repeatedly Hale eliminated passages in which, presumably, he detected the flavor of defamation, and sometimes to the author's vexation he even withheld a letter from publication. When Hale finally came to Washington and himself took over, Henry felt relieved, though his successor assured him he had done well. Samuels notes that the *Advertiser* contributions, even though not printed quite as their author wrote them, "gave proof of Adams' growing literary powers." Some of the characterizations were cuttingly effective, and details were chosen with a just sense of the dramatic.

It is possible, but at this writing far from certain, that Henry Adams was the author of a particularly intriguing literary document relating to events in Washington during these hectic months just before the Civil War: the anonymous *Diary of a Public Man*. Whoever its author, and whatever

47

the date and circumstances of its composition, it became publicly known only as late as 1879, when the *North American Review* printed it in four installments running in the issues from August through November of that year. In 1945 F. Lauriston Bullard edited the *Diary* as a book.[3] Credit for suggesting that it might be the work of Henry Adams must go to Evelyn Page, who observes in an article in the *New England Quarterly* (June, 1949) that the period covered by the *Diary* coincides almost exactly with that of young Adams's presence in Washington. Noting that it has a nicety of organization that would probably not have resulted casually, she inclines to the surmise that the *Diary* is a deliberate, later composition rather than an on-the-spot record and may have been produced by Adams during the late 1870's, when again he was living in Washington and was at work, also, on his biography of Gallatin and the anonymous novel *Democracy*. She finds significance in Adams's penchant for anonymity and feels that a careful stylistic scrutiny of the *Diary* adds plausibility to the guess that Adams wrote it. A sentence in the seventh chapter of *The Education,* referring to errors in judgment that he made at the time of the secession crisis, may have pertinent overtones: "Going over the experience again, long after all the great actors were dead, he struggled to see where he had blundered."

This interesting hypothesis can receive only the briefest

---

[3] *The Diary of a Public Man: An Intimate View of the National Administration December 28, 1860, to March 15, 1861; and a Page of Political Correspondence, Stanton to Buchanan* (Chicago: Privately printed, Abraham Lincoln Bookshop, 1945); with prefatory notes by F. Lauriston Bullard and a foreword by Carl Sandburg. There is also a popular edition (New Brunswick: Rutgers University Press, 1946).

For a detailed consideration of the *Diary* which, without mention of Adams, favors the hypothesis that its author was Samuel Ward, see Frank Maloy Anderson, *The Mystery of "a Public Man": A Historical Detective Story* (Minneapolis: University of Minnesota Press, 1948). Anderson also reprints *The Diary of a Public Man,* pp. 189–249.

discussion here. Supporting Evelyn Page, one may observe again that when young Adams wrote his anonymous series of letters to the Boston *Advertiser* he felt thwarted by Hale's overediting, as well as by the cautions imposed by Charles Francis Adams, Sr. A fuller statement, drawn up many years later, might have helped to alleviate this long-standing dissatisfaction. There is the additional point, under this heading, that Henry wrote an essay entitled "The Great Secession Winter of 1860–1861," presumably destined for the *Atlantic Monthly*, but disgustedly made a gift of it to his brother Charles in April, 1861, observing: "As you will see on reading it over, it is not worth printing." [4]

Whoever wrote the *Diary* would seem to have been well acquainted with Seward and Sumner, as Adams was, and to have entertained essentially the same estimate of them as the one envinced in *The Education*. (Almost an idolater of both men in his youth, Adams thought less highly of them, especially of Sumner, with the passing years.) Though Charles Francis Adams, Sr., was an important figure in Washington during the secession winter, he is mentioned in the *Diary* only once; such reticence in print toward members of his own family is reasonably typical of Henry and would be explainable also, if he is the author, as a calculated avoidance of hints toward his identity. On the other hand, the *Diary* tells of several interviews that its author had at the time with Lincoln; but, except for a perfunctory social encounter at the inaugural ball, Henry Adams and the President did not meet—so says *The Education*. If Adams, however, wrote the *Diary* as a historical *tour de force* almost two decades after its presumed composition—and numerous passages in it compel the conclusion that so he wrote it, if at all—he would have had little

---

[4] See Ernest Samuels, *The Young Henry Adams*, pp. 91–93. The essay was ultimately published as "Washington in 1861," *Proceedings of the Massachusetts Historical Society*, XLIII (1910), 656–689.

49

trouble in borrowing or even fictionizing appropriate episodes. In the *Diary* Lincoln is shown as remembering meeting
its author back in 1848, it is not said where. The author,
however, avers that he does not recollect any such meeting,
though he adds that it "may have been the case." Here a
tantalizing supposition can arise. In September, 1848, Congressman Lincoln campaigned in Massachusetts for the Whigs,
speaking once in Cambridge and twice in Boston as well as
in other cities. At the second gathering in Boston, Seward of
New York also spoke. Not inconceivably, Charles Francis
Adams might have sought to further his sons' political education by taking one or more of them to hear Lincoln and
Seward, though the views offered were opposed to his own,
and Lincoln might have had so distinguished a family group
pointed out to him. He might, indeed, have met them. Henry
would not necessarily have remembered, especially since in
1848, when Henry was ten years old, Lincoln's name meant
virtually nothing. "I certainly recall none of the circumstances," reads part of the *Diary* entry under February 20,
1861, "and can not place him, even with the help of all the
pictures I have seen of such an extraordinary-looking mortal,
as I confess I ought to be ashamed of myself once to have seen
face to face, and to have then forgotten." [5]

Thus, with mounting curiosity, one may speculate pro and
con. It seems to this reader that the stylistic tone of the *Diary*
is not markedly that of Adams, though doubtless he would
have labored, were he the author, to disguise his touch.
Further, it must be admitted that those few sentences sound-
ing like Adams sound very much like Adams, indeed; for
example: "I have been besieged for a week past with letters
and applications asking me every day to see a score of persons whom I hardly know, in order to oblige a score of other

---

[5] *The Diary of a Public Man*, p. 42. The diary of Charles Francis Adams, Sr.,
not available to me, might throw light on this curious little problem.

persons whom, in many cases, I know only too well. It is a shameful and humiliating state of things, none the more tolerable that it was to have been expected." [6]

When the *Diary* appeared serially in the *North American Review,* Adams and his wife were in Europe on an extended stay, collecting materials destined for inclusion in the former's *History.* Conceivably, this circumstance might be cited as lending weight to the theory of Adams's authorship: it would have pleased his wry humor to perpetrate a genteel hoax *in absentia.*

Among Adams's published letters, none is addressed to Allen Thorndike Rice, who was editor of the *North American Review* when the *Diary* was printed in it; nor is there allusion to Rice, or to the *Diary.* It is difficult to suppose, however, that Adams did not know Rice, since the latter bought the *Review* when Adams relinquished its editorship in 1876; also, Rice had been acquainted for many years with Henry Cabot Lodge, Adams's devoted student and his assistant editor.

Necessarily, despite a variety of temptations, one decides that *The Diary of a Public Man* cannot now be included in a list of the ascertained writings of Henry Adams; but the problem of its authorship is of special interest to Adams scholars. It is to be hoped that solid evidence, pointing one way or another, will soon be discovered.

In London, in late May, 1861, as private secretary to Charles Francis Adams, who by this time was American minister to England, Henry began a series of letters to the New York *Times.* The need for secrecy was even more stringent than before, and only the older brother and the editor, Henry J. Raymond, knew the identity of the author. Raymond exercised less censorship, however, than had Charles Hale.

Once more Henry's primary concern was to add strength

[6] *The Diary of a Public Man,* p. 87.

to his father's position, and thus the letters have to do mostly with the precarious problem of England's stand on the American Civil War. Now and again, however, the writer turns aside to afford a glimpse of London social life, though one can detect that he knew it mainly as an onlooker. In his first letter, dated June 7, 1861, he reports that despite the recent death of the Queen's mother, social affairs were continuing with brilliance, as shown, for example, by "the display of wealth and horse flesh in Rotten-row." On June 28 he sums up the results of the Ascot race, adding, "I indulged myself in a holiday for the purpose of seeing it, and as the weather was delightful, and the crowd very gay and summer-like, in muslins and light apparel generally, including thin coats and white hats for the men, nothing was wanting to make the day enjoyable. Those who knew said that the race was a poor one, but one race is generally to ordinary eyes so much like another, that this complaint may be considered the exclusive privilege of the jockeys and turfmen and their imitators."

On July 15: "The Queen held her last drawing-room this week, at which I see, by the way, that Mr. Motley, the historian's, wife and daughter, were presented by our Minister. . . ." This pretense of having learned indirectly something that he must have known firsthand was, of course, a typical bit of subterfuge, whereby Adams hoped to throw off the scent anyone who might try to infer the authorship.

Some passages almost achieve a gossipy, *New Yorkerish* chat. The letter printed July 19, for example, submits an anecdote concerning Monsieur Du Chaillu, author of a popular book on the gorilla ("The gorilla and Adelina Patti have been the great events this Spring"), telling how Du Chaillu spit in the face of "a Mr. Maline, a very disagreeable, unpopular, offensive man. . . ." Of greater interest to later readers, is a sentence or so noting the death of Elizabeth Barrett Browning: "She has been long a helpless invalid, and banished from

England nearly all her life. Indeed, neither she nor her husband were [*sic*] made for this country of fogs and etiquette, and awkward stiffness. They were both of warm and expansive natures, and England is hard and unimpulsive." Such a comment, and a few others like it, sufficiently betray the resentment felt by this young man toward the social coldness that any American felt some of the time in London. He was to nurse it most of his life and air it in *The Education,* though qualifying it there with an enumeration of his English friendships.

The relatively informal, genteel note is struck oftenest in the early letters. As the series proceeds, Henry shows appropriate anxiety at the increasing tolerance shown by the British public and their government for the Southern cause. At first convinced, according to his own report, that the English were making it their pride to stand neutral, though "neutrality in a struggle like this is a disgrace to their great name," he was averring by the end of 1861 that "the English people dislike us, fear us, wish to see our nation crippled, and our free institutions overthrown." The hostility of the London press and public over the Mason and Slidell incident drew forth a dictum that "the phlegmatic and dogmatic Englishman has been dragged into a state of literal madness. . . ." Toward most of the high figures in the British government he was not more gentle, though he perhaps had more respect for the talents of Lord John Russell than he was to show in retrospect in *The Education,* where it is wryly submitted that "Russell proved that he had been feeble, timid, mistaken, senile, but not dishonest." In the *Times* letter published September 24 Adams observed that his Lordship "has again and again disconcerted his colleagues by telling the truth." Palmerston, on the other hand, did not embarrass his government in that fashion. He was only a "wretched imitation of a great man."

53

Writing often in this idiom of reckless disgust, Henry rightly feared that his authorship of the letters might become known. He suddenly terminated the series with the dispatch published on January 4, 1862. The Boston *Daily Courier* had printed his account, "A Visit to Manchester," on the previous December 16, identifying him as the author, though he had asked that his name not be divulged. The result was a mocking pair of editorials in the London *Times*. As *The Education* records, Charles Francis Adams, Sr., necessarily became aware of his son's undiplomatic journalism on the subject of Southern cotton and the Northern blockade [7] but evidently did not learn of the epistolary series to the New York *Times*.

One can agree with Ernest Samuels, as with the implications of Adams's own account in *The Education,* that the New York *Times* letters must have had an effect more adverse than helpful to the American minister's efforts to keep relations between the two countries sensibly friendly. In general, the letters were not temperate and wise. With the event safely past, however, one can relish this rare instance of Henry Adams becoming repeatedly angry and veritably throwing away tact. It is stimulating proof of how little he was the son of his father—praised in *The Education* for his wonderful control, whatever the momentary stress—but seemed to draw instead from the qualities of his grandfather, whom Albert Gallatin had criticized for lacking a sound judgment.

---

7 "A Visit to Manchester—Extracts from a Private Diary" argued that the shutting down of English spinning mills resulted not from a shortage of Southern raw cotton but from a temporary glut of the market. It urged, therefore, that the Northern blockade should be intensified, so that the war might be ended before an actual shortage appeared. The editorial scorn of the London *Times,* however, was especially directed to a paragraph in which Adams rather petulantly praised Manchester society over that of London. The former reminded him of the way things were done in America: "In Manchester, I am told, it is still the fashion for the hosts to see that their guests enjoy themselves." (See Ernest Samuels, *The Young Henry Adams,* pp. 112–118.) "A Visit to Manchester" was reprinted in the *American Historical Review,* LI (October, 1945), 74–89.

To such men as John Quincy Adams and his grandson, each carrying within him a large fund of anger against that in which he disbelieved, only ripest maturity could bring at last the convincing semblance of poise.

Henry Adams's first venture into published scholarly writing was an essay entitled "Captain John Smith," appearing in the January, 1867, issue of the *North American Review,* then edited by Charles Eliot Norton. As candidly admitted in *The Education,* the young man was eager "to make a position for himself," and such an article seemed calculated for an effect, since it struck at the Pocahontas legend, particularly precious to self-conscious exemplars of Virginian chivalry. Adams had done some research on Smith as early as 1861, after hints obtained in conversation from John Gorham Palfrey, author of *A History of New England,* but he owed most to Charles Deane, whose edition of Wingfield's *Discourse of Virginia* contained notes casting doubt on Captain John Smith's veracity. Adams finished a draft of his study in 1862 but laid it aside until 1866, when at Palfrey's urging he revised and sent it to the *North American.*

In essence the article virtually establishes that the famous story of Smith's rescue by Pocahontas is not history but hoax, invented by Smith in his later years, presumably to call attention to himself so that he might mend his tattered fortunes.[8] At least it is highly suspicious that Smith's first account of the incident was that in his *Generall Historie of Virginia,* published in 1624, seven years after the death of the Indian maiden who was said to have laid her head upon his when the clubs of her father's warriors were about to fall. In his

[8] The reader may wish to consult William Wirt Henry's defense of John Smith in the *Proceedings of the Virginia Historical Society* at the annual meeting, February 24, 1882, cited by Harold Dean Cater in *Henry Adams and His Friends,* p. 41 n.

True Relation (1608) and subsequent writings, published before 1624, Smith had not mentioned the episode.

In a letter to Palfrey, March 20, 1862, Adams was apologetic about devoting himself to a "literary toy" when the Civil War had placed mightier questions at stake, but he explained gloomily that "my pen is forced to keep away from political matters, unless I want to bring the English press down on my head again, and in society I am a failure." Then more brightly: "So perhaps the thing is excusable, especially as it is in some sort a flank, or rather a rear attack, on the Virginia aristocracy. . . ." The essay made his purpose clear in this regard by initially stating, in effect, a proposal to follow Charles Deane in an argument "which aims at nothing less than the entire erasure of one of the most attractive portions of American history."

Adams always retained an affection for his monograph on Smith and Pocahontas, revising it for inclusion in *Chapters of Erie and Other Essays* (1871) and giving it further revision for its appearance in *Historical Essays* (1891). In the final version he eliminated most of the first two pages of the essay as it had been printed a quarter-century earlier, thus toning down the challenge to Southern bluebloods. For the rest, he simplified and strengthened the phrasing. A comparison of parallel passages from the two versions is offered here as instructive in showing how Adams imposed an increasing stylistic discipline upon himself as he grew older:

1867	*1891*
Captain John Smith belonged to that extraordinary school of adventurers who gave so much lustre to the reign of Elizabeth, and whose most bril-	Captain John Smith belonged to the extraordinary school of adventurers who gave so much lustre to the reign of Elizabeth, and whose most

liant leader it was one of King James's exploits to bring to the Tower and the block. Like Raleigh, though on a much lower standard, Smith sustained many different characters; he was a soldier or a sailor indifferently, a statesman when circumstances gave him power, and an author when the occasion required. He was born in Lincolnshire in 1579, of what is supposed to have been a good Lancashire family. At a very early age he became a soldier of fortune in the Low Countries, and seems to have drifted into the Austrian service, where, in the year 1600, he took part in the campaign against the Turks. Afterwards he reappears as a soldier of the Prince of Transylvania, who gave him a coat of arms, which was registered at the Herald's College in London. The extraordinary adventures which he met with during the three or four years of his life in Eastern Europe, are related in his Autobiography, or "True Travels," a work published in London in 1630, near the close of his life. There is an interesting note in Dr. Palfrey's History of New England (Vol. I, pp. 89–92) which contains an

brilliant leader King James brought to the Tower and the block. Like Raleigh, though on a much lower level, Smith sustained many different characters. He was a soldier or a sailor indifferently, a statesman when circumstances gave him power, and an author when occasion required. Born in Lincolnshire in 1579, of what is supposed to have been a good Lancashire family, at a very early age he became a soldier of fortune in the Low Countries, and drifted into the Austrian service, where he took part in the campaign of 1600 against the Turks. Afterward he reappeared as a soldier of the Prince of Transylvania, who gave him a coat-of-arms, which was registered at the Herald's College in London. His extraordinary adventures during the three or four years of his life in Eastern Europe were related in his Autobiography, or "True Travels," a work published in London in 1630, near the close of his life. Dr. Palfrey's History of New England contains the earliest critical examination of this portion of Smith's story from an historical and geographical point of view, with a examination for the first time of this portion of Smith's story from an historical and geographical point of view, with a result not on the whole unfavorable to Smith, although with reservations which admit a considerable degree of doubt as to particulars. In the absence of other authorities, however, the credit of the Autobiography must be left to stand or fall with that of the Generall Historie.

result not on the whole unfavorable to Smith.[1]

[1] Palfrey's History of New England, i. pp. 89–92, note.

The two passages help to demonstrate that Adams practiced the counsel almost invariably given to people who questioned him on the art of composition: to delete all except the essential. ("When you come to writing," he wrote in 1904 to Sarah Hewitt, "I can recommend only one rule:—Strike out relentlessly every superfluous word.") It is true, as Ernest Samuels points out, that Adams's early style was sometimes "excessively judicial and stately"; that in his essay, "British Finance in 1816," which soon followed the article on Captain Smith, the prose rhythms now and then seem to suggest Junius and Burke; and that, in the mode of his beloved eighteenth century, he showed a partiality for the periodic and the balanced sentence. Yet it remains true that his literary development followed a discernible path of clear, concise expression that did not turn aside into rhetorical bypaths. The final reward was to be the remarkable control apparent on the pages of *Chartres* and *The Education*.

An itemized, exhaustive survey of all of Adams's earlier writings is, of course, not within the scope of this study. Most of his essays published from 1867 to 1871 were reprinted, as noted of "Captain John Smith," after a revision that did not fundamentally affect them, in *Chapters of Erie* and/or *Historical Essays;* and the serious reader may supplement his own perusal of them with the analysis offered by Samuels in *The Young Henry Adams.* A pair of articles on British financial policy during the Napoleonic period are significant because they mark Henry's debut as an amateur economist and indicate the range of his mind. Written as much to instruct Americans in the wisdom of promptly resuming specie payments as to give exposition to a dramatic chapter in English financial history, they underline the author's endorsement of his family's traditional monetary views. They also show a signal talent for the lucid exposition of a technical subject.

More pertinent, however, to an understanding of Henry Adams's mind and thought is the less available essay on geology that appeared in the *North American Review* for October, 1868. Specifically a review and criticism of the tenth edition of Sir Charles Lyell's *Principles of Geology,* it has not yet been reprinted, though its readability and its philosophic implications give it more than a restricted interest, especially if read in conjunction with the chapter on Darwinism in *The Education.*

Adams opens his essay with a Latin quotation that doubtless his readers of 1868 found more familiar than do most today: " 'Nunc naturalem causam quaerimus, et assiduam, non raram et fortuitam.—In the economy of the world, I can see no traces of a beginning, no prospect of an end.' Dr. [Charles] Hutton used this language in announcing his famous theory of the earth eighty years ago." Though Hutton was vehemently cried down by pious-minded critics, Lyell in 1830 reasserted and developed his pronouncement, so that it became in a sense the basis of geologists' indifference to the problem of first causes; their assumption, in other words, that the natural influences now at work have always been so and will continue. One may add that here, also, would seem to be a clue to the older Adams's method when he tried to work out a dynamic theory of history: to the extent that it was mathematical and scientific, it did not require its proponent to speculate about ultimate origins. Probably the positivism of Auguste Comte, to which Adams as a young man adhered "within the limits of evolution," also exerted a lifelong influence.

This is not to suppose erroneously that when Adams's mind was not held voluntarily within the strict limits of the "scientific" method, it could not range boldly over metaphysical problems. It would do this in *Mont-Saint-Michel and Chartres;* and, indeed, its penchant in this respect can be observed in the Lyell review, though Adams here insisted—with somewhat greater emphasis than he would in later years— that speculation had to be tested in the light of whatever facts were at hand. "The more geology is studied," he wrote, "the more its incompleteness becomes obvious; it cannot make progress without theorizing, yet few of its theories have the proper number of legs to run upon; the facts, if not contradictory, are wanting." Thus he challenged Sir Charles in his effort to account for periods of glaciation by supposing an oscillation of the land-sea proportions at the poles and equator: "So far as there is any evidence at hand, both the depression of land and its subsequent emergence about the pole . . . took place directly in reverse of what the theory requires." Similarly Adams questioned another attempt by his author to explain glacial phenomena: the hypothesis, drawn from James Croll, that the orbit of the earth had been eccentric enough to take it as much as 14,500,000 miles farther from the sun than at other periods. Though Adams admired the brilliance and boldness of Agassiz's glacial theory, which Sir Charles had been slow to accept, he could not conclude that more had been proved than that "astonishing revolutions in climate have taken place. . . ." There remained the question of "why they have taken place, and how often." [9]

To one who had read *The Education,* it is not surprising to find in this Lyell review that the young Adams was interested in Sir Charles's attempt to calculate the age of organic life by noting the cycles of testacea. Observing the tentativeness of Lyell's estimate of 240,000,000 years as the limit of life on earth, Adams adds, "Nevertheless we may hope that scientific data for a closer calculation may possibly be discovered, and, were this once effected, that another step would enable science to fix the limits within which species have flourished, and the race of man among the rest may expect to carry on its development."

Adams concludes with a suggestion that American geologists and physiologists, adopting Lamarck's hypothesis of the transmutation of acquired characteristics ("a purely scientific matter, about which we shall certainly not venture to express an opinion"), may throw "light upon the early history of the human race, if not absolutely upon its origin. . . ."

Lyell himself was pleased with the searching, informed quality of the review, calling it the best one that had been written about his book. As symbol of his appreciation and friendship, his field compass was eventually sent to Henry.

Perhaps more than any other single piece of writing by the younger Adams, this criticism of Lyell's *Principles* looks forward to his later attitudes. Here is the careful examination into "facts," to the extent that they can be known; but here also is the candid recognition, so rare in disciplined thinkers,

---

[9] I find myself disagreeing on this point with Ernest Samuels, who feels that Adams reproached "Sir Charles' reluctance to be swept off his feet by Agassiz's glacial theory . . ." and ". . . continued to subordinate science to conventional metaphysics as completely as did Agassiz himself." To my reading Adams finds grandeur but not finality in what Samuels terms "Agassiz's curious mélange of theology and science" and did not endorse it without qualification any more than Lyell did.

that when the facts cease to be available, the mind and imagination may still venture forward in search of that synthesis which an exalted human curiosity demands. In short, with truth elusive, convenience must be made to serve, while the critical faculty stands coolly ready at need to maintain the possible distinction between the two. It was the aspiration of Henry Adams, not clearly stated until he reached old age, to discover that the "rational" and "irrational" approaches to the mystery of universal reality were not fundamentally different, in that ideally both could reach the same triumphant end: that of an unassailable unity "tying all suns and stars and worlds in one." And in this aspiration, never to be quite fully realized, lay implicit much of the torment of his spirit.

In the sixteenth chapter of *The Education,* entitled "The Press," Adams states that in the fall of 1868, several months after his return to America, he deliberately started to execute a plan formulated in England to become a journalist. What he needed, he says, was a New York daily, "and no New York daily needed him. He lost his one chance by the death of Henry J. Raymond." Raymond, however, was still living at this time: his editorship of the *Times* continued until he was fatally stricken with cerebral hemorrhage in June of the following year; probably he would have welcomed the young writer whose energy, integrity, and talent he already knew. It is possible, of course, that had Raymond lived, Adams would later have applied to him; nevertheless, one surmises that the young Adams was not as eager to become a member of the fourth estate in New York as the older Adams records. It is difficult, as a matter of fact, to imagine him adjusting himself to the hourly hurly-burly that work on a metropolitan newspaper even then entailed; and it was a family habit to gravitate toward the nation's capital.

In any event Adams went not to New York but to Washington, where the government was embarking on one of the least savory political regimes in the nation's history. Had he discovered the kind of administration he hoped for, and had he been offered a post in it, he might soon have forsaken journalistic aspirations for a career like that of his forebears; but the event as proved made him a free-lance opposition writer for two years, until he returned to Cambridge to teach history at Harvard and to edit the *North American*.

The titles of some of the articles written during this residence in Washington [10] indicate the direction of his efforts. "American Finance, 1865–1869," published in the *Edinburgh Review*, condemned Congress for not ordering the resumption of specie payments, sharply criticized the tax system, denounced the corruption of the tariff, and called for a thoroughgoing political cleansing. "Civil Service Reform," printed by the *North American*, summoned the people to disregard party organization and insist upon a return to the constitutional principle of the separation of powers, so that the spoils system could be killed. "The New York Gold Conspiracy" was refused by both the *Edinburgh Review* and the *Quarterly*, whose editors feared libel suits, and it finally appeared in the *Westminster Review*. Offering a careful but outraged account of the financial machinations of Jay Gould and James Fisk, whereby the former almost cornered the nation's supply of gold, it remains readable as a commentary on the ethical sordidness of the Gilded Age.

By the time Adams wrote the second installment of his Congressional survey called "The Session" (*North American Review*, July, 1870), he had gained an audience aware of his fearlessness and his gift for invective. As he reports in *The Education*, "The Session" was conceived as a frank imitation

[10] For a more detailed account of Adams's free-lance journalism than can be given here, see, again, Ernest Samuels, *The Young Henry Adams*, pp. 168–207, *passim*.

of Lord Robert Cecil's series of the same name, appearing in the *London Quarterly* as an annual review of politics; but the matter and style of the American adaptation belonged to Adams. The first installment, published in the *North American Review* for April, 1869, had defined the obligation of the Senate to return the numerous powers recently taken over from the executive and had asserted the need for a widely ramifying governmental reform. The second "Session" recorded the failure of Grant to live up to the expectations of those who had elected him. Thoughtful citizens had supposed, Adams protested with an innocence probably excessive, that with the termination of civil war the federal government would return to the states those reserved rights that it had taken over during the emergency. Only by so doing could it be faithful to a fundamental concept of the American founding fathers: that absolute power should not be permitted to arise in the land, whether in government or elsewhere. Grant, however, had shown himself ignorant of such a concept; he set up no affirmative policy whatever; and he surrounded himself with advisers unable or indisposed to make good the President's lack. Boutwell of the Treasury was particularly inept. "Mr. Boutwell had neither the wish nor the scope to assume the functions or to wield the power of his office; and instead of stamping upon the President and his administration the impress of a controlling mind, he drew himself back into a corner of his own, and encouraged and set the example of isolation at a time when concentrated action was essential to the Executive." So government settled more deeply than ever into its rut of patronage and corruption, and reform became a lost hope. Reconstruction was carried on with measures violative of the Constitution, with the result that "the powers originally reserved by the Constitution to the States are in future to be held by them only on good behavior and at the sufferance of Congress. . . ." By direct appeal to the people, proponents of reform managed to exert pressure so that tariff legislation was not consistently dictated by special interests; but revenue reform was impossible, and the attempt to pack the Supreme Court after its decision that the Legal-Tender Act went beyond the powers of Congress shocked every decent observer. In foreign affairs, the conflict between legislative and executive helped to strengthen Adams's bitter contention that government had ceased to govern. Attempts at betterment could only be pathetic. "While the reformers in Congress rejoice at carrying a small reduction on pig-iron, or regret the omnipotence of the steel lobbyists, they turn about in their seats and create by a single stroke of special legislation a new Pacific railway,—an imperishable corporation with its own territory, an empire within a republic, more powerful than a sovereign state, and inconsistent with the purity of Republican institutions or with the safety of any government, whether democratic or autocratic. While one monopoly is attacked, two are created. . . . The people require it, and even if the people were opposed, yet with the prodigious development of corporate and private wealth resistance must be vain." By prophetic implication he was agreeing with the observation to be made a half-century later by his brother Brooks in the introduction to *The Degradation of the Democratic Dogma,* that the tragic fallacy of John Quincy Adams had been that of supposing "that it is possible by education to stimulate the selfish instinct of competition, which demands that each man should strive to better himself at the cost of his neighbor, so as to coincide with the moral principle that all should labor for the common good." Henry Adams, like most of the other members of his family, was never to yield to either big government or big business anything but hearty detestation.

"The Session" concluded with the gloomy, eloquently stated conviction that the constitutional system of reserved powers had already submitted to the pressures of necessity, and that, in turn, "the system of separate responsibility realized in the mechanism of the American government" inevitably would submit too. A new theory for working out the problems of human society had to be evolved—a task for many generations.

Thus here again one finds presaged the Adams of *The Education:* a deeply informed, patriotic observer disgusted with the sundry ineptitudes of his countrymen and their willful flaunting of the founding ideals; an embittered prophet allegedly resigned to the coming of evil days; yet a prophet moved by an active indignation canceling out the possibility of indifference to the problems of the society into which he had been born.

For the next few years Adams's protestantism assumed a new pattern. As editor of the *North American Review* from 1870 to 1876, he tried to make that journal an implement for reform, whatever the misgivings concerning such effort voiced in "The Session." In *The Education* he laments that "for seven years he wrote nothing" and goes on to assert that "the *Review* lived on his brother Charles's railway articles." As editor, Adams could find no writer, he records—this time with anything but self-deprecation—to take his own place as a commentator on politics and other current affairs. Thus the quarterly *Review,* at that time still the first literary power in America, "became chiefly historical," and the editor "became an authority on advertising."

Characteristically, the older Adams is here belittling the achievements of the younger. Charles wrote not only about railways but about currency, and, in collaboration with Charles F. Wingate, helped to expose the Tweed Ring in New York. Brooks Adams, whose subsequent career as a writer was to show in him the forthrightness and intellectual penetration to be expected from one of his family, contributed an article ("The Platform of the New Party," July, 1874) on civil service reform. Among others who wrote for the various issues of the magazine were David A. Wasson, Francis A. Walker, David A. Wells, Simon Newcomb, J. L. Diman, William Graham Sumner, C. F. Dunbar, Daniel Coit Gilman, James Russell Lowell, and Francis Turner Palgrave. The last two helped Adams "to keep it literary"; but certainly the *Review* was less a genteel organ than an index to enlightened opinion. Fearlessly and consistently, it castigated corruption.

Henry himself wrote occasional reviews, about twenty-five in all, mostly of historical books. In his final number (October, 1876), however, he joined his brother Charles in composing "The Independents in the Canvass," an essay whose liberalism so affronted the publishers, Osgood and Houghton, that they disavowed the whole issue. Disillusioned with a campaign that had ended in the nomination of Rutherford B. Hayes, the brothers denounced the Republican party for yielding to the ascendancy of "as loud-mouthed and repulsive a set of political vagabonds as ever canted about principles or hungered after loaves and fishes." The Democratic party was not much better, but at least, in choosing Samuel J. Tilden, it had nominated its leading reformer. By implication, independent voters were urged to vote for Tilden. Adams took advantage of the publishers' displeasure to sever his connections with the *North American*. During the period of his editorship, the circulation of the magazine had doubled. Before long it was purchased by Allen Thorndike Rice, who moved its offices from Boston to New York and presently made it a monthly.

Once more Adams was savoring the bitterness of unrequited striving. Unable to tolerate an unopposed plundering of American democracy, he had been mainly responsible for the calling of a conference of Independents in New York City, April 27, 1875. Attended by E. L. Godkin, J. D. Cox, Samuel

Bowles, Charles Nordhoff, and others, this meeting produced a plan of action. The key figure among the Independents was Carl Schurz, who for a time urged that the group should try to compel the nomination of Charles Francis Adams, Sr., by one of the major parties. As it became clear, however, that the elder Adams had no relish for such a role and, further, that he lacked public backing, the Independents concluded to support Benjamin H. Bristow. Bristow was not an Independent, but as Secretary of the Treasury he had shown respectability by attacking the "Whiskey Ring." Adams organized a syndicate to purchase the Washington *Post,* which would be the journalistic weapon of the Independents. Horace White, Charles Nordhoff, Francis Walker, and Carl Schurz were successively asked to accept the prospective editorship.

All this, of course, came to nothing. Bristow lost out in the caucus, the newspaper was never purchased, and Schurz returned to party traces to support Hayes, receiving as eventual reward the secretaryship of the Interior. Though Adams could still express hope in the October *North American* that the Independents would continue active after the election, whoever the winner, and would insist that promised changes be carried out, his despairing annoyance with them appeared in the observation that after the nominations they "resembled nothing so much as a group of discreetly clad clergymen caught out in a thunder-storm without any umbrellas."

It was, for him, the end of another chapter, one in which he had proved—to anyone sufficiently sympathetic to make the observation—that he had high energy and could be a person of action. His efforts had been devoted, however, to the languishing cause of intelligence and decency in politics, and the upshot was inescapable. He was satisfied, he wrote to his assistant editor and student, Henry Cabot Lodge, that things could not be changed much in his generation. "When the day comes on which it will be considered as disgraceful to be seen in a caucus as to be seen in a gambling house or brothel, then my interest will wake up again and legitimate politics will get a new birth."

He was tired of being an editor, and he was tired of Harvard. He had learned much as a teacher, and his pretense, set forth in *The Education,* that he had taught his pupils nothing has permanent rebuttal in the volume *Essays in Anglo-Saxon Law* (1876), which collects the scholarship of his graduate students and offers one of his own studies, "Anglo-Saxon Courts of Law." Another product of this period was *Documents Relating to New England Federalism,* a volume which he edited in 1877, mainly as a labor of love in behalf of his grandfather, since it consisted for the most part of a documented vindication of John Quincy Adams from the slanderous accusations of some of his Massachusetts enemies—a vindication that the old President himself had written but never published. Certainly, many of Henry's labors at Harvard had not been empty of reward. Nevertheless, he could feel the force of an observation he was to make many years later: that ten years as a college professor would disqualify one from being anything else. Not that he could foresee or desire, under the circumstances, anything other than that "quiet literary life" which at twenty he had defined as his ideal. Possibly only another college professor is able to realize, as some of the ungowned critics are not, that one seldom discovers a quiet literary life in an academic squirrel cage, fashioned in part by trustees, regents, or other administrators who often have little but self-conceit to fortify them for regulating minds better than their own. Adams's decision in 1877 to avail himself of his independent income, and that of his wife, and leave Cambridge for Washington, there to pursue according to his own schedule the scholarly tasks that interested him most, was not spectacular or heroic, but it was reasonable. And in Washington the happiest eight years of his life lay before him.

69

I'VE been trying to read my brother Charles's Life of our father. Now I understand why I refused so obstinately to do it myself. These biographies are murder, and in this case, to me, would be both patricide and suicide. They belittle the victim and the assassin equally. They are like bad photographs and distorted perspectives. Luckily no one knows the difference, and the modern public is as dead to the feeling of historical atmosphere as it is to the color of the Chartres windows. I have sinned myself, and deeply, and am no more worthy to be called anything, but, thank my diseased and dyspeptic nervous wreck, I did not assassinate my father.—To Elizabeth Cameron, March 5, 1900

III

Photographs and Perspectives

The Life of Albert Gallatin

IN 1877, his last year as Harvard professor and editor of the *North American Review,* Henry Adams came into possession of the letters and papers left by Albert Gallatin to his son. Supplementing them with material from the government archives and elsewhere, Adams edited a three-volume edition of Gallatin's *Writings* and wrote a one-volume *Life.* All four volumes were published in Philadelphia in 1879.

Of the reviews that greeted *The Life of Albert Gallatin,* many contained unfavorable comment, while acknowledging that an impressive amount of information was presented. Characteristically affecting indifference, Adams nevertheless admitted (in a letter to young Henry Cabot Lodge) that he was irked at the ignorance and unfairness of the reviewers. None of them knew anything of the subject except, obviously, what they had learned from the book they were reviewing; one can urge for them that there was almost no other source from which they might have learned, but they could have been honest enough to say so; and when in January, 1880, the New York *Nation* stated that in the field of American history the only volume worth noting for the year just past was a translation of von Holst, Adams protested to E. L. Godkin, editor of that magazine, that he felt hurt.

Time has justified the author. Historians of such rank as David S. Muzzey, James Truslow Adams, and Henry Steele Commager point out that the Gallatin biography has been authoritative from the moment it appeared, and that there is slight chance it will be superseded. Indeed, Commager designates it as probably the supreme work of political biography in this country. One can say further of it that, apart from its strictly literary qualities, which are high, it deserves distinguished rank as an American document. The hundreds of letters and official utterances contained in it prove impressively that Albert Gallatin in his quiet way was a great man, and, one may add, a particularly valuable American, though in his day his political enemies shamefully made what capital they could out of his Genevan birth and rearing. An appreciation of his character and career as Congressman, Secretary of the Treasury, and diplomat ought to be a constructive part of the national heritage, and it is not to the nation's credit that he has been virtually forgotten. It is not the fault of Henry Adams.

That *Gallatin* has been reprinted but once may be only an unfortunate accident. More likely, however, it reflects the fact that to the unscholarly reader the book presents a formidable solidity, which many of the early reviewers mistook, out of their own ineptitude, for dullness. "The book," lamented a writer in the *Nation*, "resembles in appearance a volume of cyclopedia—it measures nearly ten inches by six, and weighs nearly four pounds." [1] Actually the book is not stupendous, and its solidity derives, of course, not from its bulk but from its contents and method. Rejecting the casual narrative tech-

[1] Evidently this reviewer, who did not append his name, was Charles Francis Adams, Jr., writing partly in brotherly amusement. Whether the irked Henry ever learned the writer's identity is not known. See Evelyn Page, " 'The Man Around the Corner': An Episode in the Career of Henry Adams," *New England Quarterly*, XXIII (Sept., 1950), 401–403.

nique of most historical biographers of his period, Adams chose the one that would keep him closest to his subject: that of letting Gallatin, wherever possible, tell his own story and present his own ideas through private and official letters. Thus Adams became the first important American biographer to write objectively and pointed the way to a discountenancing of the excessively laudatory style popularized by George Bancroft and other relatively uncritical authors.

Not that Adams lacked admiration for his subject.

To do justice to Gallatin [wrote Adams to Samuel Jones Tilden] was a labor of love. After long study of the prominent figures in our history, I am more than ever convinced that for combination of ability, integrity, knowledge, unselfishness, and social fitness Mr. Gallatin has no equal. He was the most fully and perfectly equipped statesman we can show. Other men, as I take hold of them, are soft in some spots and rough in others. Gallatin never gave way in my hand or seemed unfinished. That he made mistakes I can see, but even in his blunders he was respectable.

I cannot say as much for his friends Jefferson, Madison, and Monroe, about whom I have been for years hard at work. In regard to them I am incessantly forced to devise excuses and apologies or to admit that no excuse will avail.

It is perhaps typical of Adams's restraint that in this passage he does not compare Gallatin with either John or John Quincy Adams. In the book, however, he does not hesitate to show, as he must, his grandfather and great-grandfather in their historical roles, often in a light less than glorious. Nor does his respect for Gallatin seem much affected by that statesman's occasional criticism of Adams's forebears. "Mr. Adams left the city yesterday at four o'clock in the morning," wrote Gallatin to his wife, concerning the outgoing President's embittered refusal to attend Jefferson's inauguration. "You can have no idea of the meanness, indecency, almost insanity, of

his conduct, specially of late." Henry Adams leaves this remark without specific rebuttal,[2] though on the next page he
observes that "the new political force of which Mr. Jefferson
was the guide had no word of sympathy for the vanquished"
and adds that Gallatin "had yet to pass through his twelve
years of struggle and disappointment in order to learn how
his own followers and his own President were to answer his
ideal, when the same insolence of foreign dictation and the
same violence of a recalcitrant party presented to their and
to his own lips the cup of which John Adams was now drain-
ing the dregs." Later pages reveal the courage and dignity,
however, with which Gallatin ultimately met defeat and disillusion. In this respect he seems to have been a more finely
poised person than either Thomas Jefferson or, one infers,
the fiery John Adams.

Of Henry Adams's grandfather, Gallatin wrote to Jean
Badollet: "John Q. Adams is a virtuous man, whose temper,
which is not the best, might be overlooked; he has very great
and miscellaneous knowledge, and he is with his pen a powerful debater; but he wants to a deplorable degree that most
essential quality, a sound and correct judgment." Gallatin
goes on to say that he has had complete and repeated proofs
of this serious defect in John Quincy Adams. The comment
would seem to apply, however, to John Quincy's treatment
of people, rather than to his weighing of ideas. Gallatin may
have had especially in mind his experience with Adams at
Ghent in 1814, when both served on the commission that
conferred with the British in drawing up the treaty of peace
for the War of 1812. Several quarrels by the impetuous young

[2] In the second volume of the *History,* Adams was to comment as follows: "In
Jefferson's eyes a revolution had taken place as vast as 1776; and if this was his
belief, perhaps the late President was wise to retire from a stage where everything was arranged to point a censure upon his principles, and where he would
have seemed, in his successor's opinion, as little in place as George III would
have appeared at the installation of President Washington."

Adams with the equally impetuous young Henry Clay, also a member of the commission, came near to wrecking the negotiations. Only the steady head and temper of Gallatin achieved compromise and saved the day. The Treaty of Ghent was Gallatin's triumph, and Henry Adams accords him full honor for it, though it may be added that John Quincy Adams had also paid tribute to Gallatin's qualities. Indeed no one ever recognized more clearly than John Quincy himself that his indignation sometimes overrode his calmness, and one of the best sources of information about the internecine bickerings at Ghent is his own diary and letters. It may be added, too, that in their old age Albert Gallatin and John Quincy Adams were mutual admirers and warm friends. The differences between them were, in many ways, those naturally arising between a calm realist with high standards and an uncompromising, explosive idealist.

To one in some respects more interested in the author than in his subject, *Gallatin* is worth careful reading for reasons apart from historical study; it reveals its author's own attitudes and ideals. It is doubtless but another sign of Adams's atypicality that, for a model of political and personal conduct, he should select not a New Englander but a Pennsylvanian; furthermore, a Pennsylvanian who had once been so roundly despised by New Englanders that one of the resolutions of the famous Hartford Convention had been aimed specifically against him. Though it would be extravagant to say that the older man was the *alter ego* of the younger, it is inescapable that much of what Henry Adams believed and felt, both at the time he wrote the book and later, had already been believed and felt by Albert Gallatin.

Both men, for example, were quiet and thoughtful and showed a tendency toward constant self-depreciation. Despite his astounding capacity for work, Gallatin accused himself of a constitutional indolence that "makes me more fit to think than to act." Similarly, Adams berates himself in *The Educa-tion* for his hesitation, even as a small boy, "to act except as a choice of evils" and avers that as a young man he "had no need to learn from Hamlet the fatal effect of the pale cast of thought on enterprises great or small."

With the same strength as that shown in John and John Quincy Adams, both men held to an a priori belief in the need for absolute honesty, in government as in private life. Gallatin's attachment to the Jeffersonian dogma of a small and weak central government as insurance against tyranny had already had, ten years before the biography appeared, a perhaps accidental echo in Adams's pair of essays on Con-gress entitled "The Session." Like Gallatin, Adams was a small-navy man and, again like Gallatin, he was opposed to tariff legislation. When the controversy over gold and silver reached its climax in the 1890's, Adams surprised some of his friends by standing up for bimetallism. Brooks Adams ob-serves that his brother Henry had "instincts" that inclined him toward silver; Henry may have been influenced, too, by the fact that Brooks's historical studies led the same way. It may be noted in addition, however, that bimetallism was the economic doctrine of Albert Gallatin.

Both men, shy of revealing themselves emotionally, favored understatement. Adams has been criticized for writing of his future wife, to his friend Gaskell, with such apparent lack of ardor: "She is certainly not handsome; nor would she be quite called plain, I think. She is twenty-eight years old. . . . Her manners are quiet. She reads German—also Latin—also, I fear, a little Greek, but very little. She talks garrulously, but on the whole pretty sensibly. She is very open to instruction. . . . She dresses badly. She decidedly has humor and will appreciate *our* wit." There is no reason to presume that when Adams wrote this, in March, 1872, he had yet read Gallatin's remarks made in similar circumstances, and so the parallel in tone is especially noteworthy: "I am contracted with a girl about twenty-five years old, who is neither handsome nor rich, but sensible, well-informed, good-natured. . . ." The young lady, Hannah Nicholson, was Gallatin's second wife. At the loss of his earlier wife he had suffered the sense of desolation that his biographer was to experience in 1885 at the sudden death of Marian Hooper Adams.

"Social amusements . . . Mr. Gallatin regarded very much as he did good wine or good cooking,—things desirable in themselves, but ending with the momentary gratification." Adams might well have made this observation of himself, adding that both he and his subject found congenial companionship almost a necessity. Probably Gallatin's most enjoyable years were those he spent as a diplomat in Paris savoring the talk of such men as Alexander von Humboldt, Alexander Baring (Lord Ashburton), and Pozzo di Borgo. One thinks of Adams's satisfaction in the company of men like John Hay, Clarence King, and Cecil Spring-Rice.

The most impressive similarity between Gallatin and Adams, however, was one that the latter must have begun to sense when he was writing the biography. He must have perceived that Gallatin's fall, in 1813, from political position, and the ruination of his ideals offered a curious likeness to the blasting two generations later of young Henry Adams's political hopes by the administration of President Grant. In the second instance as in the first, the personal failure could be called "the result of forces which neither he nor any other man or combination of men . . . could control." He might have reflected, also, that the reactions of the two men to the spectacle of government being run in deference to ideals that they detested was curiously similar. Both essentially quit the field and cultivated scholarly obsessions: Gallatin to become the father of American ethnology and Adams to become a leading historian. Adams could only have guessed, however, that with the deepening of time he was to feel even more keenly than Gallatin that isolation which is perhaps the inevitable plight of the sensitive modern mind. Already Adams had learned, as Gallatin's life seemed to prove, that opportunity and circumstances have more influence toward giving weight to a man and rendering him useful to his time than talents alone. But like his predecessor he was to discover that frustration and disillusion may be partially combated by an assertion of private integrity and by a rigorous defining of one's own position in a world he never made.

As a further parallelism, which time was to reveal, one may note that Gallatin's faculties grew sharper as he grew older. The period of his intellectual prime, asserts his biographer, came after his seventieth year (he lived to be eighty-eight). Even before his retirement from government he had conceded the defeat of his hopes, born out of the French Enlightenment and the democratic aspirations that animated the first years of Thomas Jefferson's administration; and as he observed events his disillusion deepened. Certain passages in his later letters seem almost prophetic of *The Education of Henry Adams*. In 1834 he speaks of

this most energetic country, where the strong in mind and character overset everybody else, and where consideration and respectability are not at all in proportion to virtue and modest merit. Yet I am so identified with the country which I served so long that I cannot detach myself from it. I find no one who suffers in mind as I do at the corruption and degeneracy of our government. . . . There is something wrong in the social state.

"But," he added, "I do not despair. . . ." As his physical strength declined, his intellect became more excitable. "I am a bold speculator," he said defiantly a few months before his death. "Such has been the habit of my mind all my life long." Only readers coming late can appreciate how, in his unfailing

PHOTOGRAPHS, PERSPECTIVES

zest for understanding, in his contemptuous but not utterly despondent estimate of society's condition, in his loneliness, and in his open-eyed acceptance of the joy and tragedy of individual existence, Albert Gallatin pointed the path that his biographer would follow.

John Randolph

"I am bored to death," wrote Adams to John Hay in September, 1882, "by correcting the proofs of a very dull book about John Randolph, the fault of which is in the enforced obligation to take that lunatic monkey *au serieux.* I want to print some of his letters and those of his friends, and, in order to do so, was obliged to treat him as though he were respectable."

A month later he complained again to Hay: "Do you know, a book to me always seems a part of myself, a kind of intellectual brat or segment, and I never bring one into the world without a sense of shame. . . . This particular brat is the first I ever detested. He is the only one I never wish to see again; but I know he will live to dance, in the obituaries, over my cold grave. Don't read him, should you by chance meet him. Kick him gently, and let him go."

It is the usual needless self-depreciation. *John Randolph* is scarcely dull: it would be difficult, indeed, to write an utterly dull book about the man who was probably the most startling figure ever to appear upon the American political stage. Nevertheless, Adams's lack of warmth for his subject can be detected on practically every page. If *Gallatin* was a labor of love, *John Randolph* was a labor of contempt.

Some of this contempt may have had an ironic, almost funmaking motive. Henry Adams liked to annihilate social pretensions. A comparison of the third and fourth chapters of the first volume of his *History,* soon to be written, might be invoked to show that in some ways he had less reverence for the respectable traditions of his own part of the country, New

79

England, than for those of the South. At the same time he liked to jar the family complacency of Southern blue bloods. The Randolphs, it will be remembered, proudly claimed descent from Pocahontas. Twenty years before his biography of Randolph, Adams had written the essay, already noted, that debunked the legend of Captain John Smith and Pocahontas. The Virginia aristocracy, he had commented then, "will be utterly gravelled by it if it is successful. I can imagine to myself the shade of John Randolph turn green at that quaint picture which Strachey gives of Pocahontas 'clothed in virgin purity' and 'wanton' at that, turning somersets with all the little ragamuffins and 'decayed serving-men's' sons of Jamestowne." And when *John Randolph* was published, Adams wrote gleefully to Henry Cabot Lodge: "The Virginians are red-hot at my introductory chapter." Doubtless he would have been disappointed at any other reaction.

Still, much of the contempt he felt was real and deep, with thick ancestral roots. There was scarcely a public figure of his time that the picturesque Randolph had not, on one occasion or another, denounced; but he seems to have reserved a special hatred for John Adams and his son, John Quincy Adams, whose principles and way of life contradicted his own. Toward the close of the book, Henry Adams dryly concedes that in certain respects this hatred was legitimate: "It was not for an instant imagined or imaginable that either of the Yankee Presidents ever entertained any other feeling than contempt for him; they had no possible intellectual relation with such a mind, but were fully prepared for his enmity, expected it, and were in accord with Mr. Jefferson's opinion, in 1806, that it would be unfortunate to be embarrassed with such a *soi-disant* friend." Evidently Henry Adams felt that he, too, had no possible relation with such a mind as Randolph's. Indeed, he seems scarcely to have conceded that Randolph had a mind at all, since, looking to the impeachment trial of Justice Samuel Chase as the only instance when Randolph was "compelled to follow a long and consecutive train of thought within the narrow bounds of logical method," Adams concludes simply that Randolph's failure was "decided." It may be observed incidentally that regarding this episode even such a friendly biographer of Randolph as William C. Bruce does not offer a fundamentally different judgment.[3]

Adams's book does make clear, however, some of the sources of its subject's impressiveness to his contemporaries and even yields him, here and there, a kind of admiration. Tribute is paid, for example, to Randolph's amazing powers as a rhetorician, his indifference to chances for individual gain, his fearlessness in repeatedly attacking the majority, whether in or out of his own party, his personal charm when he chose to exert it, and (though on this point Adams has qualifications) his honesty. If Randolph contradicted himself about such matters as the American Navy and the Negro problem, he seems in the main to have been loyal to those republican aspirations of 1800 which Jefferson himself for a time relinquished, and Adams concedes this. At the same time he accords Randolph nothing but obloquy for the part he played, according to his biographer, in laying the ground for eventual civil war:

The doctrine of states' rights was in itself a sound and true doctrine; as a starting point of American history and constitutional law there is no other which will bear a moment's examination;

---

[3] See *John Randolph of Roanoke, 1773–1833: A Biography Based Largely on New Material* (New York and London: G. P. Putnam's Sons), 1922. The subtitle refers to various letters and to Randolph's diaries, unavailable to Adams. Bruce deals more richly and sympathetically than Adams with Randolph as a person but shows less historical grasp. With justice, he accuses his predecessor of New Englander and Adams family bias. He is not innocent of bias of his own, however, arising from the fact that he was a native Virginian, born and reared in the very county where Roanoke is situated. Some of the problems of biographical interpretation presented by John Randolph are still to be dealt with.

it was as dear to New England as to Virginia, and its prostitution to the base uses of the slave power was one of those unfortunate entanglements which so often perturb and mislead history. This prostitution, begun by Randolph, and only at a later time consummated by Calhoun, was the task of a man who loudly and pathetically declared himself a victim to slavery, a hater of the detestable institution, an *ami des noirs*. . . .

I cannot agree with Mason Wade that *John Randolph* is poorly written; Henry Adams was not capable of writing poorly, at least at any length, and this book on Randolph is distinctly readable. Shorter and less scholarly than *Gallatin,* it can be taken more easily. Though the eccentric Virginian who is his subject would have appeared more vividly in a more sympathetic portrait, he is certainly far from lifeless in the passage in the final chapter from which, as a further example of Adams's treatment, this sentence is taken:

Not once or twice, only, but day after day, and especially during his short senatorial term, he would take the floor, and, leaning or lolling against the railing which in the old senate chamber surrounded the outer row of desks, he would talk two or three hours at a time, with no perceptible reference to the business in hand, while Mr. Calhoun sat like a statue in the Vice-President's chair, until the senators one by one retired, leaving the Senate to adjourn without a quorum, a thing till then unknown to its courteous habits; and the gallery looked down with titters or open laughter at this exhibition of a half-insane, half-intoxicated man, talking a dreary monologue, broken at long intervals by passages beautiful in their construction, direct in their purpose, and not the less amusing from their occasional virulence.

From this bit of description, and others like it, one can infer another important basis of the author's antipathy. To a person of Adams's temperament, garrulity was a species of sin. His letters and books frequently praise the hard virtue of "holding one's tongue." All the Adamses honored this virtue, as they deemed it, and often they achieved it, at least in public. Randolph's very existence seemed to depend on his ability to loose a brilliant, invective tongue, and doubtless he would have treated with withering scorn any suggestion toward controlling it.

The dissatisfaction with which the reader is likely to close the book perhaps comes from a fundamental dilemma in treatment that the author did not solve and may not even have recognized. He evidently believed, with most biographers before and since, that during much of his career Randolph was not strictly sane. Both logic and charity would say at once, that, on the basis of this belief, Randolph should not be held morally accountable for his varied aberrations: he was, in short, more ill-fated than reprehensible. But here seems to be a point concerning which the Puritan inheritance in Henry Adams asserted itself too strongly. He could not forgive this proud, physically unfortunate, and intellectually unbalanced Southerner for "habitual want of restraint." "Myriads of other men," proclaims the final sentence of the book, "have suffered as much without showing it in brutality or bitterness, and he himself never in his candid moments pretended to defend his errors: 'Time misspent, and faculties misemployed, and senses jaded by labor or impaired by excess, cannot be recalled.' "

It is a less than chivalrous summation, this apt employment of an unhappy, broken man's words against himself, and one must say at last that *John Randolph,* though historically informative and stylistically skillful, is deficient in pity. Had Henry Adams written it a decade later, when life had more fully revealed to him its somber intractability, he might have been less unforgiving and might have produced a book which he could acknowledge to his friends without apology.

The Life of George Cabot Lodge

As already observed, George Cabot Lodge, son of Senator and Mrs. Henry Cabot Lodge, was one of Adams's favorite younger friends. Though more than a generation separated the pair, their backgrounds were significantly similar, and they shared an approach to life at once ironic and idealistic. Adams relished Lodge's energetic and erudite conversation; admired, with perhaps a shade of envy, his boyish, near-pagan delight in nature; respected the frankness with which he made poetry his single goal in life; and encouraged him in the endless self-discipline and industry with which he worked toward it.

When "Bay," as young Lodge was familiarly called, died suddenly at Tuckanuck, Massachusetts, in August, 1909, Adams was in Paris. The death was a major blow, and one of Adams's more moving letters is that which he wrote at the time to Bay's father. Presently the grief-stricken family asked him to compose a memorial biography, to serve as a companion piece to a collection of Bay's poems, and Adams at once consented. The resultant volume, *The Life of George Cabot Lodge,* which appeared in 1911, was Henry Adams's last formal piece of writing.

For different reasons, he felt toward it, however, much as he felt toward his *John Randolph.* "If they will only let me keep my name off it!" he exclaimed confidentially to Elizabeth Cameron in a letter written February 7, 1911, a few months before publication. He had previously explained to her much of the basis of this wish, which was simply a recognition that "Cabot [Bay's father] will do it, and will not let anyone else do it, however he may try to leave it alone." True, in a letter to Bay's mother, Adams tried to stipulate that, whatever changes or insertions the parents might make in the manuscript, it should be sent to him for final editing. Nothing altered the fact, however, that the book could not be in any full sense his own. "So Cabot came to dinner last night," he wrote Elizabeth Cameron, "to talk about Bay's publication, and of course I was beautiful and approved everything, and said that I agreed with everybody, which I always do because nobody cares. Sometimes I do it once too much, as in the case of John Hay's *Letters*.[4] Bay's will be another case of the same sort, but not so lurid."

Beyond his annoyance at the friendly restrictions, Adams may well have felt that silence would have been the aptest comment on the career of a poet who—despite considerable talent, cultivated with an inconclusive ardor almost heart-wrenching—never struck a major chord. Aside from any question of ability, three circumstances might be cited to explain Bay Lodge's failure: first, most obviously, his premature death; secondly, as the biography occasionally hints, the sheltered quality of his life, which tended to keep his art from reaching vigorous maturity; and, thirdly, the lack in Boston as elsewhere in America of a human environment hospitable to poetry. Adams alludes to the second of these points but does not develop it. Had he possessed literal foresight, he might have defended himself from the implied accusation made by Edith Wharton in *A Backward Glance* (1934) that Adams, at his house in Washington and elsewhere, helped to furnish the protective atmosphere that kept Bay "in a state of brilliant immaturity." The letters, edited in 1947 by Harold Dean Cater, passing from Adams to young Lodge show

[4] Adams had refused to write a memorial of John Hay, "not on my account but on his. All memoirs lower the man in estimation" (To Elizabeth Cameron, March 13, 1907). At the instance of Mrs. Hay, however, he collected the letters and diaries of her husband so that they would make a continuous autobiography. Without consulting Adams, except to inform him what she was doing, Mrs. Hay suppressed all proper names, even those of places, except for the initial letter. Keys to the names are available at the Illinois Historical Society, Springfield; the University of Chicago Lincoln Library; and the Massachusetts Historical Society.

the older man treating the younger as an equal both in terms of friendship and artistic interest, and it is hard to believe that Bay could have found Adams's mind and personality anything but an antidote to the near-poisonous influence of staid Boston society.

This influence—the third of the circumstances cited to explain Bay Lodge's failure—must have interested Adams more than either of the others. Probably Mr. and Mrs. Henry Cabot Lodge, however, would have been perplexed had he proceeded to explain it in full. He states it unmistakably, nevertheless, and with admirable conciseness, at the end of the first chapter:

The gap between the poet and the citizen was so wide as to be impassable in Boston. . . . The Bostonian of 1900 differed from his parents and grandparents in 1850, in owning nothing the value of which, in the market, could be affected by the poet. Indeed, to him, the poet's pose of hostility to actual conditions of society was itself mercantile,—a form of drama,—a thing to sell, rather than a serious revolt. Society could safely adopt it as a form of industry, as it adopted other forms of book-making.

Thus had the average New England mind changed from that of fifty years earlier, when it dared not dismiss as literary elegance the animadversions of Emerson and Whittier, Longfellow and Lowell. In 1900, continues Adams (the idiom is surely his, not that of Henry Cabot Lodge): "Society was not disposed to defend itself from criticism or attack. Indeed, the most fatal part of the situation for the poet in revolt, the paralyzing drug that made him helpless, was that society no longer seemed sincerely to believe in itself or anything else; it resented nothing, not even praise. The young poet grew up without being able to find an enemy."

Plainly, Bay Lodge and his biographer had in common the fact of having been born into an uncongenial era, with gifts that society had ceased to honor. As the memorial took shape, Adams might well have reflected, however, that Lodge's plight had been more galling than his. Completely faithful to an artistic ideal, Lodge staked his total upon a precarious talent —though his chances might have been little better had he been Shakespeare—and he necessarily lost. Adams had distributed his own capacities with more luck or shrewdness than he was wont to admit; he had been amateur diplomat, journalist, teacher, and scholar-philosopher; and in each endeavor he had gained distinction enough to appease the discontent of most gifted human beings. He could call each of his endeavors a "failure," but at the same moment he had to present evidence that made most of his readers disbelieve him. The failure of Bay Lodge, on the other hand, was real, and so stood the fact, whatever the consolation of blaming Boston more than the poet.

It should be said, then, that if *The Life of George Cabot Lodge* lacks eloquence and warmth, and probably most readers find it does, one must refrain from condemning its writer before appreciating his embarrassments. To please a father who would not only read but revise, Adams had to pay almost higher tribute to his subject than the record permitted; at the same moment conscience forced him to make clear that Lodge's career was not, and probably could not have been, anything better than a disheartening stalemate with the world.

In view of the brevity and the sheltered quality of Bay Lodge's life, the biography could have little narrative movement. Nevertheless, Adams sets up, as in the books on Randolph and Gallatin, a chronological framework, often letting the subject speak for himself through his letters. These letters reveal an honest and fundamentally serious young man, liberally gifted, however, with cynical wit. They show him profoundly studied and intellectually brilliant, certainly possessing those qualities of modesty, fidelity, and congeniality that make for worthy friendship. Adams presents the letters skillfully, and, partly no doubt because they show so much of Lodge, tends himself to play the role of editor rather than that of author, usually refraining from direct characterization. *The Life* is not a cheerful and lively account: Adams could hardly have been happy when he wrote it, and certainly he was engaged in anything but a happy task. Nevertheless, he produced a book that, to say the least for it, can still be examined as a lucid, sympathetic record of the career of a very appealing minor poet.

One learns from *The Life* that Bay Lodge was born in 1873 in Boston; went to school there and at Harvard; rounded out his education in Europe; never turned from his calling as a poet except to serve actively in the Navy during the Spanish-American War; married fortunately and became the father of children; and died, evidently of heart trouble complicated by ptomaine poisoning, in August, 1909. Author of sonnets and long poems, he published *The Song of the Wave* (1898); *Poems* (1902); *Cain, A Drama* (1904); *The Great Adventure* (1905); *Herakles* (1908); and *The Soul's Inheritance* (1909). To a present-day reader the earlier poems, especially, contain an alliterative and rhythmic quality too strongly suggestive of Swinburne, who was perhaps Lodge's favorite author, and not enough realistic awareness of human experience. Adams concentrates his critical attention on the verse plays, *Cain* and *Herakles,* summarizing both and offering an encomium that could be taken as less extravagant four decades ago, when Eugene O'Neill, Maxwell Anderson, and others had yet to make their appearance and bring a significant body of American drama into being, than if it were submitted today: "He [the reader] will search long, and probably in vain, through American literature, for another dramatic effort as vigorous and sustained as that of *Cain,* and, if he finds what he seeks, it is somewhat more than likely that he will end by finding it in *Herakles.*" At this date, certainly, one cannot endorse such praise. Nevertheless, one can agree that both of these compositions show a matured sense of poetic structure (neither of them, it would seem, was meant to be acted) and a philosophic awareness of moral issues; and one can second Adams's annoyance, expressed in a letter to Henry James, that the appearance of *Herakles* did not even draw mention from the literary press. One can do this while noticing that the phrasing is often consciously exquisite or, at moments less lucky, flatly banal.

Again, in many ways Lodge was a younger, though probably lesser, Henry Adams, as Gallatin had been an older one. Driven by the same need for discovering value and coherence in life, and beset by many of the same obstacles to doing so, Lodge suffered similar torments. Adams quotes a passage from *Herakles* that reads like an adolescent simplification of his own periodic pessimism:

> Have we not learned in bitterness to know
> It matters nothing what we deem or do,
> Whether we find the false or seek the true,
> The profit of our lives is vain and small?
> Have we not found whatever price is paid,
> Man is forever cheated and betrayed?
> So shall the soul at last be cheated after all!

And then the answer, which Adams might deem too theatrical for his own stylistic taste, while conceding for it some application to his own life:

> I am resolved! And I will stand apart,
> Naked and perfect in my solitude
> Aloft in the clear light perpetually,
> Having afforded to the uttermost
> The blood-stained, tear-drenched ransom of the soul!

Here and there the author briefly reinforces the observation made in his opening chapter that the poet could not have expected to succeed, since the audience he wrote for did not exist. Early in his career, Lodge had struggled to write a successful stage play; for like Adams before him, filled with contempt for the world, he nevertheless felt the need of proving himself in it and was prey to chronic discouragement. Writing to Sturgis Bigelow, April 28, 1900, he asserted: "I've got to write another play before June. I have written several this winter, all on a steadily decreasing scale of merit, and I hope this one will be bad enough to be successful. The trees are full of leaves, and the air full of sun, and only I am vile. I wish I could pretend it was all somebody else's fault, but I can't. *Voila!*" On this passage Adams comments curtly: "A successful play needs not only to be fairly bad in a literary sense, but bad in a peculiar way which has no relation with any standard of badness Lodge could reach. He toiled in vain." The last sentence might well be taken as a summarizing comment by Henry Adams on the life and endeavors of George Cabot Lodge—an honest if bitter dictum, susceptible to general application. Too often, twentieth-century America lavishes her rewards on chipper mediocrity while talent accumulates the venom of neglect.

Edmund Wilson correctly points out, in his preface to *The Life of George Cabot Lodge,* included in *The Shock of Recognition,* that "the sole interest of Lodge today is a sad typicality which lends itself to the purposes of historians and critics"—that plus the fact that Henry Adams (with the senior Lodge looking over his shoulder, a distraction to which Wilson does not refer) wrote of him. Bay Lodge was one of a whole group of young Harvard poets of generous but unfulfilled promise. Wilson quotes a letter from George Santayana to William Lyon Phelps, explaining that in drawing the tragedy of the central figure in *The Last Puritan* Santayana had in mind the frustrations of young artists, during the 1880's and 1890's, like Sanborn, Savage, McCulloch, Stickney, and Lodge.

Now all these friends of mine [writes Santayana] . . . were visibly killed by lack of air to breathe. People individually were kind and appreciative to them, as they were to me, but the system was deadly, and they hadn't any alternative tradition (as I had) to fall back upon; and of course . . . they hadn't the strength of a great intellectual hero who can stand alone.

This comment, closely parallel to that of Adams concerning the mercantile, unpoetic environment against which Bay Lodge had to contend, surpasses it in emphasis by asserting the almost literal deadliness of that environment. One may say in passing that Santayana seems here to adopt too easily the seldom tenable opinion that poets of protest are physically killed and die young because of the world's opposition or indifference. The brain tumor of Stickney and the injured heart of Lodge, like the infected lungs of Keats, are best given a physiological rather than a literary or sociological explanation, though it is doubtless true that a discouraged man is less likely than a hopeful one to fight for life. Also, Adams may be on sound factual ground when he suggests in *The Life* that Lodge overworked himself. He offers this hypothesis at the end of the seventh chapter in a passage rightly praised by Wilson as a revelation of "the rare sensitive-cynical Adams who is himself a kind of poet":

The insidious weakness of literary workmen lies chiefly in their inability to realize that quiet work like theirs, which calls for no physical effort, may be a stimulant more exhausting than alcohol, and as morbid as morphine. The fascination of the silent midnight, the veiled lamp, the smoldering fire, the white paper asking to be covered with elusive words; the thoughts grouping themselves into architectural forms, and slowly rising into dreamy structures, constantly changing, shifting, beautifying their out-lines,—this is the subtlest of solitary temptations, and the loftiest of the intoxications of genius.

A passage so meaningful might be allowed to terminate these reflections on *The Life of Lodge*. It remains to say, however, that Adams contrasts with his subject in having, to use Santayana's phrase, "the strength of a great intellectual hero who can stand alone." Luckier than Lodge in having a physique that could survive and return to the most dragging midnight toil, he was also stronger in warding off any real danger of having his creativity stifled, which may be the kind of stifling to which Santayana ambiguously refers. As repeatedly suggested within this work, it is idle to speculate on what might have been the course of Adams's career in a world more harmonious with his sensibilities. One can simply note that finally, in such books as *Chartres* and *The Education*, Adams dramatized his opposition and left himself and his writings to symbolize an untouchable integrity. *The Life of Lodge* can be read as a moving annotation on the human plight that its author himself represented.

IF AMERICANS were right in thinking that the next necessity of human progress was to lift the average man upon an intellectual and social level with the most favored, they stood at least three generations nearer than Europe to their common goal. The destinies of the United States were certainly staked, without reserve or escape, on the soundness of this doubtful and even improbable principle, ignoring or overthrowing the institutions of Church, aristocracy, family, army, and political intervention, which long experience had shown to be needed for the safety of society. Europe might be right in thinking that without such safeguards society must come to an end; but even Europeans must concede that there was a chance, if no greater than one in a thousand, that America might, at least for a time, succeed. If this stake of temporal and eternal welfare stood on the winning card; if man actually should become more virtuous and enlightened, by mere process of growth, without Church or paternal authority; if the average human being could accustom himself to reason with the logical processes of Descartes and Newton!—what then?—*History of the United States*

IV

Of Temporal

and Eternal Welfare

History of the United States

BEFORE writing the *History of the United States during the Administrations of Jefferson and Madison,* Henry Adams paid scrupulous deference to two preliminaries: first, as presumably all historians must, he assembled his facts; and, secondly, as few historians do, he sought to define the character of the people whose story he intended to tell.

The first preliminary involved the labor of five years or more in scrutinizing all pertinent materials, official and private, available in this country and in sifting various archives in Europe. Most of the period between May, 1879, and October, 1880, was divided among London, Paris, and Madrid; at each of the three capitals Adams put copyists to work transcribing documents from the files of the Foreign Office; he himself worked with books and newspapers. "I foresee a good history," he wrote to Henry Cabot Lodge from London, May 13, 1880, "if I have health and leisure the next five years, and if nothing happens to my collections of materials. My belief is that I can make something permanent of it. . . ." An unusually confident and zestful statement from Adams, it can, nevertheless, be taken for its full worth, despite his fear expressed in the same letter that he was indifferent to completing and publishing. When all the European materials had been gathered he was appalled, and yet excited, at their mass. The finished work, he estimated, would fill six volumes —a guess that fell three volumes short.

Back in America in the fall of 1880 he continued the preliminary task of assembling the facts. Letters written the following summer to Justin Winsor, the librarian at Harvard, indicate the dogged thoroughness with which Adams perused files of old American newspapers. He had the carpenter of the College construct him a stoutly hinged, double-locked box, in which successive volumes of the Boston *Advertiser* and other journals could be shipped back and forth between Cambridge and Beverly Farms.

I return today the box of newspapers for a new load [he wrote to Winsor, September 27, 1881]. It is astonishing how very little information is to be found in them. I want to learn all I can about the social and economical condition of the country in 1800. Can you send me a few books on the subject in the return box with the newspaper volumes? I want the Memoirs of Lindley Murray by himself. New York. 1827. John Fitch's Biography by Westcott, Phil. 1867. Golden's Life of Fulton, 1817. There is, I believe, a History or Memoir about the Middlesex Canal which I want to see; and I want to find out how much banking capital there was in the U.S. in 1800, and how it was managed. I want a strictly accurate account of the state of education and of the practise of medicine. I want a *good* sermon of that date, if such a thing existed, for I cannot find one which seems to me even tolerable, from a literary or logical point of view.

By the first month in 1882 most of the materials had been gathered, and Adams could report to his English friend Gaskell: "I write for five hours every day, and ride two, and do society for the remainder. . . ." Some years had to pass before he would seriously feel the pressure of time.

The second preliminary, that of determining and appraising the composite character of the American people, the protagonist of his narrative, required a synthesizing imagination and high literary skill. As the letter to Winsor indicates, Adams did not want his characterization of Americans in 1800 to be a mere feat of fiction. What exactly were their circumstances, he evidently asked himself, their abilities and attainments, their interests and ideals? The answers to these and similarly stubborn questions he put down in the first six chapters of his opening volume. Taken together, these chapters form what Herbert Agar praises as the best interpretation ever written, with the possible exception of Tocqueville's, of the American character. Adams deals first with physical conditions in America of 1800. American readers may feel that they already have a general awareness of the magnitude of the task, defined in this opening, which still confronted their countrymen at the beginning of the nineteenth century. They can well be reminded of the fact, however, that two-thirds of the small population (5,308,483 persons, of whom nearly one-fifth were Negro slaves) lived within fifty miles of the Atlantic tidewater; also, that the country beyond the Alleghenies, soon to be incremented astoundingly by the Louisiana Purchase, was notable mainly for its wildness and inaccessibility. Bad roads and difficult rivers were the only means of communication and transport; hence that physical and psychological sectioning of the country that made national patriotism so precarious. The way of life was still overwhelmingly rural; Philadelphia, the largest city, numbered 70,000 souls.

Not until Adams begins to deal with habits and attitudes of living, submitting with scant comment whatever information bears on the point, may chauvinistic readers experience a shock. Traditionally, it has been too easy to infer from grammar-school textbooks a highly roseate picture of the early

Americans, living off the lush abundance of their land and enjoying physical health, mental keenness, and spiritual grace. Actually, Adams makes clear, life was generally harsh and shabby. The typical American diet, for example, consisted of salt pork and whisky, with dyspepsia the universal consequence. Except to some extent in the cities, and on a few of the Southern plantations, where a latter-day feudal pattern was observed, Americans did not aspire to grace or even cleanliness. Literature and the arts were virtually unknown. A common diversion was the free-for-all fight, which featured maiming and eye gouging.

This near-barbaric coarseness of American life, by no means dissipated a century and a half later, might be explained, if not defended, by reference to history and environment. Not so readily accounted for is the typical attitude of mind in 1800, which was conservative in the least admirable sense. With all their need for scientific enlightenment as a weapon for overcoming the imposing natural obstacles before them, Americans were consistently indifferent or inimical to new inventions and ideas. As but one of many instances, Adams cites the nearly impenetrable skepticism concerning the steamboat. As early as 1789 John Fitch had constructed a steam-propelled vessel that for an entire summer he operated successfully on the Delaware River in plain sight of Philadelphia. Yet he could secure no financial backing. Rebuffed similarly in New York and out west in Kentucky, he finally committed suicide. Another inventor of perhaps equal genius, Oliver Evans, was no more fortunate. Robert Fulton at length succeeded, in 1807, in compelling the acceptance of his *Clermont* mainly because he enjoyed the monetary support of Robert R. Livingston.

Touching broader questions of politics and economic life, American thinking was similarly conservative. Presumably radical leaders like Gallatin and Jefferson were content, says Adams, "with avowing no higher aim than that America should reproduce the simpler forms of European republican society without European vices; and even this their opponents thought visionary."

Following this estimate of American popular characteristics, Adams offers three chapters dealing respectively with the main geographical sections of the country in 1800: New England, the Middle States, and the South. Readers who expect him to reveal bias in favor of the first must be disappointed. Indeed, Adams shows a fine zest in his often withering delineation of the state of mind of New England, which harked back to the clergy-ridden eighteenth century and set the people against the democratic liberalism of the man who became President in 1800: "Every dissolute intriguer, loose-liver, forger, false-coiner, and prison-bird; every speculator, scoffer, and atheist—was a follower of Jefferson; and Jefferson was himself the incarnation of their theories." Americans today, seized with terror at the mention of anything Russian, might experience a salutary mental purgation by considering the monomania of New England's leaders, who mortally feared whatever might suggest France and the French Revolution. Jefferson's worst sin was that he had lived in France and was tainted with the attitudes and thought set forth in the opening phrases of the Declaration of Independence.

Adams withholds his approval from the educational system of New England in 1800, which, though excellent in principle, was badly antiquated. Concerning the point, Adams makes one of his many remarks about Harvard that may help to explain a subsequent depreciation of him by C. W. Eliot. "The college," reads the *History*, "resembled a priesthood which had lost the secret of its mysteries, and patiently stood

99

424360

holding the flickering torch before cold altars, until God should vouchsafe a new dispensation of sunlight." The stricture is softened, however, by the observation that the spirit of science was already making itself felt in the College.

Boston was culturally poor, a stronghold of the "resolute sons of granite and ice. . . ." The typical entertainment (though here other American cities could qualify as well) "was the state dinner—not the light, feminine triviality which France introduced into an amusement-loving world, but the serious dinner of Sir Robert Walpole and Lord North, where gout and plethora waited behind the chairs; an effort of animal endurance." More than once, disrespectful ironic chuckling emerges from the early pages of the *History*.

The South had a society that was picturesque but not in many ways encouraging. Though the gentry lived a life of relative refinement and were perhaps better educated than any other social class in America, their number was small, and the gap between them and the populace was enormous. Of the latter Adams says: "Wherever courage, activity, and force were wanted—they had no equals; but they had never known discipline, and were beyond measure jealous of restraint. With all their natural virtues and indefinite capacity for good, they were rough and uneducated to a degree that shocked their own native leaders. Jefferson tried in vain to persuade them that they needed schools. Their character was stereotyped, and development impossible; for even Jefferson, with all his liberality of ideas, was Virginian enough to discourage the introduction of manufactures and the gathering of masses in cities, without which no new life could grow."

Yet Adams concludes his observations on Virginia's society with a compliment. Lacking church, university, schools, or literature—at least in any form that fostered intellectual life —the Virginians concentrated on politics. "And this concentration produced a result so distinct and lasting, and in character so respectable, that American history would lose no small part of its interest in losing the Virginia school."

South of Virginia, Charleston was an oasis in the wilderness. Its small society of rice and cotton planters had cultured tastes and hospitable habits; and their way of life, founded on European models, had charm. As in Virginia, however, the cultural and economic contrasts between the highest class and the bulk of the population made the social pattern less democratic than aristocratic.

North Carolina was the most democratic region of the South. "Neither cultivated nor brilliant in intellect, nor great in thought, industry, energy or organization, North Carolina was still interesting and respectable." It is curious and perhaps unfortunate that Adams has little to say of Georgia except to call it "turbulent."

Of the Middle States, New York in 1800 impressed Adams in retrospect for its vigor and its freedom from the kinds of conservatism that often exerted, respectively, a depressing influence in New England and Virginia. On the other hand, the moral tone set by New York political leaders like Aaron Burr, De Witt Clinton, Edward Livingston, and others, was not high. It is on Pennsylvania and her way of life that Adams expends most of his praise:

The value of Pennsylvania to the Union lay not so much in the democratic spirit of society [of which, Adams asserts, it had more than any other state] as in the rapidity with which it turned to national objects. . . . Too thoroughly democratic to fear democracy, and too much nationalized to dread nationality, Pennsylvania became the ideal American State, easy, tolerant, and contented. If its soil bred little genius, it bred still less treason. With twenty different religious creeds, its practice could not be narrow, and a strong Quaker element made it humane. If the American Union succeeded, the good sense, liberality, and democratic spirit of Pennsylvania had a right to claim credit for the result. . . .

Philadelphia was not only the country's most populous city; it was also the most intellectual. "For ten years Philadelphia had attracted nearly all the intelligence and cultivation that could be detached from their native stocks. Stagnation was impossible in this rapid current of men and ideas." This was not to forget the Philadelphians' neglect of John Fitch with his steamboat, or their virtual banishment of William Cobbett when he denounced the practice still common among physicians of bleeding their patients, including those suffering of old age. Nevertheless, it was Philadelphia that proved relatively congenial to the varied talents of Charles Brockden Brown, H. H. Brackenridge, William Bartram, Philip Freneau, and Gilbert Stuart.

All told, the American character in 1800 thus seemed to show a not particularly happy mixture of strength and weakness, of enlightenment and ignorance.

This quick summary, with quoted excerpts, of Adams's appraisal has been offered, first, to suggest his methods and his historian's style, and, secondly, to give setting to his comment on American ideals which appears in his sixth chapter. Whatever he may have conceded in earlier chapters about the limitations of the average American, Adams is quick to uphold him against the condemnations of visiting European critics. These critics could seldom, then as now, discover any motivation in American conduct beyond that of money-grubbing. Freely admitting this practical economic drive, Adams berates observers who could not discern that beyond the eagerness for wealth there was also an eagerness toward an ideal. America did, after all, represent a fundamental protest against Europe. Englishmen could feel the force and excitement behind their own legend of Dick Whittington and yet seemed unable or unwilling to feel the larger excitement of the emigrating European peasant, which turned him into a new man within half an hour after landing at New York. With ample opportunity to be cynical, Adams chooses not to be cynical at all about the "silent influence" that Englishmen, almost against their will, found at work in America, "which had nothing to do with avarice or with the dollar, but, on the contrary, seemed likely at any moment to sacrifice the dollar in a cause and for an object so illusory that most Englishmen could not endure to hear it discussed." And how define this object? "Every American," writes Adams, "from Jefferson and Gallatin down to the poorest squatter, seemed to nourish an idea that he was doing what he could to overthrow the tyranny which the past had fastened on the human mind. Nothing was easier than to laugh at the ludicrous expressions of this simple-minded conviction, or to cry out against its coarseness, or grow angry with its prejudices; to see its nobler side, to feel the beatings of a heart underneath the sordid surface of a gross humanity, was not so easy."

The present study is directed, of course, much less toward Englishmen and their almost chronic reluctance to detect the nobler element in American life than toward Henry Adams and his feeling for America's possibilities. It is true, as seen earlier in his report on the Garibaldi episode, that an impulsive liking of "the people" was not inherent in Adams's temperament. The democratic sympathy found in the *History* may have been deliberately conceived as a concession to necessity. The early family ideal of government by the educated best had gone down to crushing, permanent defeat in 1828, when John Quincy Adams had lost the Presidency to Andrew Jackson. The grandson could recognize that from that point on America's chances lay with the common people or nowhere. Hence the intensity of his effort to appraise their qualifications for a civilized destiny and hence, also, the significance of whatever praise he found it possible to accord them. The average citizen is glad to bask in the unrestrained commendation of democratic idealists like Jefferson and Lincoln, not realizing that, with all its sincerity, it carries less weight than the cautious approval of an Adams, congenitally impelled to require more of people than heaven gave them. The tone of even the more hopeful pages of the *History* is one of marked contrast with that of, say, Whitman's "Democratic Vistas"; yet Henry Adams was more than willing to acknowledge the existence of human virtues when he found them. This willingness is something to keep in mind as one works toward a final estimate of the man and his attitudes. Knowing too much history to confuse the accomplishment with the ideal, he observes, nevertheless, with real if controlled excitement that "the instinct of activity, once created, seemed heritable and permanent in the [American] race." With all his admiration for the accomplishments at this time of individual European geniuses—of men like Scott, Wordsworth, Shelley, Heine, Balzac, Beethoven, Hegel, Oerstad, Cuvier, Turner, and Watt —Adams can assure his reader that in the effort to lift mankind itself to a higher level Europe's inheritance of class distinctions and prejudice placed her in a posture of decrepitude beside the "lithe young figure" of America. Looking back from the Gilded Age, probably the most corrupt period politically in American history, he realizes that the philosophic idealism of Thomas Jefferson largely failed when it had to meet the *machtpolitik* of Canning and Napoleon, not to mention the near-treasonous hostility of the New England Federalists. A President whose passion was peace, who believed that "his task in the world was to establish a democratic republic, with the sciences for an intellectual field, and physical and moral advancement keeping pace with their advance," was as much of an anachronism among leaders of nations in 1800 as he would be today. Nevertheless, Adams pays tribute to him and to the people who believed in him. This essential fidelity to the difficult human cause never entirely left Henry

Adams, though with the passing years his cynical and pessimistic manner so grew that many who knew him, like many
who now read him, refused to call him anything except a
defeatist. The concluding pages of this study will deal more
fully with this accusation; it is sufficient to say now only that
most defeatists do not strive from youth to old age to define
and understand the complicated predicament of their countrymen and, indeed, of all mankind. Such a preoccupation is
of itself evidence of some identification with the actors in
that predicament; and it will appear that Adams's later pessimism, which he expressed often enough, was always tentative,
qualified by a basic hope.

The introductory section of the *History* concludes with a
laying down of the great, challenging questions which, Adams
avers, had to be answered affirmatively for American society
if it were to win complete success. When he wrote them,
about 1882, he necessarily knew that most of them remained
outstanding, and one may add that they so remain six decades
later. They help gauge the extent to which this country has
persistently and appallingly fallen short of the near-Utopian
goals originally envisioned for her by Thomas Jefferson. Also,
however, they can be taken as an implied statement of the
ultimate national ideal of Henry Adams, and perhaps, too,
as explanation of why, as more and more he felt himself inclined to set actuality against dream, he found cynicism so
tempting and why he experienced increasingly a sense of isolation in a world different from the one he would have chosen,
if he could, to fashion. The kind of society implied in these
questions will probably not soon be found this side of a philosopher's heaven:

Could American society transmute its social power into the higher
forms of thought? Could it provide for the moral and intellectual
needs of mankind? Could it take permanent political shape?

Could it give new life to religion and art? Could it create and maintain in the mass of mankind those habits of mind which had hitherto belonged to men of science alone? Could it physically develop the convolutions of the human brain? Could it produce, or was it compatible with, the differentiation of a higher variety of the human race?

The manner in which Adams adverts to these questions in the final chapters of his ninth volume will presently be noted.

In the intervening pages he tells the story of America between 1800 and 1805, the main episodes of which are familiar in outline to most readers. It was the period of the Lousiana Purchase, with its constitutional problems; of the impeachment trial of Justice Samuel Chase, the failure of which left the judiciary virtually unassailable in time to come; of the Tripoli pirates, chastised by a small but daring American Navy; of accumulating insult from England under the leadership of Canning and from France under the leadership of Talleyrand and Napoleon; of the shabby but dangerous conspiracy of Aaron Burr; of trouble with the western Indians, led by Tecumthe; and, finally, of the War of 1812, that conflict which, waged with bravery but also with occasional and noteworthy blundering on both sides, ceased without a declared victory for either contestant but left Americans with their first valid sense of national unity.

The narrative moves easily and brilliantly, with ample suggestion, however, of the anxiety felt by the men who were the chief actors. If Adams imparts a central theme to the story, it is the relentlessness of events in proving the impracticability of the resolve of Jefferson, Gallatin, Madison, and others to establish a government dedicated to peace and opposed to taxes except for a peaceful purpose: "a wise and frugal government," as the President affirmed in his 1800 inaugural, "which shall restrain men from injuring one another, which shall leave them otherwise free to regulate their own pursuits of industry and improvement, and shall not take from the mouth of labor the bread it has earned." It is the theme, as Robert E. Spiller indicates in his chapter on Adams in the *Literary History of the United States,* of the individual's virtual help-lessness to compel history, of the tragic disparity—later to be dramatized in *The Education*—between ideal and fact. In terms of the ideal, perhaps, the government of Jefferson was wise, since no government ever stood more consistently for the principle of international peace or showed itself more willing, for the sake of harmony, to absorb the most wounding insult. Judged, however, in terms of its earthly results, affecting the people directly concerned, the government of Jefferson fell short of wisdom. Such measures as the Non-Importation Act, the Embargo Act, and the Non-Intercourse Law had economic effects, especially in the agricultural areas, almost as disastrous as war; and yet in the end war was not avoided. Further, in being forced to promulgate such acts, following the Louisiana Purchase, Jefferson relinquished many of the republican principles of government that he undoubtedly held dear.

Adams's few comments are essentially realistic. Perhaps as the great-grandson of the man whose political life Jefferson helped to terminate, he may be suspected of a quiet exultation in observing the difference between the respective tones of Jefferson's first and second inaugural addresses. Such a comment as the following, though the attitude it sets forth is skillfully and correctly attributed to Randolph, can hardly be said to show a fully objective stand on the part of its author:

That Jefferson was willing not only to assume powers for the central government, but also to part from his States-rights associates and to gratify the Northern democrats by many concessions of principle, his first Administration had already proved; but John Randolph might wonder to see him stride so fast and far toward what had ever been denounced as Roman imperialism and corruption; to hear him advise [in his second inaugural address] a change in the Constitution in order to create an annual fund for public works, for the arts, for education, and even for such manufactures as the people might want—a fund which was to be distributed to the States, thus putting in the hands of the central government an instrument of corruption, and making the states stipendiaries of Congress.

Yet Adams goes on to say that in announcing his broader theory of statesmanship, "Jefferson proved the liberality and elevation of his mind; and if he did this at some cost to his consistency, he did only what all men had done whose minds kept pace with the movement of their time." Caught in a fluctuating pattern of shifting forces, the rational human being tries not to escape it, for he cannot, but to act within it as usefully as he can even while he disapproves it. By bringing the will to a working acquiescence, intelligence saves it from a sense of being overwhelmed.

This progress from a central government small and humble, "wise and frugal," to one of greater strength and assertion— not to say menace—is the historical path that Adams traces. In his Annual Message of December 5, 1815, President James Madison laid down views pointing definitely in the direction of strong government. "Madison seemed to take his stand, beyond further possibility of change, on the system of President Washington." And the Fourteenth Congress, by a vigor and initiative "in contrast with the imbecility of many previous Congresses," endorsed this position. But to show that the states'-rights question was far from dead, and that history might always contain surprises, Madison vetoed the bill for internal improvements that had been introduced by young Calhoun. This action, however, almost Madison's last before his retirement, by no means reversed the political current toward increasing centralization already set in motion. Federalism, defeated as a political party, succeeded as a principle.

The literary impressiveness of the *History* resides not alone in its reasonable organization, allowing for a highly readable essay of analysis and appraisal at both opening and conclusion, but in the ease with which explanations and characterizations combine with the narration. Without loss of the sense of forward movement, the reader is invariably given necessary backgrounds and usually obtains an understanding of the personages on the historical stage that can be imparted only by a writer with a strong dramatic sense reinforcing his historical knowledge. However large or small the event, the human being is always present, and both his intrinsic individual quality and his place in the general scene receive attention. Consider, as one example out of scores, Adams's treatment of Joel Barlow, a personage by no means impressive, observes the author, since men like Dwight, Trumbull, Alsop, and Hopkins—themselves minor enough—"were Miltonic by the side of Joel Barlow."

Yet Barlow was a figure too important in American history to be passed without respectful attention. He expressed better than any one else that side of Connecticut character which roused at the same instant the laughter and the respect of men. Every human influence twined about his career and lent it interest; every forward movement of his time had his sympathy, and few steps in progress were made which he did not assist. His ambition, above the lofty ambition of Jefferson, made him aspire to be a Connecticut Maecenas and Virgil in one; to patronize Fulton and employ Smirke; counsel Jefferson and contend with Napoleon. In his own mind a figure such as the world rarely saw,—a compound of Milton, Rousseau, and the Duke of Bridgewater,—he had in him so large a share of conceit, that tragedy, which would have thrown a solemn shadow over another man's life, seemed to render his only more entertaining. As a poet, he undertook to do for his native land what Homer had done for Greece and Virgil for Rome, Milton for England and Camoens for Portugal,—to supply America with a great epic, without which no country could be respectable; and his "Vision of Columbus," magnified afterward into the "Columbiad," with a magnificence of typography and illustration new to the United States, remained a monument of his ambition.

This characterization, at once ironic and compassionate, gives depth to the passage later in the *History* where Adams submits the episode ending in Barlow's death. When French-American relations were at their worst, Barlow accepted an appointment as American minister to France. Striving with characteristic fearlessness, and in vain, to win an audience with the evasive and deceitful Napoleon, Barlow set out across the wastes of Poland during the winter of 1812 as the Grand Army was retreating from Moscow; and at a small village near Cracow he contracted and died from an acute inflammation of the lungs.

Of major figures presented by Adams, none is more challenging to the resources of literary art than Thomas Jefferson, initially a dire political enemy but finally a warm personal friend of John Adams. Henry Adams evidently had some fear that his own judgment on Jefferson might be warped, a fear expressed in a letter to George Bancroft, April 25, 1879. In this letter Adams also observed: "My own opinion is that J. was a coward, as he proved by resigning his governorship of Virginia in the face of a British invasion. C'était son seul défaut." In the *History,* however, this condemnation of Jefferson does not appear (its presence in a personal letter does not, of course, prove that Adams could not have departed from it later), and the third President is treated without either eulogy or censure. Only a few excerpts can be offered to suggest the solicitude with which, at various points in the *History,* Adams attempts this characterization:

According to the admitted standards of greatness, Jefferson was a great man. After all deductions on which his enemies might choose to insist, his character could not be denied elevation, versatility, breadth, insight, and delicacy; but neither as a politician nor as a political philosopher did he seem at ease in the atmosphere which surrounded him. As a leader of democracy he appeared singularly out of place. As reserved as Washington in the face of popular familiarities, he never showed himself in crowds. . . . The rawness of political life was an incessant torture to him, and personal attacks made him keenly unhappy. His true delight was in an intellectual life of science and art. To read, write, speculate in new lines of thought, to keep abreast of the intellect of Europe, and to feed upon Homer and Horace, were pleasures more to his mind than any to be found in a public assembly. He had some knowledge of mathematics, and a little acquaintance with classical art; but he fairly revelled in what he believed to be beautiful, and his writings often betrayed subtle feeling for artistic form,—a sure mark of intellectual sensuousness. He shrank from whatever was rough or coarse, and his yearning for sympathy was almost feminine. That such a man should have ventured upon the stormy ocean of politics was surprising, the more because he was no orator, and owed nothing to any magnetic influence of voice or person.

. . . . .

For eight years this tall, loosely built, somewhat stiff figure, in red waistcoat and yarn stockings, slippers down at the heel, and clothes that seemed too small for him, may be imagined as Senator Maclay described him, sitting on one hip, with one shoulder high above the other, talking almost without ceasing to his visitors at the White House. His skin was thin, peeling from his face on exposure to the sun, and giving it a tettered appearance. This sandy face, with hazel eyes and sunny aspect; this loose, shackling person; this rambling and often brilliant conversation, belonged to the controlling influences of American history, more necessary to the story than three-fourths of the official papers, which only hide the truth.

Adams's meticulous artistry in the treatment of individuals, whether of major or minor stature, does not prevent him from having a sense of the vast sweep of events and imparting

that sense to his chapters. Since the United States, despite all
of Jefferson's and Madison's attempts to achieve for her an
ennobled isolation, was drawn even then into the European
maelstrom, the story has world breadth. Adams writes of the
Napoleonic struggle in terms that suggest the epic treatment
of a Tolstoi or a Hardy: "Spain, France, Germany, England,
were swept into a vast and bloody torrent which dragged
America, from Montreal to Valparaiso, slowly into its movement; while the familiar figures of famous men—Napoleon,
Alexander, Canning, Godoy, Jefferson, Madison, Talleyrand;
emperors, generals, presidents, conspirators, patriots, tyrants,
and martyrs by the thousand—were borne away by the stream,
struggling, gesticulating, praying, murdering, robbing. . . ."

The *History* has, in short, those qualities of comprehensiveness and delicacy, of scholarship and readability, of power
and ironic humor, that befit a significant segment of the universal drama. It has already survived the test of more than
half a century of subsequent historical research, and it should
survive much more. One foresees no need of revising the high
compliments paid it in the 1930's by such scholars as Carl
Becker and Henry S. Commager. The former referred to the
History as a work "which for clarity, tight construction, and
sheer intelligence applied to the exposition of a great theme,
had not then, and has not since, been equalled by any American historian." "It is not an exaggeration, indeed," affirmed
Commager, "to insist that the *Gallatin* is the best political
biography, the *Administrations of Jefferson and Madison* the
finest piece of historical writing, in our literature."

More recently the *History* has been accorded two practical
tributes. During World War II, Major H. A. DeWeerd edited
for *The Infantry Journal* those portions of the *History* relating
to the War of 1812. Entitled *The War of 1812* (1944) the
resultant volume was intended especially for instructional purposes among the armed forces. Then in 1947 Herbert Agar,

performing a task of skillful editing, condensed the bulk of the *History* by two-thirds, so that its essential passages may now be perused in a pair of volumes. In responding thus intelligently to the requirements of busy readers, Agar has undoubtedly done Adams a service. The *History* will now be read in part by many who would never otherwise have touched it. A condensation or digest, however, must fail in certain important respects to take the place of its longer original, and Agar gladly concedes that his edition is "the truncation of a work of art," and that "the balance which the author gave to his work has been destroyed." It is to be hoped that the condensation will lead many readers on to the study and enjoyment of the complete *History*. Unfortunately that has long been out of print. A new edition of it at this time would be a deserved compliment to the memory of its author, who, with all his auguries about the future, could perhaps not foresee how richly his work was destined to add to a comprehension of the American democratic ideal.

It bears repeating that at various points in his narrative Adams indicates admiration for the aspirations that animated American foreign policy in the opening years of the nineteenth century. It was a policy consonant with the theory of a wise and frugal government and with that resolve, approvingly defined by young Henry Adams in his second journalistic review entitled "The Session," that power should not be permitted to arise in the land. In 1870, when "The Session" was written, he would seem to have clung to some hope that modest government was still possible even in the post-Civil War period; but in the *History,* written more than a decade later, he recognizes that the seeds of political giganticism and overbearance were present and quick almost from the first. Not without regret he records how Jefferson's popularity came to an end with the near-ruin of the country economically by the Embargo Act and observes that it was then that "America began slowly to struggle, under consciousness of pain, toward a conviction that she must bear the common burdens of humanity . . . ; that she could not much longer delude herself with hopes of evading laws of Nature and instincts of life. . . ." Caught in the implications of an international existence, government had to ramify and to gather in richness and power. Even by the time of the Louisiana Purchase, says Adams, it should have been clear that government could not be restrained.

Must the people, then, become resigned forever to the occasional or constant tyranny of political power? The answer, of course, resides within themselves. Adams emphasizes the alternative by asserting that the hopes of mankind lay thenceforward "in raising the people themselves till they should think nothing necessary but what was good." Hence, again, his preoccupation with the character of the American people and his anxiety that they show themselves to be energetic and wise. Even leaders as brilliant and persuasive as Jefferson and Gallatin are relatively powerless except as they prove that their own enlightenment is representative of one to be discovered in the electorate.

One turns with interest to the final pages of the *History* where, recalling the logic of Adams's plan, one expects to find at least tentative answers to those salient questions propounded in the first volume. One is prepared for a pessimistic conclusion; for if Adams's account of American history between 1800 and 1815 shows anything, it shows, surely, that our society would not soon "transmute its social power into the higher forms of thought"; "provide for the moral and intellectual needs of mankind"; "take permanent political shape"; "give new life to religion and art"; "create and maintain in the mass of mankind those habits of thought which had hitherto belonged to men of science alone"; "physically

develop the convolutions of the human brain"; and "produce
. . . the differentiation of a higher variety of the human race."
Adams, however, virtually ignores these specific questions,
which on earlier pages he labels fundamental; he seems almost
to pass them by as being too stern; and if his doing so is a
failure in logic and organization, it is also a triumph in idealism. Refusing to be caught in the dilemma of his own creation,
he finds in certain national conditions and attitudes the glim-
mer of hope which evidently was the only conclusion he could
tolerate.

Materially, the country had made an amazing advance between 1800 and 1817; population had increased more rapidly
than was usual in human experience, and wealth had accumulated still faster. On these points Adams submits a simple
calculation suggestive of some of the historical hypothesizing
he was later to set forth in *The Education:* "From such statistics as the times afforded, a strong probability has been
shown that while population doubled within twenty-three
years, wealth doubled within twenty." Thus, he suggests, the
American people could read in advance, "with almost the
certainty of a mathematical formula," their economic history
for at least a hundred years.

By 1817, certain Americans had become distinguished:
Calhoun and Clay in Congress; Pinkney and Webster at the
bar; Buckminster and Channing in the pulpit; Bryant and
Irving in literature; Allston and Malbone in painting. These
men varied considerably in character and qualities but showed
in common "a keen sense of form and style." All in all they
did not prove, Adams concludes, that Americans were artistic;
they proved, rather, that American intelligence "in its higher
as in its lower forms was both quick and refined."

This quickness of American intelligence did not show itself, Adams concedes, in political terms, though the inefficiency
of the government during the War of 1812 might be explained

by the fact that "the party of Jefferson and Gallatin was founded on dislike of every function of government necessary in a military system." Further, the people had as their chief trait an antipathy to war. There is perhaps an element of contradiction in Adams's going on from this point to affirm that a high degree of national intelligence was shown—despite antipathy to war—by the performance of Americans in the naval battles which they won. (Earlier he has cited in detail certain naval battles that they lost. Is it patriotic obliquity that makes him ignore these now?) In designing the fast-sailing schooner or skipper and in perfecting their gunnery markmanship, the Americans revealed, he avers, an astonishing superiority to the English and to any other nationality that might reasonably be named for comparison. The same superiority seemed to be demonstrated by the statistics of land battles like Chippewa and New Orleans; also by the remarkable efficiency in the war of American scientific engineering, a branch of the military service that developed at once when circumstances required it.

Having thus inferred from their actions an unusual practical intelligence in the American people, Adams goes on to predicate, in his conclusion, two other significant national traits: quickness and mildness. The conservatism that had still been so strong in 1800 was largely dissipated in 1817. The steamboat, formerly laughed at, was honored now at its full value as the most significant agency in a rapid internal expansion and development. Quickness was apparent, too, in the political development—the shift from a less to a more centralized governmental form. "In politics, the American people between 1787 and 1817 accepted greater changes than had been known in England since 1688." The same speed of development could be observed in religion; the Unitarian movement of Boston and Harvard College swiftly brought a virtual end to the older churchly forms and attitudes. A comparable religious movement in England would have shaken church and state to their foundations, but in America it arrived easily.

The American people evinced their mildness in relaxing orthodox severity. The contrast between Jonathan Edwards, the Puritan, and William Ellery Channing, the Unitarian, was enormous, both in doctrine and method. Religion became increasingly cheerful. "For the first time in history," observes Adams with a characteristic tinge of irony, "great bodies of men turned away from their old religion, giving no better reason than that it required them to believe in a cruel Deity, and rejected necessary conclusions of theology because they were inconsistent with human self-esteem." Optimism and mildness also marked political developments. Weary of strife, the people acquiesced in a system of government that left the old disputed constitutional points undetermined; they were ready to prefer workability to theory and to promote whatever encouraged ease and enjoyment.

Though Adams does not expressly laud the American people for the alterations in national character that had evidently taken place by 1817, the generally tolerant tone of his treatment indicates that, in his eyes, life had become better. He seems glad to share some of the ease and mildness that he found in his countrymen.

Yet in the final paragraph of the *History* much of the old moralistic sternness suddenly reasserts itself. As though recalling belatedly the stiffly challenging questions posed in Volume I, he bids farewell in Volume IX with a passage that essentially revives them. The American people, he avers, had shown themselves to be intelligent,

but what paths would their intelligence select? They were quick, but what solution of insoluble problems would quickness hurry? They were scientific, and what control would their science exercise over their destiny? They were mild, but what corruptions would their relaxations bring? They were peaceful, but by what machinery were their corruptions to be purged? What interests were to vivify a society so vast and uniform? What ideals were to ennoble it? What object, besides physical content, must a democratic continent aspire to attain? For the treatment of such questions, history required another century of experience.

Interest in this passage, and in the final chapter to which it strikes the ultimate note, can be twofold. One may observe, first, that by the date of its writing (1888) Adams was already weighing the hypothesis that history might be studied in scientific terms. Much of his narrative, it is true, concerns itself simply with the relations between man and man; his conception of history in terms of physics, as an interplay between force and force, awaited fuller formulation in *The Education*. Nevertheless, in his conviction that the American people, more distinctly than any of the peoples of Europe, were a uniform social entity, Adams was pursuing the suggestion he had submitted to Francis Parkman in a letter dated December 21, 1884: "Democracy is the only subject for history. I am satisfied that the purely mechanical development of the human mind in society must appear in democracy so clearly, for want of disturbing elements, that in another generation psychology, physiology, and history will join in proving man to have as fixed and necessary development as that of a tree; and almost as unconscious." Americans had their heroes, but not as Thomas Carlyle might have demanded; for these heroes —unlike most of those of earlier cultures—stood out, paradoxically, by their typicality, by their emphatic embodiment of the very traits most characteristic of the society that had temporarily elevated them. The historian could mark the steady growth of a vast population unaffected by the social distinctions confusing to other historians—"without kings, nobles, or armies; without church, traditions, and prejudices. . . ." More than half a century after Jefferson, such a society was to appall an artist like Henry James and drive him to Europe; but the story of its development seemed to lend itself to a scholar intent on observing the operation of defined forces. The history of the American population seemed indeed to be a better subject for the scientist than for the dramatist or poet. Adams was to say later, in *The Education,* that he wrote the *History* "for no other purpose than to satisfy himself whether, by the severest process of stating, with the least possible comment, such facts as seemed sure, in such order as seemed rigorously consequent, he could fix for a familiar moment a necessary sequence of human movement"—and the result had not satisfied him. It is not for the critic, at least at the moment, to decide more readily than Adams whether he was right or wrong in his delineation of the American people, or whether he utilized a valid method. One can regret, certainly, that he was not blessed with the phenomenal ambition and long life that might have enabled him to write a careful study of his country's progress in time between 1900 and 1917 and thus to have carried out in detail the implication of his ultimate sentence: "For the treatment of such questions, history required another century of experience." Fortunately *The Education of Henry Adams* suggests much that he might have said in the more meticulous study, which must now be undertaken—if at all—by some scholar of comparable interests and gifts.

One may emphasize, secondly, the caution in the note with which the *History* terminates. Adams did not know, and refused to say, whether the American democratic experiment might succeed. Such tentativeness is only proper in one who had discovered, through the volumes of his labor, so many appalling limitations in the people; in one who, further, wrote out of the Gilded Age and could bitterly observe the kind of "progress" revealed in the contrast between Presidents

119

Washington and Grant. As he finished his toil, he turned aside to write with grim jocularity to John Hay: "All my stupid people, including my readers, will be put to sleep for a thousand years; and when they wake up, they will find their beards grown to their waists, and will rub their eyes, and ask: 'Do the crows still fly over Washington?' "

Yet he was not, in the *History* any more than elsewhere, a prophet of unalloyed doom; and, to repeat, in a hypercritical observer like Adams, the qualifications to his pessimism are often more weighty than another's optimism. Not only did he want the American people to win; he thought they had a chance to do so—though that chance, as he had granted in the first volume of the *History,* might be no better than one in a thousand. At least, Americans had demonstrated that in certain respects they could improve: they could reveal qualities of intelligence, quickness, and mildness, which might be serviceable in bringing them at last to the point of thinking "nothing necessary but what was good." Referring to his native land in a letter to Gaskell written March 25, 1883, he had said simply: "I confess to thinking it the only country now worth working for. . . ." One can look ahead, also, to the old man during his last days in Washington, railing to the young Owen Wister against the swarming evils of the time, then suddenly pausing to lean forward and lay his hand upon him, exclaiming with intensity in eyes and voice: "Keep the faith!"

Of course, one asks, without demanding a sure answer, What would Adams think of Americans today? He would probably observe that history continues to ordain for them a government that is strong because a weak one is impossible, and that the goal of a central authority worthily great through responsiveness to the will of an enlightened majority remains a dim hereafter light. Some of his phrasing could well be used to designate how pitiably short the American people still fall of that state of civilization which alone can make them, in the end, worth saving. Who but a genius in invective could sufficiently denote the blatant imbecility that shouts down quiet wisdom, whether in the halls of Congress or in the market place, while few seem to care? That mildness of which Adams wrote seems now to verge on a disastrous indifference to intellectual and ethical issues; to have brought a widespread tacit concession that the only surviving morality is political—a morality badly askew, since it represents the ancient stupidity of trying to make a part serve for the whole. And who but Adams might adequately state the fear that through such indifference America may cease trying to be America and let herself become a military state, bellowing love of peace and justice while exerting the rule of blood and iron in a world rendered, partly by her people's quickness and intelligence, somewhat less delectable than Dante's hell?

Yet one can infer also that Adams's mind would be as active as ever in trying to discover a way out. "I am a dead duck, but still quack questions and want to know," he wrote in his seventy-fifth year to Elizabeth Cameron. If he could still be here, one would see him discerning the present near-disastrous cheapness of government and society and according it its merited contempt, but, nevertheless, not denying humanity and his inescapable share in it. He would not approve, surely, of those who turn from democracy with its myriad blemishes to espouse a dictatorial scheme that can only be worse. Nor would he bless those intellectuals who avowedly turn from life entirely to cultivate bitter herbs in their gardens or mutter objurgations in their ivory towers. Not that he would ever withhold the right and necessity of the individual to fashion his own universe, to live a sane life within to resist insanities without; but from his example one learns the wisdom of not failing to treat as real that which the eyes behold, and so the resolution to make the inner and the outer vision at last coincide.

Tahiti

Tahiti was an unpremeditated result of Adams's visit to the Society Islands in 1891 with John La Farge. Although the travelers had meant to remain only a week, the vagaries of steamship schedules kept them four months, during which they became intimate with the ranking Tahitian family, late-fallen on evil days. Titular head of this family was Marau Taaroa, a middle-aged lady of European education and good manners who would have been "queen" had native autonomy survived. The actually dominating personage, however, was Marau's mother, the matriarchal Arii Taimai, who invested the two Americans with a kind of feudal enfeoffment whereby they took Tahitian names and became sons of the family. Before them, Robert Louis Stevenson had been similarly honored in another district of the island; but Marau and her mother, who had extended no share of this tribute, were not entirely pleased. Surviving letters show that Adams was serious about his own adoption and that he was touched by the hospitality and human fineness of his hosts. "The whole thing was done quite simply but quite royally," he wrote, "with a certain condescension as well as kindness of manner. For once my repose of manner was disturbed beyond concealment." It is perhaps worth observing incidentally, for the enlightenment of certain reviewers who assume racial snobbery in Adams, that the younger generation in this family was half Tahitian and half Jewish. It was the fine old chiefess, however, the widow of an Englishman who bore the surname of Salmon, that especially drew Adams's affection. When time came for parting, she "kissed me on both cheeks—after all, she is barely seventy, *va!*—and made us a little speech, with such dignity and feeling, that though it was in native, and

I did not understand a word of it, I quite broke down. I shall never see her again, but I have learned from her what the archaic woman was." In such vein he wrote to Elizabeth Cameron, who would understand.

Probably the last person able to give an accurate account of Tahitian legend and history from the native point of view, Arii Taimai had proved to be informatively loquacious and had graciously co-operated with Adams's design, conceived when it became plain that his stay must lengthen, to put her memoirs into writing. The son and daughter, Tati and Marau, had translated her discourse while Adams took notes. *Tahiti* is thus in essence the old matriarch's narrative, organized and composed by Henry Adams. It has had little chance for attention, since it has only recently become easily accessible. Of the first edition, somewhat inaccurately entitled *Memoirs of Marau Taaroa, Last Queen of Tahiti* and privately printed in Washington, 1893, two copies are in the Adams collection in the Massachusetts Historical Society.[1] Copies of the second edition are to be found in the same collection and also in a number of university libraries; more accurately named *Memoirs of Arii Taimai*, it was privately printed in Paris, 1901, with revisions, rearrangements, and additions. The latest readily available edition, with the convenient main title simply of *Tahiti,* was edited in 1947 for the Scholars' Facsimiles and Reprints by Robert E. Spiller, who contributed a helpful introduction. The map drawn according to the 1769 survey by Captain James Cook forms a frontispiece, as in the second edition, and the seven genealogical tables prepared by Adams intersperse the text. Unfortunately, however, an index has not been supplied.

As Professor Spiller observes, *Tahiti* is a book for study rather than entertainment. Perhaps the most serious obstacle

[1] Professor Robert E. Spiller informs me that other copies of this first edition, of which probably about ten were printed, are now in private hands.

to readability is the welter of native proper names, rendered phonetically in spelling often differing from that employed by Captain Cook, Herman Melville, and others who have interested themselves in the same general subject. If one patiently pursues his way, however, through the first several chapters (there are eighteen in all), he gains enough comprehension of persons and places to follow the story with interest, sensing as he does so its parallelism with more famous histories in chronicling the rise, decline, and fall of a people.

In general, it is the elaborated story of Arii Taimai's family or "clan," the Tevas, traditionally the most distinguished and influential in Tahiti. (One may risk calling them the Adamses of the Society Islands.) Descended, according to ancient supposition, from a demigod, the Tevas achieved dominance and somewhat precariously maintained it by a series of intertribal wars still waging when the English expedition under Captain Samuel Wallis reached Tahiti in June, 1767, and introduced European complications into native politics. Much of the narrative from this point forward is drawn from or supported by the miscellaneous accounts of Wallis, Cook, Banks, Bougainville, Commerson, Bligh, Edwards, and numerous missionaries, with annotations furnished, of course, by Adams. In their intercourse with the natives, the Europeans' worst blunder—aside from the casual one of introducing white man's diseases and ethical corruptions—was that of forcing their own interpretation of "kingship" upon this traditionally kingless society. In upholding the "royal" claims of Tu, or Pomare, Captain Cook and others lent their support to an otherwise unsanctioned ruler for the whole island whom the majority of the natives would not accept. The result was almost unintermittent civil war until the French, with political manipulations even then familiar, outplayed their indifferent English competitors and finally placed Tahiti under a protectorship in 1846. The signal contribution of Chiefess

Arii Taimai was to persuade her people, including the then "Queen" Pomare, to leave off a hopeless resistance and to submit without extensive bloodshed. Also, Taimai subsequently arranged a marriage between her daughter Marau and "King" Pomare V, though by the time Adams arrived this union had been dissolved by divorce. Pomare had sold his rights, such as they were, to the French, whose protective benevolence was double-edged, and was devoting himself to drink.

Writing to Elizabeth Cameron, February 6, 1891, Adams characterized the Tahitian atmosphere as "more than tinged with a South Sea melancholy, a little sense of hopelessness and premature decay"—particularly challenging, perhaps, to an artist like La Farge, who, if he could catch it in color, would do something "uncommon delicate." Behind the melancholy, however, lay not only memory but disease, and "the old Hawaiian horror" cropped up to make Adams frequently sick with pity and disgust, though the serene La Farge busied himself with his paints and seemed unaffected. The natives had preserved some of their ancient songs but no longer danced to them. "People who wear clothes," Adams gloomily observed, "can't dance." At first he suffered keenly from his old intellectual's curse of ennui and called Tahiti "an exquisitely successful cemetery," but the longer he remained the less he was bored. As his fortuitous task as recorder of Tahitian legend and history grew upon him, he became frankly excited.

One can agree with the editor of the Scholars' Facsimiles and Reprints volume that *Tahiti* has a symbolic quality. It is, in a sense, the human story in miniature, with passage from an exalted, half-divine beginning to a degraded, all-too-human conclusion. Presumably Adams was not disposed to analyze Tahitian society as an entity, at least with attention to the dispersion and leveling out of its energies. What application he might have discovered here for Newtonian physics, or Lord Kelvin's second law of thermodynamics, can hardly be suggested. In any event, the point of view he selected for his narrative did not lend itself precisely to the imaginative kind of scientific-historical theorizing to appear later in *Chartres* and *The Education*.

One result of the stylistic presumption that *Tahiti* is Arii Taimai's narrative is that Adams probably omits certain allusions and anecdotes, hinted at in one of his letters as being at least mildly scandalous, that might have lent greater conventional zest to the reading. Another result is that certain passages have a curiously dual tone, mingling observations that may have come from Taimai with some that could have come only from Adams. The old Chiefess' knowledge of her own family history might have enabled her to say, for example, that Bougainville touched on the eastern side of Tahiti in April, 1768; but it is less certain that she could add casually that he "returned to Europe with such glowing accounts of Tahiti as created lively interest." The narrative proceeds in a slightly awkward, amusing idiom wherein the voice is Taimai but all else is Adams:

At that moment Europe, and especially France, happened to be looking for some bright example of what man had been, or might be, in a state of nature, and the philosophers seized on Tahiti to prove that, if man would only rid himself of restraints, he would be happy. This is an account of our family, not a history of the island, and I am not well acquainted even with the names of the philosophers who brought about the French Revolution by trying to apply to France the state of nature which Bougainville described in what he called the island of New Cytherea; but I know that Diderot wrote a "Supplement to Bougainville's Travels" in the form of a dialogue between the ship's chaplain and a Tahitian supposed to be named Orou, and that Orou overwhelmed the chaplain by showing the superiority of Tahiti over Paris, and the immorality of constancy in marriage.

One of my friends has pointed out to me another French book, printed in 1779, an "Essai sur l'isle d'Otahiti," which offers a pleasant jumble of Montesquieu, Rousseau, and Hawkesworth. . . .

There is, almost inevitably, cutting irony at the expense of Westerners and the institutions that produced them. On the other hand, there is no attempt to uphold the Romantic heresy and to point to life in virginal Tahiti as proof of the innate goodness of the human heart:

The real code of Tahitian society would have upset the theories of a state of nature as thoroughly as the guillotine did; but when seen through the eyes of French and English sailors, who had not the smallest sense of responsibility and would not have been sorry to overthrow all standards, Tahiti seemed to prove that no standard was necessary, which made the island interesting to philosophers and charming to the French people, never easy under even the morality recognized at Paris.

All told, the English are more severely censured than the French. The notorious Captain Bligh, for one, is condemned primarily in terms of his nationality: "Had he been a Frenchman, he might perhaps have enjoyed discovering the mistakes of his predecessors, and trying to correct them by mistakes of his own, but when the English once saw what they took to be a fact, they saw nothing else forever." Both European nationalities, however, behaved with cupidity and blindness, and in surveying the consequences of their conduct Adams, perhaps unwittingly, moves out of irony into direct denunciation. Probably nowhere else in his writings—not even in the Senate bill that he wrote for Senator Don Cameron, upholding freedom for Cuba—does one find him so directly assuming the cause of a plundered and betrayed people:

When England and France began to show us the advantages of their civilization, we were, as races then went, a great people. Hawaii, Tahiti, the Marquesas, Tonga, Samoa, and New Zealand made a respectable figure on the earth's surface, and contained a population of no small size, better fitted than any other possible community for the conditions in which they lived. Tahiti, being first to come into close contact with the foreigners, was first to suffer. The people, who numbered, according to Cook, two hundred thousand in 1767, numbered less than twenty thousand in 1797, according to the missionaries, and only about five thousand in 1803. This frightful mortality has often been doubted, because Europeans have naturally shrunk from admitting the horrors of their own work, but no one doubts it who belongs to the native race. . . .

No doubt the new diseases were the most fatal. Almost all of them took some form of fever, and comparatively harmless epidemics, like measles, became frightfully fatal when the native, to allay the fever, insisted on bathing in cold water. Dysenteries and ordinary colds, which the people were too ignorant and too indolent to nurse, took the proportion of plagues. . . . The virulent diseases which had been developed among the struggling masses of Asia and Europe found a rich field for destruction when they were brought to the South Seas. . . .

For this, perhaps, the foreigners were not wholly responsible, although their civilization certainly was; but for the political misery the foreigner was wholly to blame, and for the social and moral degradation he was the active cause.

The accent here is perhaps less impassioned than that of John Quincy Adams, but the grandfather's moral indignation still shows its vitality in the grandson. It is this quality of pity and anger that, for students of Adams, helps to make *Tahiti* something more appealing than a minor historical document on the Society Islands. When one remembers, too, that the work is partly a labor of dedication to a woman— evidently not unworthy to evoke in her own way that reverence for dignity, beauty, and power that Adams was wont to discover in the presence of the feminine ideal—the importance of *Tahiti* as a symbolic link between the *History* and *The Education* becomes inescapable. They are, no doubt, a strange triumvirate: Marian Hooper Adams, Arii Taimai, and the Virgin of Chartres; but each of them brought something of the meaning of life to Henry Adams, and he was one compelled to accept such meaning and prize it wherever he found it.

MY FAVORITE figure of the American author is that of a man who breeds a favorite dog, which he throws into the Mississippi River for the pleasure of making a splash. The river does not splash, but it drowns the dog.—To Barrett Wendell, March 12, 1909

V

American Author

Democracy

WHEN in 1880, during the administration of Ruther-ford B. Hayes, there appeared an anonymous satiric novel on American government, few people in Washington or elsewhere in America paid much attention. In 1882, how-ever, two separate editions of the book were brought out in London and raised a lively discussion that reverberated back across the Atlantic; and then for several seasons it stood among the best sellers.

Any sophisticated reader could detect that whoever had written *Democracy* knew Washington and the government in-timately, and it is interesting that suspicion lighted scarcely at all on Henry Adams, though his wife and several of his friends—John Hay, Clarence King, and Emily Beale, among others—were accused. The New York *Nation* surmised that it was "the work of some clever Englishwoman long resident in Washington and a practiced writer, carefully revised and edited by an American." Most other guesses were syntactically better but substantially as wrong. Only Mrs. Humphry Ward, writing in the *Fortnightly Review* at the time of the English editions, showed accurate acumen. Praising the ease of the dialogues in the book, she observed that the style was not unlike that of Howells and Henry James (who had not yet reached his "later manner"), and then reasoned that the author must be an American male. Might he not be one Henry Brooks Adams, she asked, who thirteen years earlier had written an article on "Civil Service Reform" for the *North American Review?* [1]

Fortunately for Adams's abhorrence of publicity, her question was ignored. The secret of authorship was not openly disclosed until 1921, three years following Adams's death. At that time Henry Holt, whose firm had published the first edition, told the full story in an article in the *Unpartisan Review.* To date *Democracy* has been issued in five American editions with nineteen reprintings; and there have been several editions in England and one each in France and Germany.

To one who has the advantage of knowing the idiom of Henry Adams through his later writings, the identifying stylistic marks of authorship are plain. Every chapter has his cultivated pessimism and the usual duality of deftness and solidity in phrasing. Who else in the late 1870's would be likely to refer with such contempt to the Senate chamber of the United States "with its code of bad manners and worse morals," or calmly observe that "the capacity of women to make unsuitable marriages must be regarded as the cornerstone of society"? Who else would be likely to have his heroine chastise Boston by saying: "I suppose you have there a brilliant society; numbers of poets, scholars, philosophers, statesmen, all up and down Beacon Street. Your evenings must be sparkling. Your press must scintillate. How is it that we New Yorkers never hear of it? We don't go much into your society; but when we do, it doesn't seem so very much better than our own. You are just like the rest of us. You grow six inches high, and then you stop. Why will not somebody grow to

[1] See Edmund Wilson, "Novels of Henry Adams: Democracy," *New Republic,* XLIV (Oct. 14, 1925), 203.

be a tree and cast a shadow?" Henry James was capable of treating America's self-nominated elite with as little respect as this, but his *Bostonians* was not to be written until 1885; and it would show here and there an interesting indebtedness to the novel of his friend Henry Adams.

Mrs. Humphry Ward had wisely linked *Democracy* with its author's earlier "Civil Service Reform." That essay had been written out of the violated ethical sense of a reformer, and this novel expressed, though with a different emphasis and motive, Adams's deeper disillusion with what had happened to government since the Civil War. Unlike the essay, it seems to conclude that corruption has become intrenched and chronic and that improvement is impossible. True, one particular passage may seem to show that the author's inherited faith in democracy had not utterly vanished. Edmund Wilson cites in this connection the rather elaborate declaration of Mr. Nathan Gore of Massachusetts, one of the older and more gentlemanly minor characters in the book. At the heroine's insistence, Gore declares his political faith with "almost the energy of despair":

"I believe in democracy. I accept it. I will faithfully serve and defend it. I believe in it because it appears to me the inevitable consequence of what has gone before it. Democracy asserts the fact that the masses are now raised to a higher intelligence than formerly. All our civilisation aims at this mark. We want to do what we can to help it. I myself want to see the result. I grant it is an experiment, but it is the only direction society can take that is worth its taking; the only conception of its duty large enough to satisfy its instincts; the only result that is worth an effort or a risk."

The appearance and background of Nathan Gore (he is a handsome man with a gray beard; in his youth he was a successful satiric poet and had been a student in Europe for many years) strongly suggest James Russell Lowell. He obviously represents an older order, and the significance that one might like to attach to his courageous but inconfident remarks is rendered suspect by the fact that the author presents him with more than a hint of contempt: "He was abominably selfish, colossally egoistic, and not a little vain; but he was shrewd; he knew how to hold his tongue; he could flatter dexterously, and he had learned to eschew satire." Further, the flippancy with which Gore concludes makes clear how lonely he is in his stand: "There! have I repeated my catechism correctly? You would have it! Now oblige me by forgetting it. I should lose my character at home if it got out." Hoping vainly to be reappointed minister to Madrid, Gore later in the story comes to resemble Adams in his conclusion that one of the most foolish things a qualified citizen can do is to ask for a diplomatic post: such plums are usually handed out to incompetents as a reward for political lackeying.

For students of Adams, the interest in Gore's little speech is that it concisely summarizes Adams's feeling toward democracy and the American people as he was setting it down, even as he wrote his novel, in the various volumes of his *History*. One may doubt the ultimate triumph of the founding fathers' dream, but one must, nevertheless, assume a certain working belief in it, for what other belief deserves one's devotion? The tone of weary but firm defiance belongs to Adams as unmistakably as to the character he created: "Let us be true to our time. . . . If our age is to be beaten, let us die in the ranks. If it is to be victorious, let us be first to lead the column."

The story of *Democracy* is not spectacular, but by a reasonably adroit and persuasive creation of his characters, Adams gives it genuine interest. Mrs. Madeleine Lee, an attractive and well-to-do young widow, changes her residence from New York City to Washington, resolved to study the political world. In her fundamental seriousness and her belief that life should have a definable moral purpose, she is prophetic of Isabel Archer in Henry James's *Portrait of a Lady,* to be published one year later than *Democracy.* Madeleine Lee's satiric wit may have been drawn in part from Mrs. Henry Adams, and various elements in her character from Mrs. Bigelow Lawrence, but her motives most strongly suggest the author himself. "She wanted to see with her own eyes the action of primary forces; to touch with her own hand the massive machinery of society; to measure with her own mind the capacity of the motive power. She was bent upon getting to the heart of the great American mystery of democracy and government." She does this in a manner she had hardly foreseen, by becoming an object for marital conquest by the dominating political figure in Washington, Senator (and, later, Secretary of the Interior) Silas P. Ratcliffe of Peonia, Illinois, a gentleman morally entitled to the first syllable of his name. Though by no means enamored of this pompous and forceful personage, she considers marrying him as a sacrifice of herself for the betterment of democracy, and as a means of making another suitor, a middle-aged Virginian named John Carrington, available to her younger sister, Sybil. Actually, Sybil is not in love with Carrington but is in league with him to balk Ratcliffe's wooing of Madeleine. Since the Senator's wooing is as obstinate and ruthless as his politics, this is not easy to do. The crisis occurs when Madeleine reads and presents to Ratcliffe a letter from Carrington accusing the great statesman of bribery. Forced to a statement, Ratcliffe concedes the truth of the accusation but argues oratorically that he has committed this and other breaches of ethics for the high cause of party; and he still asks her to marry him, on the plea that she can help him to purify politics. Outraged, she reflects that

. . . the audacity of the man would have seemed sublime if she had felt sure that he knew the difference between good and evil,

135

between a lie and the truth; but the more she saw of him, the surer she was that his courage was mere moral paralysis, and that he talked about virtue and vice as a man who is colour-blind talks about red and green. . . . Was it politics that had caused this atrophy of the moral senses by disuse? Meanwhile, here she sat face to face with a moral lunatic, who had not even enough sense of humour to see the absurdity of his own request, that she should go out to the shore of this ocean of corruption, and repeat the ancient role of King Canute, or Dame Partington with her mop and her pail. What was to be done with such an animal?

She contemptuously withdraws from his presence, and as he leaves her house he is accosted by an old Continental roué, a member of the Hungarian legation, who strikes him across the face with his cane. The blow would seem to symbolize the righteous anger of both heroine and author with political indecency. The book closes with Madeleine's leaving on a trip to Europe, after which she will presumably return to marry Carrington and seek no further intimacy with the men and the animating forces behind government.

There would seem to be little point in trying to invoke, say, Nathan Gore's expression of faith in democracy as full antidote to the bitterness of this conclusion. The heroine, an intelligent and honest person, has found little but pollution within the framework of American political life and is convinced that the individual is helpless to cleanse it. One may argue that the book itself is evidence that the author hoped to achieve reform, but it is possible to rejoin that in writing *Democracy* Henry Adams had simply utilized some of his leisure time to announce, in the form of fiction, his disillusion and disgust. As already noted, he had written to Henry Cabot Lodge, June 24, 1876: "Politics have ceased to interest me. . . . The Caucus and the machine will outlive me, and that being the case, I prefer to leave this greatest of American problems to shrewder heads than mine." In October, 1902, he wrote to his brother, Brooks Adams: "I bade politics good-bye when I published *Democracy*." Emphatically though forlornly, he still wanted decency to win. His contributions to the cause would be made in the study, however, not on the platform or in the smoke-filled room.

Much of the force of *Democracy* is an affronted patriotism. Behold, Adams seems to exclaim bitterly, what has happened to us! In his sixth chapter he gathers the characters for an outing at Mount Vernon, where their conversation inevitably turns to the father of their country. His limitations are more than conceded: "George Washington," expounds Victoria Dare, "was a raw-boned country farmer, very hard-featured, very awkward, very illiterate and very dull; very bad tempered, very profane, and generally tipsy after dinner." Her remarks are calculatedly violent, for Miss Dare likes to shock people; yet no one seriously contradicts her. Mr. Gore presently observes, however, with phrasing that is meaningful despite a quaint pretentiousness: "For all that, we idolize him. To us he is Morality, Justice, Duty, Truth. . . ." Carrington seizes the chance to offer little-known anecdotes emphasizing Washington's inveterate honesty. Whatever else the first president was, he was honest to the point of obsession. Adams becomes heavily ironic in letting the rodential Senator Ratcliffe offer the appropriate historical comment: "Washington was no politician at all, as we understand the word. He stood outside of politics. The thing couldn't be done today. . . . If Washington were President now, he would have to learn our ways or lose his next election. [Could the author have avoided having in mind here the political fate of John Quincy Adams?] Only fools and theorists imagine that our society can be handled with gloves and long poles. One must make one's self a part of it. If virtue won't answer our purpose, we must use vice. . . ."

So the point is made. The great Republic was founded

137

by men virtuous; it is now controlled by men vicious, by men abominable in their shabby pride. *Sic transit.* . . .

This particular bitterness, with the protest implied is found in almost all the writings of Henry Adams. Ever and again he asks whether complexity must mean corruption and, unable to accept the almost inescapable answer, asks the question once more. His first novel is, like the *History* only more so, a pessimistic indication of fact and probability, to be contemplated more searchingly in his later works. Seven decades later one can only commiserate his disheartened ghost as it hovers over a national capital where words like "idealism" and "truth" so often meet with pitying smiles, while "realism" and "expedience" are impressively mouthed; where fear has outlawed tolerance, and intelligence is subjected to loyalty investigations. *Democracy* is at once a record and a prophecy of official shamelessness.

The novel contains much denunciation of American life in general, as well as of politics specifically, but not without qualification. Thus, although the heroine scathingly condemns the stupidity of life in centers like New York, Philadelphia, Baltimore, and Boston, she abuses Europe too, after several visits there, and "frankly avowed that she was American to the tips of her fingers. . . ." Both the President and his wife, as well as Senator Ratcliffe, seem to represent among other things the dispiriting boorishness of the Middle West. Baron Jacobi, the much-lived old Hungarian roué, asserts in a genteel and impressive speech that he has found no society as corrupt as that of the United States. "The children in the street are corrupt, and know how to cheat me." As his remarks continue, however, he emphasizes political somewhat more than personal corruption: "Everywhere men betray trusts both public and private, steal money, run away with public funds." He regrets that he cannot return in a hundred years, at which time the United States will be "more corrupt

138

than Rome under Caligula; more corrupt than the Church under Leo X; more corrupt than France under the Regent!" On the other hand, a more hopeful note for society in general seems to be sounded when the heroine, finally disillusioned with her quest for decency in government, gladly contemplates returning "to the true democracy of life, her paupers and her prisons, her schools and her hospitals." One recalls the comment of Anthony Trollope in his *Autobiography* (1883) that Americans—whom he praised for "their personal generosity, their active and far-seeking philanthropy, their love of education, their hatred of ignorance, the general conviction in the mind of all of them that a man should be enabled to walk upright"—usually spoke of public life as a thing apart from their own existence, as a state of dirt in which it would be an insult to suppose they resided.

Readers interested in refuting to whatever extent they can Adams's indictment of American political corruption during the post-Civil War period may well point out that James G. Blaine, the presumed original of Silas P. Ratcliffe,[2] probably was denied the Presidency through the operation of an ethical

---

[2] "Gossip and conjecture have pretty well settled, for the original of the main characters, upon Mrs. Bigelow Lawrence [Madeleine] and her sister Miss Fanny Chapman [Sybil], James Lowndes [Carrington], James G. Blaine [Ratcliffe], and Emily Beale [Victoria Dare]." (Robert E. Spiller, Introduction to *Esther*, Scholars' Facsimiles and Reprints edition, p. v.) The President seems to be a composite portrait of various Middle Western politicians; he is not specifically, surely, Rutherford B. Hayes, though in a letter to Gaskell written June 14, 1876, Adams denominated Hayes as "a third-rate nonentity whose only recommendation is that he is obnoxious to no one." The President's wife may be drawn partly from Mrs. Hayes, with her strong sentiments for conventional virtue, and partly from Mrs. U. S. Grant, of whom Adams wrote to Gaskell, December 7, 1869: "She squints like an isosceles triangle, but is not much more vulgar than some Duchesses." Harold Dean Cater suggests (*Henry Adams and His Friends*, p. 128 n.) that the original for Baron Jacobi, the diplomat, was Aristarchi Bey, Turkish Minister to the United States in the 1880's. Born in 1843, this friend of the Adamses was a much younger man, however, than the old Hungarian in the novel is shown to be.

principle. Blaine enjoyed favors from a railroad company somewhat as Ratcliffe, in *Democracy*, enjoys them from a steamship company; and the famous "Mulligan Letters," supposed to contain proof of Blaine's ethical dereliction, played in history much the same role as that played in the novel by the private papers of Samuel Baker, which establish the guilt of Ratcliffe. *Democracy* contains no hint of the existence of that influential, relatively independent group headed by Carl Schurz, which had Henry Adams for a time as one of its most industrious members and over several decades helped to make men like Blaine (or Ratcliffe) an anathema to an important segment of the American population.

So one may contend that Adams's strictures in *Democracy* are somewhat too stern. His prognostications in the novel are certainly less cautious and more gloomy than those in his *History*, though one may note that in the latter work they pertain more specifically to the people than to the government and deal, of course, with an earlier period. Also, it seems likely that in an anonymous novel he was more likely to strive for sensation than in a documented scholarly study. Nevertheless, one must concede the essential truth of the picture presented in *Democracy* and must agree, too, that a humble, "unsuccessful" human being like John Carrington—whose political chances, like those of Henry Adams, had been annihilated along with many of the eighteenth-century ideals of the founding fathers—was more admirable than all the grasping boors whose shoddy standards became triumphant.

It is interesting that the moral struggle of *Democracy* is shown to take place in a woman, and that her decision in favor of decency seems to be her feminine repudiation of a man-made world she cannot approve. Robert E. Spiller observes that the book can thus be regarded as "an examination of the moral force resident in the feminine soul." This is true perhaps only in part, since much the same moral force resides within the soul of the hero, John Carrington, though the defeat of the Southern cause, to which he gave his youth, has led him to withdraw from active effort and become a quietly cynical onlooker who appreciably resembles the author that created him. One must note, too, that Madeleine is virtually unique among women. Her sister Sybil is her temperamental opposite and is not in the least concerned about moral issues in government. For a more thorough consideration of this conflict between masculine and feminine modes of feeling and thought, one must turn, as Spiller says, to Adams's second novel, *Esther*.

For its satiric force and for its artistic merits, *Democracy* deserves to be rescued from the near-oblivion it has suffered during the present century. This writer cannot agree with Harold Dean Cater (in his Biographical Introduction to *Henry Adams and His Friends*) that it is "written in poor literary style." The composition has a high level of excellence, as the brief passages already quoted tend to show. The phrasing is at once polished and robust, and the organization is careful. The characters do tend to fall into types, and if one sets the book beside the *Bostonians,* one sees at once that the psychological fabric provided by Adams is much thinner than that provided by Henry James. Such a comparison, however, is not entirely just, as Adams was attempting a much simpler thing, in terms of esthetic creation, than his friend usually was. It is enough that the men and women in *Democracy* are believably alive and are placed in a significant, vivid setting, achieved with intelligent economy. Certain scenes especially, such as that of the ball at the British embassy, or that of Madeleine's final dismissal of Ratcliffe, bring the reader that satisfaction which comes only from honest and meticulous art. It is too much to ask that *Democracy* should again be popular, but it can be read for pleasure as well as study, and it can be part of the basis for the literary reputation that Henry Adams is at last being accorded.

Esther

Esther appeared in March, 1884, under the pseudonym of Frances Snow Compton,[3] and was offered for sale at one dollar a copy. According to a statement made almost forty years later by Henry Holt, who undertook the publication, "the result was *nil*." Adams had stipulated that the book should not be advertised and that copies of it should not be sent to the press. His ostensible motive for such prohibitions was that he wanted to see whether a book could make its own way without "pushing." One can infer that the more genuine reason was his usual distaste for publicity. Only 527 copies were sold in this country during the eleven years that the book remained in print; 28 copies were sent to England. If *Democracy* had been an astonishing success with the reading public, *Esther* was an unspectacular failure, though it is an instance of time's revenges that in 1948 a first edition of this failure was offered for sale in New York City (by Biblo and Tannen) for four hundred dollars.

As in his earlier novel, Adams chose a woman as the central figure for *Esther*. For reasons relating to her personal happiness, Esther Dudley is searching for the truth, if any, embodied in the institution of religion as Madeleine Lee, in *Democracy*, searched for it in the institution of government. Even more signally than for Madeleine, the result for Esther is failure and near-despair.

The conflict in *Esther* wages between the heroine's love for

[3] The title page of the Scholars' Facsimiles and Reprints edition (New York, 1938) erroneously bears the masculine form, "Francis." Though the point is hardly major, I think it of definite significance that Adams, with his admiration for the nineteenth-century woman and his contempt for her male consort, should have chosen a feminine nom de plume.

a young Episcopalian divine, Stephen Hazard, and her conviction of her unfitness, because of her lack of churchly faith,
to become his wife. Artistically gifted, she is employed by
Wharton, the artist who has been engaged to paint the murals
in Hazard's church, St. John's on Fifth Avenue. As she helps
Wharton in this task, she becomes increasingly conscious of
her deficiency in any true religious emotion, notwithstanding
her growing love for Hazard, much of whose decorous court-
ship is pursued while she plies her brush. Esther's father, a
Federal veteran of the Civil War who dies before Esther's
conflict reaches its crisis, has been careful to allow his daughter
entire freedom in forming her own convictions and attitudes.
She is, thus, again like Madeleine in *Democracy,* somewhat
like Henry James's Isabel Archer, at liberty to make what she
can of life. Womanlike, she appeals for guidance to a trusted
masculine friend, her cousin George Strong, a college professor of geology, but he cannot impart to her a certainty and
strength that he himself lacks. A tentative subplot results from
the presence of Esther's high-spirited, unspoiled young friend
from Colorado, Catherine Brooks, with whom the artist
Wharton falls in love; his passion, however, can reach no
conclusion, especially in view of the reappearance of his
strangely malignant wife, whom he had left many years earlier
in Europe. Mrs. Murray, Esther's aunt, contributes to the
action by opposing Hazard's interest in Esther; she attempts
to direct events by removing her niece from New York City
to Niagara Falls; with characteristic resolution, however,
Hazard follows. The book ends with Esther's sadly assuring
him that she can never accept his faith and his church and
so dismissing him. The personal struggle is more nearly tragic
for Esther than for Madeleine Lee, for whereas Madeleine
virtually loathes her suitor, Esther loves hers.

As most summaries are, this one is unfair. It contains no
hint of the skill with which Adams has brought certain

characters—especially Esther and George Strong—genuinely into being, and it naturally must omit the wisely sardonic touches in the writing that heighten readability. True, as Robert E. Spiller has pointed out in his introductory essay to the Scholars' Facsimiles and Reprints edition, a distinctly "costume" quality has attached to *Esther* with the passing of time. Most of the so-called realistic novels of Howells and James, however, to name no lesser writers, have suffered in the same fashion, and Adams's work stands up astonishingly well in artistic comparison with theirs. One can repeat essentially what has been said in connection with *Democracy:* one should not attempt to elevate Adams to the first rank among American novelists: his higher excellence lies elsewhere; but his undoubted contribution to the art of serious fiction in our country should now receive its belated acknowledgment.

In reading *Esther,* the student of Henry Adams is likely to be drawn to other matters of interest beyond its strictly artistic values. In the essay already cited, Spiller observes: "Adams had read Esther aright. Woman is vested with a greater power of understanding of life than is man, but she has no answer to its riddle: what to do? The novel ends, as does Johnson's *Rasselas,* with a conclusion in which nothing is concluded. In this sense only is Marian [Adams] the original of Esther. And when the final chapters of the real story were being written, its fictional counterpart was dying a death of inertia." One may essentially accept this observation without fully endorsing the dictum—repeatedly submitted in one guise or another by Adams—that it is woman, not man, who understands life. It is perhaps easy to forget momentarily that Esther is, after all, the creature of Henry Adams: he did not "read" her, he created her. His habitual insistence on the superior ability of the female to apprehend basic issues intuitively was, in the main, a convenient sardonic means of calling attention to his point: that whatever the modern world retains of form, it has lost the spirit and has surrendered itself to materialistic values. It is a sound inference, surely, that his success in delineating the sensibility of a remarkable woman depended partly on his intimate knowledge of one, but it must also be observed that his own approach to reality was often emotional as well as analytical. He became more sensitive in this respect as he got older; yet some of his early letters, such as one addressed to Senator Charles Sumner on December 22, 1858, after the latter's physical breakdown,[4] show that even as a very young man he possessed an ample fund of feeling. Thoroughly "masculine" in his persistent cultivation of an informed, logical mind, he had ways of reacting to experience that were always distinctly "feminine." He and his writings would be less often misunderstood if this particular versatility in him were consistently taken into account.

In any event, Mrs. Adams's suicide—though all the causes of it can hardly be known—compel one to believe that she was tormented by contradictions that for her, as for Esther, made a satisfying existence impossible and pointed, indeed, to an inconclusive conclusion. This general parallelism may have been part of what her husband had in mind when, in a letter to John Hay in 1886, he referred to *Esther* as a book "written in one's heart's blood" and acknowledged that it meant more to him than all the volumes of his *History*.

The contrasts are probably more revealing than the specific comparisons that are often drawn: as, for example, that neither Esther nor Mrs. Adams was remarkably beautiful; or that both women had a close, perhaps unfortunate, emotional dependence on their respective fathers and felt pathetically isolated when death deprived them of parental companionship. Notably, the central narrative question, whether Esther can achieve an orthodox religious faith and thus conscientiously marry

4 See Harold Dean Cater, *Henry Adams and His Friends*, pp. 1–3.

the possessive young clergyman with whom she has fallen in love, could not have been taken from the career of "Clover" Adams. Indeed, the scholar-artist with whom she cast her lot would seem to have been like her, rather than different, in needing though lacking religious consolation, and was able to survive, where she failed, mainly through superior personal resources that gave his life a degree of esthetic and intellectual coherency. Also, he would have been the last to assert control over another person's existence in the unimaginative, dogmatic manner of Stephen Hazard.

Still on the question of "sources," it is interesting if not signally important that the minor characters in *Esther*, as in *Democracy*, frequently suggest ascertainable acquaintances of the author. There is much of Clarence King in George Strong, the geologist, and much of John La Farge in Wharton, the artist. Here and there in Wharton one can also detect a trait of Augustus Saint-Gaudens. It was the supposition of William Roscoe Thayer that Hazard may have been drawn from Phillips Brooks. Catherine Brooks, Esther's young friend and companion, surely has much in her of the author's various "nieces."

Each character, however, is also essentially the creation of Henry Adams and embodies some of his comment on human experience. When the dying Mr. Dudley whispers to his daughter, "Laugh, Esther, when you're in trouble! Say something droll! then you're safe," he is speaking at the direction of a man who usually managed to disguise the innermost pain of his life behind an ironic façade and thus made a mystery of his true personality that is not yet solved.

What he was later to assert or imply repeatedly in *The Education* concerning the high but never quite fulfilled promise of himself, of Clarence King, and of many brilliant others of their generation, seems to emerge from the petulant feminine observation of Mrs. Murray to George Strong: "You and Hazard and all your friends are a sort of clever children.

We are always expecting you to do something worth doing, and it never comes. You are a sort of water-color, worsted-work, bric-a-brac, washed-out geniuses, just big enough and strong enough to want to do something and never carry it through. I am heartily tired of the whole lot of you. . . ." On this point one can think, also, of the retrospective analysis of Van Wyck Brooks, who characterizes the post-Civil War culture of New England as an Indian Summer.

Other passages in the book reveal rather strikingly that Adams's thinking was assuming the shape that was finally to appear in *Chartres* and *The Education*. "Is science true?" asks Esther of George Strong. His reply is something of a surprise to the heroine but, then, she had not the advantage of knowing Henry Adams:

> "No!"
> "Then why do you believe in it?"
> "I don't believe in it."
> "Then why do you belong to it?"
> "Because I want to help in making it truer."

And he goes on to assure her that the axioms of science are as difficult to accept as the miracles and mysteries of religion: "There is no science which does not begin by requiring you to believe the incredible." "Mystery for mystery," he has already remarked, "science beats religion all hollow."

Speaking so, George Strong resembles Adams more than Clarence King. Strong admits to Esther that he does not care much whether or not his favorite study of geology is "true." He might have explained, in a manner implying Adams's later attitude toward the various scientific concepts invoked in working out his theory of history, that where truth is elusive, convenience must serve.

Though George Strong, sympathetic with Esther in her fight to attain happiness, is willing for a moment to urge her to believe what she cannot mentally accept, much of his *raison d'être* in the novel is his exemplification of the plight of the sophisticated modern mind that cannot, with whatever will, remove the misgivings of reason. His surname is a tribute to the honesty of his attitudes, his free admission of how little he knows.[5] He cannot and therefore will not convince himself of the existence of a personal God or regard the doctrine of future rewards and punishments as anything more than old women's nursery tales. Does he then believe in nothing? asks Esther. He responds slowly that there is evidence, amounting to strong probability, of the existence of two things, call them mind and matter.

"Do you expect to convert any one to such a religion?" she asks.

"Great Buddha, no! I don't want to convert any one. . . . No one ever took up this doctrine who could help himself."

A little bit later he adds somewhat Socratically: "Hazard and I and everyone else agree that thought is eternal. If you can get hold of one true thought, you are immortal as far as that thought goes. The only difficulty is that every fellow thinks his thought the true one. Hazard wants you to believe in his, and I don't want you to believe in mine, because I've not got one which I believe myself." They are the accents of Henry Adams, prematurely summing up his lifelong quest and disillusion. To get hold of one true thought—but where, and how?

The intellectual position of the Reverend Mr. Hazard is something else. He is one of those strong-minded men who, "seeing that there was no stopping-place between dogma and negation . . . preferred to accept dogma." He avers stiffly to Esther that he believes, for example, in the resurrection of

5 "For it is a sign of strength," wrote Herman Melville to Nathaniel Hawthorne, "to be weak, to know it, and out with it. . . ."

the body. Doubts have always been laid provided the doubter wanted to lay them. "It is a simple matter of will." Simple, possibly, for Hazard but not for Esther, whose will is not noticeably inferior to her lover's; and not simple for the man who created them both. The precariousness of the young clergyman's attitudes is indicated, if not defined, by the noun that constitutes his surname. Despite his fortitude and integrity, Hazard seems to be presented deliberately as a rigid, somewhat repellent figure; he is an able and high-minded young cleric, but scarcely a human being on whom the heroine can stake her happiness in life. He believes that he loves Esther, but she is right in discerning that his primary allegiance is to his church, whatever the difficulties of sustaining its dogmas; that he conceives of her as a potential ornament for it; and that he is incapable of taking her for her own sake and so of loving her as she, pathetically enough, loves him.

As for Esther, her pathos belongs to Mrs. Henry Adams and to almost every sensitive woman in modern Western society. "All the contented women are fools," adumbrates Mrs. Murray, "and all the discontented ones wish to be men. Women are a blunder in the creation and must take the consequences. If Esther is sensible she will never marry; but no woman is sensible. . . ." The ending of the book, however, shows the niece acting with the firm good sense that the aunt was so sure was lacking. Whatever her love for Hazard, Esther could not believe as he did; nor would she submit herself at last to the persistent tyranny that she felt emanating from him. Not sufficiently resolute or, more plausibly, not so fortunately situated as to be able to reach happiness by following her own nature, she could at least cling to her woman's refusal to submerge her identity in a dogmatic, man-fashioned world.

The problem of Esther Dudley is thus closely similar to that of Madeleine Lee. Exploring, respectively, the institutions of churchly religion and of democratic government, both reach disillusion. Of the two novels, *Democracy* is the more readable, but *Esther* is the more profound.

"The trail from Esther to the Virgin of Chartres," writes Spiller, "is a long and intricate one, but it is straight." Twenty years later Adams was to discover a still more impressive symbol of valor and tenderness.

LETTERS

By no means have all the letters of Henry Adams been published, but to date they fill four separate volumes [6] as well as appearing here and there in a dozen or so other books. They establish their author as probably the foremost epistolarian in American literature.

He belonged to about the last generation in this country congenitally inclined to accept fully and seriously the obligations of personal correspondence. Beginning with Abigail Adams, wife of the second President, successive members of his family had written letters admirable for solidity, force, and polish. John Adams's skill in this respect increased as he grew older, so that his correspondence with Thomas Jefferson, already cited, some of it set down when the Quincy patriarch was over ninety, is incomparable. John Quincy Adams and his son, Charles Francis, carried on the habit of epistolary excellence. It was an eighteenth-century mode. One forms a mental image of Henry Adams retiring almost every morning for several hours to the privacy of his desk, no matter in what part of the world he found himself, and rapidly cover-

[6] *Letters to a Niece and Prayer to the Virgin of Chartres, by Henry Adams, with a Niece's Memories,* ed. Mabel La Farge (Boston: Houghton Mifflin Co., 1920).

Letters of Henry Adams, 1858–1918, ed. Worthington C. Ford (2 vols; Boston and New York: Houghton Mifflin Co., 1930–1938).

Henry Adams and His Friends: A Collection of His Unpublished Letters, ed. Harold Dean Cater (Boston: Houghton Mifflin Co., 1947).

ing white sheets of paper with those rounded, steel-clear characters that were his unmistakable mark. Anyone receiving an envelope so indubitably superscribed could be certain that the contents would be rich with information, whether grand or trivial, and zestful with ironic commentary from one of the strongest and wittiest of minds. Despite their distinct readability in our own generation, the letters were almost certainly not composed, as were those of Horace Walpole and some others, with an eye toward posterity. Worthington C. Ford observes that about 1885 (the year Mrs. Adams died) Adams destroyed his available correspondence, as well as all his diaries and notes, and from time to time thereafter would recall such letters as he could and burn them. He might be amazed and annoyed to learn how many of them nevertheless survived; but readers may be grateful.

The earliest letter in print is dated November 3, 1858; the last one, February 19, 1918. The first one, addressed to his brother Charles, opens jauntily: "With that energy of expression and originality of thought for which you are so justly celebrated, you have remarked in your last that the pleasures and pains of life are pretty equally divided. Permit me in the particular instance before us to doubt the fact." The final letter, written to his English friend Charles Milnes Gaskell, concludes quietly: "Perhaps our next letters will grow more cheerful with the improvement of the world." He thus began with the unaffrighted pessimism of youth and attained, at last, the forlorn hopefulness of age. In the almost sixty years that fell between these two passages, Henry Adams had not lived a career of high adventure in the usual sense, but he had probably absorbed as much of experience as any human being of his time. Always moving near, and often among, the leading events and personages of the moment, his quick eye observed much on the surface and still more beneath; and his quick pen usually made a record. Gloomy and aspiring, solemn and puckish, the letters form a fascinating annotation to his own life story and to history.

From 1858 to 1918: America moved out of a culture in which, North and South, strong traces of the eighteenth century still lingered, into the epic tragedy of her Civil War. Her greatest President martyred, she dreamed less deeply the ideals of the founding fathers and tended to prize industrial wealth as the highest human value. She built the transcontinental railway and laid the Atlantic cable. Partly because of her mildness and hospitality, partly because she needed their laboring strength, she welcomed millions of immigrants from northern and southern Europe but considerably fewer from the Orient. She fought the last of the Indian wars and, with some twinges of a conscience not quite dead, reserved a few unwanted acres and still fewer human rights to the defeated race. Challenging the dying might of Spain in Cuba and the Philippines, she asserted her claim to international power and, a few years later, confirmed it beyond doubt by contributing the winning stroke to a World War that was to be but the first act in a tragic drama yet playing. In Europe, when Adams was a student in Berlin, the unification of Italy was under way; it has been noted how he went down to Palermo and interviewed Garibaldi. Ten years later saw the triumph of a new-born Germany and the fall of France's Second Empire. In the next generation Russian Tsarism acknowledged its moribundity in defeat by Japan, which rose to power in Asia; and virtually all nations joined in the conflict that broke with the assassination of Archduke Ferdinand in 1914. Before it had subsided, the Russian peoples took their astounding step from feudalism into Communistic modernity that implied the portentous East-West dichotomy now haunting present and future. Against such a background one reads the letters of Henry Adams.

A full listing of his correspondents would reach several

score. Among men, however, he seems to have written oftenest to his brothers, Charles and Brooks, and to intimates like Charles Milnes Gaskell and John Hay. Unfortunately, in the printed volumes his letters to Clarence King do not appear; but one finds letters addressed to such acquaintances as Charles Sumner, William H. Seward, James Russell Lowell, John Gorham Palfrey, Charles Eliot Norton, Oliver Wendell Holmes—both father and son—William and Henry James, Edwin L. Godkin, Samuel Jones Tilden, Carl Schurz, Francis Parkman, George Bancroft, Barrett Wendell, Henry Holt, Henry Osborn Taylor, William Roscoe Thayer, William Sturgis Bigelow, Charles W. Eliot, Whitelaw Reid, John Franklin Jameson, Henry Cabot Lodge, Theodore Roosevelt, and many others. Though almost any letter one turns to is likely to contain a variety of matter, Adams tended to comment on politics, economics, science, and the general state of the world most directly when he wrote to men. Letters to women often touched more distinctly on art, religion, or social matters and were especially notable for a chivalrous grace. His feminine correspondents included Elizabeth Cameron, niece of William Tecumseh Sherman and wife of Senator Don Cameron of Pennsylvania; Elizabeth Chanler, half-sister of Francis Marion Crawford and author of *Roman Spring;* his many "nieces," especially Mabel Hooper La Farge; Rebecca Gilman Rae; Isabella Stewart Gardner; and Mrs. Henry Cabot Lodge, whom he usually called his "Sister Anne."

If any one group of letters may be called exceptional, they probably are those written to Elizabeth Cameron. Her friendship was closely meaningful to Adams in his later years because she had been intimate with him and his wife during their residence in Washington. Rightly regarding her as a person of remarkable intelligence and sympathy, he wrote freely to her of what was next to his mind and heart. An instance is the excerpt, already quoted in the first chapter, from a letter written to her in his sixty-third year as he sailed along the Norwegian coast toward the North Cape. Probably to no one else would he have so frankly confessed his emotions, caught in the impingement of a weird Götterdämmerung beauty: "I've no one to talk to but you, and I do want to talk about it, though I don't want to talk. No one understands. I'm only a bore."

He was seldom, if ever, that. Whether abroad or at home, he always had much to say that was diverting, and if he sometimes ran the danger of talking too much about himself, he tempered egotism with playful self-depreciation. In March, 1898, for example, he wrote to Mrs. Cameron of his visit to Damascus:

. . . brute of selfishness that I am, there is no doubt in my mean mind that I am uncommonly happy in this absurd mode of life. Damascus is, and always must have been, a mere shop, without political or intellectual leadership—just the sort of place that Chicago is, or St. Louis, or Lyons; yet Damascus amused me for a week as neither London nor Paris can. . . . There, once more, I seemed to meet people and exchange something. . . . I've not talked to so many strangers for forty years as I have this last ten days; and it proved to me that the times, not I, have changed. But what was more curious was the atmosphere of the rascally Syrian town, made of Moslem scoundrels, Christian thieves, and Jew moneylenders, all of types that blanch Chicago white. Yet what bores one in Chicago, intensely amused me in Damascus. They cheated me out of my eye-lids, stole my letters, lied ten times to the word, and made me live like a swine, and I only laughed. You would have laughed too, had you seen me, on my last afternoon, sitting in what they call a garden, under flowering almonds and apricots, with the willows just showing green, munching dry pistache and fresh almonds, and puffing violently at a nargileh that would not get lighted—I never could learn to smoke a nargileh—while I watched the Moslem men in their robes and

turbans, and the Christian or Jewish women, unveiled, and tried
to imagine what it looked like to Bedreddin—or whoever it was
—when the Djinn dropped him at the gates of Damascus,—probably close to where I sat,—and he took to making tarts. The city
is still full of these tarts!

This is Adams not quite at his best. For that, one must go
to the letters written from the South Seas and from Japan,
while he was journeying with John La Farge. This episode
has already been noted in some detail, and little more can
be done here than refer the reader to the various letters. Any
brief quotation must fail to be truly representative, though
the following excerpt, taken from a letter to Rebecca Gilman
Rae in November, 1890, suggests a tone frequently present:

Hawaii was pleasant, but Samoa is more amusing than fifty
Hawaiis. We have found here the true Polynesia, natives and
cocoanuts, coral reefs and bread-fruit, thatched huts and old-gold
girls, all in profusion, hardly touched by white improvement.
Here are no horsecars or electric lights, and not many clothes.
The young women whom I love are fifteen inches round the arm,
and can carry me like a child. Their backs are brown and glisten
with cocoanut oil. They have a lovely ball-dress consisting of
a girdle of green and purple leaves, and a garland of green leaves
and hibiscus flowers round their heads. They dance the siva,
which is something that would set Paris wild with delight, and
they smoke cigarettes with perfect ease, not to mention cigars
and pipes. They are extremely well-behaved, as far as I know, and
the chief belles have regular duennas, elderly married women
who are with them day and night. The duenna is present at all
one's flirtations, and is not particular about trifles, such as putting
one's arm round her neck, or going to sleep with one's head in
her lap; but if my young love were to show a disposition to be
more affectionate, she would get a very instructive beating with
a club, and would lose her social position. . . . Society is a complete communism; no one suffers from want; children are wealth

to the family; and as for white people, the child of a foreigner whose social position was good, would be envied. The Samoans are aristocratic beyond the dreams of a Washington newspaper correspondent, and detect instantly the shades of difference among whites.

Liberal as this system is, neither La Farge nor I have yet taken wives.

And so on. Adams was a good traveler: his zest for new scenes and people usually survived all manner of inconvenience and even hardship; and though his letters contain plenty of characteristic growling, it was basically good-humored. In the letter from which the Damascus passage has been quoted, he observes, with an air of surprise: "In a given situation, I generally am more comfortable than my neighbors."

Almost always, in fact, the air of comfort, or simply of an unobtrusive self-possession, is present. He holds in mind the tastes of his particular reader, and he knows just how many details to present without inflicting tedium. By shifting the topic frequently, by varying mood and structure and interspersing facts with commentary, by always injecting a bit of ironic fun, and by offering much but seldom all of himself, he achieves not only form but vitality—that *sine qua non* which Kate O'Brien aptly denominates "the first and the only unfakeable element in literature." Stylistically, the early letters are not fundamentally different from the late. He evidently decided, perhaps unconsciously, that his idiom was that of correctness and formality, and he never noticeably departed from it. Within it he found play for amusement and disgust, approval and denunciation, tenderness and anger, and laughter and solemnity. Though he worked at the problem of avoiding monotony—a letter to Henry Cabot Lodge tells of the need of deliberately varying the word order in sentences —he did not ever, so far as known, experiment with his skill as did Stevenson, by playing the sedulous ape, or as did Henry

James, by studiously fashioning a complex architecture of language to house the nuances of thought. One finds in the letters the increasing tendency toward simplicity and forcefulness, however, which Adams exhibited to its fullest in *Chartres* and *The Education*. Over the decades, the letters played the role, in short, of a perpetual self-schooling in expression.

In the letters as in his other writings one comes upon swift strokes of prophecy that show how persistently he kept his mind at work on the immediate raw material of history. He consistently averred that loathing for national and international politics expressed in his first novel and of course never took a direct part in them, but he was always snooping at the keyhole. Sometimes his guesses were astonishingly right, as when he wrote to Mrs. Cameron, January 10, 1904: "I am half crazy with fear that Russia is sailing straight into another French revolution which may upset all Europe and us too." Earlier (April 10, 1889) he had given the same correspondent a still more sweeping summary, which rings with truth for today: "The world is abjectly helpless. It is running a race to nowhere, only to beggar its neighbors. It must either abolish its nationalities, concentrate its governments and confiscate its monopolies for social economics, or it must steadily bump from rock to rock, and founder at last, economically; while it will founder socially if it does not concentrate and economise." In November, 1898, he observed to Worthington C. Ford: "The declining condition of British trade promises nothing good for England. Sooner or later we must come to her assistance economically . . . but it is impossible for us to hold her up economically without also holding her up politically; and the mere question of whether or how that should be done, sends a cold chill down my back. If our manufactures are to take her markets, and our capital is to merge with hers in developing joint interests, our fleets and armies must hold and defend the common wealth."

Occasionally, however, he could be wrong, as when he assured Mrs. Cameron in April, 1903, that Wall Street would see to it that Theodore Roosevelt would not win the coming election: "Unless the invariable experience of a century is to be reversed, Theodore will be crushed. . . ." Also, he was consistently too dire in his assessment of the economic state of the world around the turn of the century. His letters of that period repeatedly assert the imminence of a general collapse. Concerning Germany he could say, again in 1903, "The idea of a wretched little power like Germany, with no coast, no colonies, and no coal, attacking us, seems to me too absurd for a thought. . . . My limited view sees Germany as out of the race. I think she is a busted concern. . . ." He was prone, especially at this time, to reckon too high the role played by strictly economic resources; his definition of "force" was not yet comprehensive enough. Nevertheless, he was sufficiently cautious to add: "She [Germany] may have one more fight left in her. . . ."

As his wife was in her letters, he was usually entertaining in his when he summed up human character, often too acidulously for complete truth. One can suppose, for example, that he had some respect for the energy and ability of Theodore Roosevelt, but he never spared his political obsessions or his personality. Adams found him "a bore as big as a buffalo." "Of all Presidents that ever lived, Theodore thinks of nothing, talks of nothing, and lives for nothing but his political interests. If you remark to him that God is Great, he asks naïvely at once how that will affect his election. . . . He writes all his state papers, and ridiculous enough they are, so that I am far from flattered when people come down from New York, the most ignorant parochial spot I know, for its size, and charge me with them."

One account of a White House dinner, attended in January, 1904, by Adams, Elihu Root, Jacob Gould Schurman, Edward Everett Hale, a certain English lady, and others, is not easily forgotten:

You can see me! Desperate at the outlook, I flung myself—*à la* Wayne—into the mad stream, trying to stem it, and Root tried to help me; but we were straws in Niagara. Never have I had an hour of worse social *malaise*. We were overwhelmed in a torrent of oratory, and at last I heard only the repetition of I—I—I— attached to indiscretions greater one than another until only the British female seemed to survive. How Root stands this sort of thing I do not know, for it is mortifying even beyond drunkenness.

Roosevelt's successor, William Howard Taft, came off differently but not better: "Apparently we are to face a fat mush for three years . . . ," wrote Adams to Mrs. Cameron in September, 1909. Nevertheless, he had a liking for Taft and hoped he would be a competent President; but he was disappointed, as he later stated more than once.

He relished the company of Wayne MacVeagh, onetime ambassador to Turkey and Italy and Garfield's Attorney General. In 1883, Adams wrote to James Russell Lowell: "McVeagh [*sic*] is a man of extraordinary ability and character; the only man in American politics who says what he thinks, and thinks honestly." By 1901 MacVeagh's political hopes had become very dim. Adams wrote of him with affection, but also with an awareness of his limitations:

Apropos to extinct saurians. Wayne is back here, and, in half an hour's stroll last evening, he sprinkled me with a mass of political misinformation after his usual kind. Wayne is now a very long-passed article. He would like to be an anarchist like me, but he daren't. His soul is saurian,—which means Pennsylvanian,—and he clings to the skirts of the corporations with a just sense of wrong that the corporations, who have no soul, can give him only money. He takes the money, and he daren't kick the corporations, but he sasses them in the form of the individuals who run them. He is very bitter against everybody, and justly, no doubt; but he still admires England and the Church. After all, a Pennsylvanian is a wonderful thing; like an anthracite coal-bed; dark and dirty in itself, but the cause of light. . . .

Concerning the industrial great: "I attended a large dinner last night at the Embassy given to Andrew Carnegie," he wrote in May, 1909, from Paris, "with a half dozen ministers and diplomats all trying to look as though they took Andrew seriously, and worshipped heroes at a million francs apiece. It was a hazy dream, fantastic and grotesque, like a lot of monkeys in the Ceylon jungle, with Andy more monkeyish than any."

The letters confirm the affection for John Hay revealed in *The Education*. Adams was constantly concerned over Hay's failing health and the ordeal that his friend had to undergo as Roosevelt's Secretary of State. "Of course my chief visitor is John Hay," he wrote to Mrs. Cameron from Washington in January, 1902, "who comes to take me to walk at four o'clock, and in the absence of his family in New York, occasionally dines here. John seems to be quite well, for him, and in good spirits; but he is singularly detached. His attitude toward Theodore is that of a benevolent and amused uncle. He has usually some story to tell, or some outburst to repeat, partly with fun and occasionally with surprise or even astonishment, but never as though he felt any responsibility." These daily walks taken by Hay and Adams may have had distinct influence on the course of public events. Letters passing between the two friends at this time show that Hay had high trust in the political acumen of Adams and depended on him continually for counsel, both in regard to Spain and, later, Far Eastern affairs. It can even be surmised that Hay would have been glad to secure an official appointment for his friend. "Poor Hay has got a fearful mire to wade through," wrote Adams to Gaskell in September, 1898, "and I am a gilded butterfly on his cart-wheel. . . ." Then about a month later: "All my life I have lived in the closest possible personal relations with men in high office. Hay is the first one of them who has ever expressed a wish to have me for an associate in his responsibilities. . . . If he called on me, I should no doubt be obliged to do whatever he wished; but he will never be given that amount of liberty. Nothing short of a cataclysm in America could throw up men without political backing into offices of cabinet rank." It was the old diffidence and the old bitterness.

Henry Cabot Lodge fares less well in the letters than John Hay. The relationship between Lodge and Adams was, of course, almost lifelong. He had been one of Adams's most devoted students at Harvard and later helped him edit the *North American Review.* He was to sign the editor's preface of the 1918 edition of *The Education,* which, however, Adams evidently did not wish him to write. Some of Adams's best letters were written to Lodge with unmistakable good will. Yet as the years passed, Lodge became deeply immersed in factional politics and betrayed an egomania that drew the older man's contempt. "The true type of successful cant, which rests on no belief at all, is Cabot," wrote Adams in February, 1901, "who grabs everything and talks pure rot to order. . . ." A little later: "Then comes Cabot, whose methods exceed the endurance of a coral reef. No known form of polyp, fossil or living, equals Cabot for robbing the elements to secrete his store of gain."

Perhaps the Bostonian in him came forth a bit when he considered Robert Louis Stevenson, whom he and La Farge met in Samoa. The travelers called on Stevenson one October evening in 1890 after riding four or five miles up the hills, where they "struck a clearing covered with burned stumps with a very improvised house in the middle and a distant sea-view over the forest below":

There Stevenson and his wife were perched—like queer birds—mighty queer ones too. Stevenson has cut some of his hair; if he had not, I think he would have been positively alarming. He seems never to rest, but perches like a parrot on every available projection, jumping from one to another, and talking incessantly. The parrot was very dirty and ill-clothed as we saw him, being perhaps caught unawares, and the female was in rather worse trim than the male. I was not prepared for so much eccentricity in this particular, and could see no obvious excuse for it. Stevenson has bought, I am told, four hundred acres of land at ten dollars an acre, and is about to begin building. As his land is largely mountain, and wholly impenetrable forest, I think that two hundred acres would have been enough, and the balance might have been profitably invested in soap. . . .

I shall never forget the dirty cotton bag with its sense of skeleton within, and the long, hectic face with its flashing dark eyes, flying about on its high verandah, and telling us of strange men and scenes in oceans and islands where no sane traveller would consent to be dragged unless to be eaten.

Whatever his views on the emaciated Scotsman's untidiness, however, Adams held him in awe for his extraordinary energy and was glad to report him as being "extremely amusing and agreeable." In a later letter he alludes to him again—"human, not to say genial. . . . His talk is lively, agreeable, and almost quiet." [7]

7 "We have had enlightened society: La Farge, the painter, and your friend Henry Adams: a great privilege—would it might endure. I would go oftener to see them, but the place is awkward to reach on horseback. . . . They, I believe, would come oftener to see me but for the horrid doubt that weighs upon our commissariat department; we have *often* almost nothing to eat; a guest would simply break the bank . . ." (Robert Louis Stevenson to Henry James, December 29, 1890, in Sidney Colvin, ed., *The Letters of Robert Louis Stevenson* [New York: Charles Scribner's Son, 1907], II, 258 f.). This is all that Stevenson has to say of the friends' visit.

In 1900, he read Stevenson's *Letters* and could not agree with Henry Cabot Lodge that they were the best ever written. He expressed, indeed, a general distrust of all personalized talk and writing: "No one can talk or write letters all the time without the effect of egotism and error. They are like a portrait by Sargent; they betray one's besetting vices in youth and one's worst selfishness in middle-life, and one's senility in Joe Choate."

The reader of Adams's letters is not likely to have such a reaction. He will find that within their established pattern of formality they become stylistically more nimble as their author grows older, that they have less of the air of self-consciousness, and that they show an increasing sadness, tenderness, and wisdom. The cynicism of his final years that they so often express might become wearing were it not given, in terms of his own experience, a positive, dramatic quality. The letters are most meaningful, finally, when read in connection with *The Education*—not because they essentially contradict or alter the self-portrait Adams there draws of himself, but because they confirm it. They show again a man deeply conscious of the obligations of friendship and evidently grateful for the devotion of those who could comprehend, if not necessarily share, his own attitudes. They show him interested from first to last in the human race but almost totally disinclined, even in his youth, to succumb to its inveterate tendency to overrate itself. They show him swift to appreciate life's absurdities, small as well as large; indeed, they constitute full answer to the accusation made by one critic (J. T. Adams) that he lacked a sense of humor: in the tradition of Smollett, rather than that of Mark Twain, his wit is virtually omnipresent. They show him as a man of many interests and enjoyments; a student of history, politics, geography, mathematics, science, art; a man of feeling as well as thought. They show him increasingly convinced of modern society's desperate

plight, having tapped more power than it knows how to control and probably fated to reach a violent *impasse* by the
middle of the present century. Always, however, they show
him striving ceaselessly to discover an excuse for hope and in
the very assertion of his effort, however despairing the indicated conclusion, becoming the unconscious symbol of a possible salvation.

POEMS

Since Adams was widely read in ancient and modern poetry,
and was versatile in his accomplishments, it is easy to hypothesize that, like his grandfather, he tried frequently to
express himself in verse. If he did, however, it is easy to hypothesize further that he was his own severest critic and destroyed most of his efforts. In any event, aside from a few
translations only two examples of poetry from his hand are
known.

The first of these, "Buddha and Brahma," evidently was
written in late September, 1891, under circumstances that
the author summarizes in a letter of April 26, 1895, to John
Hay:

Once La Farge and I, on our rambles, stopped for an hour to
meditate under the sacred Bo-tree of Buddha in the ruined and
deserted city of Anuradjapura in the jungle of Ceylon; and, then,
resuming our course, we presently found ourselves on the quiet
bosom of the Indian Ocean. Perhaps I was a little bored by the
calm of the tropical sea, or perhaps it was the greater calm of
Buddha that bored me. At all events I amused a tedious day or
two by jotting down in a notebook the lines which you profess to
want. They are yours. Do not let them go further.

When the *Yale Review* printed the poem, in November, 1915,
Adams wrote to Elizabeth Cameron that he ought to have
sent her a copy, "but it would not amuse you. Mabel La
Farge, who now lives at New Haven, discovered it, and sent

it to my family, who only said: '*Tiens!* il se croit poëte!' which he don't. . . ."

It is true that as poetic art "Buddha and Brahma" is in no way remarkable. The blank verse pattern is for the most part accurately, even monotonously, observed; few lines contain any rhythmic subtlety. There is little attempt at wit, and images seldom occur, so that the general effect is esthetically unexciting. Though the ideas in it are challenging, the failure in form easily persuades one to believe the author when he says that he wrote in boredom. The following passage, taken from a point about one-third of the way through the poem, is fairly typical:

> Silent they sat, and long. Then slowly spoke
> The younger: "Father, you are wise.
> I must have Wisdom." "Not so, my son.
> Old men are often fools, but young men always.
> Your duty is to act; leave thought to us."
> The younger sat in patience, eyes cast down,
> Voice low and gentle as the Master taught;
> But still repeated the same prayer: "You are wise;
> I must have wisdom. Life for me is thought,
> But, were it action, how, in youth or age,
> Can man act wisely, leaving thought aside?"

The slender narrative takes its cue from the tradition that Gautama refused express answer to four salient questions, of which the first was whether or not the universe is eternal. As Adams treats this question in the poem, he throws emphasis on the immediate problem of objective reality. The perplexed youth, a devout but puzzled Buddhist, seeks out his father—who has dedicated his life to deeds, as Gautama has dedicated his to contemplation—to learn from him what justification can be offered for a career of action. The father's emphatic counsel, "*Think not! Strike!*" is, paradoxically, both final and tentative. A warrior, for example, need not question his blow, for it forms part of that outer visible world that he is committed to treat as real. Nevertheless, there is also the inner metaphysical world of thought, and in this he dwells separately, behind a veil not to be lifted. The wise man, thrown by circumstance onto the battlefield or into the market place, adjusts himself to the dichotomy. He acts, yet never loses the "one sole purpose: . . . a perfect union with the single Spirit." Thus, although action is a seeming and workable reality, to be automatically acknowledged, Thought is the true and ultimate reality, in which the Universe and all its parts silently find beginning and end. As a careful statement of philosophic dualism, with autobiographical implications, "Buddha and Brahma" merits close reading.

As suggested earlier, the poem can be taken, whether or not so intended, as explication of the memorial statue in Rock Creek Cemetery prepared by Saint-Gaudens at Adams's direction. Adams himself once referred to the passive, seated figure as "the peace of God." Without necessary reference to any specific creed, it is the peace that passeth all understanding, comprising ". . . Beginning, Middle, End,/Matter and Mind, Time, Space, Form, Life and Death."

A copy of the "Prayer to the Virgin of Chartres," reprinted in the Appendix of the present volume, was found in its author's wallet after his death early in 1918, but the poem had been composed many years before. "By way of relief from boredom," wrote Adams, February 25, 1901, to Elizabeth Cameron, "I have returned to verse, and have written a long prayer to the Virgin of Chartres, which I will send you presently, to put in your fire. It is not poetry, and it is not very like verse, and it will not amuse you to read; but it occupies me to write; which is something—at sixty-three. . . ." About seven years later he sent a copy also to

166

Margaret Chanler. "It is sad stuff," he told her, "but felt, as you see."

The "Prayer" rises to a distinctly higher artistic level than do the lines on Buddha and Brahma, technically as well as in the power of its emotion. Though the main rhythmic pattern is, again, iambic pentameter, it is often varied with trochaic openings, with spondees, and with a skillful use of run-on lines and distribution of internal pauses. The opening stanza is an instance of the variety achieved by Adams within a firm design:

> Simple as when I asked your aid before;
> Humble as when I prayed for grace in vain
> Seven hundred years ago; weak, weary, sore
> In heart and hope, I ask your help again.

Some rhythmic tedium finally intrudes despite the variations within lines because, with one exception, the syntax is brought to a full stop at the conclusion of each stanza. The shorter lines and slightly different stanzaic form of the "Prayer to the Dynamo," however, inserted in almost precisely the middle of the main poem, provide a structural relief. Throughout the entire composition the imagery is rich and appropriate. Regarded simply in technical terms Adams's accomplishment is considerable; and the total effect is so impressive that one can wish the author had been less diffident of his talent, so that he might have sought oftener to express himself in poetry.

The "Prayer" is comprehended more readily after a reading of *Mont-Saint-Michel and Chartres* and the twenty-fifth chapter of *The Education,* where Adams contrasts the highly animate, emotional, "inner" (as Robert E. Spiller calls it) force symbolized by the Virgin to the cold, inanimate, "outer" force symbolized by the dynamo. The Virgin was loving and creative; the dynamo is indifferent and catastrophic. In the final stanza of the interjected "Prayer to the Dynamo," Adams points metaphorically to the consequence of continued scientific development, and the language is particularly meaningful today:

> Seize, then, the Atom! rack his joints!
> Tear out of him his secret spring!
> Grind him to nothing!—though he points
> To us, and his life-blood anoints
> Me—the dead Atom-King!

The first part of the "Prayer to the Virgin" is a tribute to Mary's power at Chartres during the Middle Ages, a tribute which Adams makes impressively personal by identifying the dramatic speaker (as often in *Chartres*) with one who then knew and worshipped her. The concluding part is an assertion that this power must revive, after modern science has wrought its worst calamities and men have realized that there is no solace in machinery, even machinery of infinite force, but only in infinite love.

Almost beyond doubt the dramatic speaker is Henry Adams, who affirms to have learned, without having actually to travel full length the disastrous path indicated by the dynamo, that now as seven hundred years ago he belongs at the Virgin's feet. The final stanzas, with parallel structure building to climactic strength, read as a personal cry: "Help me to see! . . . Help me to know! . . . Help me to feel! . . . Help me to bear! . . ." A reader may feel that he has unwittingly intruded on a secret anguish whose privacy, beyond possible companionship, he has no right to violate.

Nevertheless, it is the anguish not alone of one man but of the contemporary human spirit at its most sensitive, unable to believe—knowing the failure of God's light, knowing the "futile folly of the Infinite," and so striving to erect again a symbol of limitless compassion that once compelled not a few minds but all.

Was Adams's self-dedication to the Virgin complete? One dare not say that it was not so when he wrote this poem. Surely its statement, as he himself says, was "felt." When he sent it to Margaret Chanler, however, who was a devout Roman Catholic, he counseled: "Throw it into the fire when done. You pray in another spirit." Though concerning so intimate a problem one might be wisest and most tactful to avoid speculation, one feels impelled to say that the "Prayer" seems to have come from a profound mood that Adams usually wanted to reach but seldom did. His letters and his later books show the sadness of one who, despite his deepest wish, had often to realize that his devotion to the Virgin was not an act of impulsive, unchallengeable religious faith (as he suggests the faith of Mrs. Chanler was) but a metaphorical and finally secular performance. Possibly, indeed, sometimes, as when he wrote his poem, the Virgin seemed real enough to give meaning and order to his life, but when he took his eyes from her face—and too often he had to—there were chaos and near-despair. He, too, belonged to the twentieth century, not really to the twelfth, nor to that future moment when men in their self-disgust and weariness would fall down again and believe.

IT was very childlike, very foolish, very beautiful, and very true—as art, at least: so true that everything else shades off into vulgarity, as you see the Persephone of a Syracusan coin shade off into the vulgarity of a Roman emperor; as though the heaven that lies about us in our infancy too quickly takes colours that are not so much sober as sordid, and would be welcome if no worse than that. Vulgarity, too, has feeling, and its expression in art has truth and even pathos, but we shall have time enough in our lives for that, and all the more because, when we rise from our knees now, we have finished our pilgrimage. We have done with Chartres. For seven hundred years Chartres has seen pilgrims, coming and going more or less like us, and will perhaps see them for another seven hundred years; but we shall see it no more, and can safely leave the Virgin in her majesty, with her three great prophets on either hand, as calm and confident in their own strength and in God's providence as they were when Saint Louis was born, but looking down from a deserted heaven, into an empty church, on a dead faith.—*Mont-Saint-Michel and Chartres.*

VI

A Deserted Heaven

IF HENRY ADAMS'S name as a writer were to stand or fall by one volume, *Mont-Saint-Michel and Chartres* might well be the one for his admirers to invoke. He himself accorded it a somewhat excessive preference: "If you will read my *Chartres*," he advised William James, "—the last chapter is the only thing I ever wrote that I almost think good—you will see why I knew my *Education* to be rotten."

Privately printed in 1904 and again in 1912, *Chartres* was given to the public in an edition sponsored by the Institute of Architects in 1913. By its presentation of the main features of churchly architecture during the eleventh, twelfth, and thirteenth centuries, its account of the medieval mystics and scholastics, and its dissertation on the cult of the Virgin, it has won an acclaim in the academic and literary world that might well gratify its author.

The book opens with a disarmingly simple preface in which Adams, prone as always to exalt the sensibility of the female over that of the male, asserts that the listener he chooses for his discourse on medieval art and thought is a "niece" rather than a "nephew." This preference is not entirely hypothetical, for especially as Adams grew older he assembled around him by mutual attraction a group of talented young or middle-aged women. Some of them were nieces by blood, others by wish. All of them seem to have adored him, and to one of them—Mabel Hooper La Farge, the daughter of his wife's brother—readers owe the valuable little book *Letters to a Niece and Prayer to the Virgin of Chartres.*

In passing it might be noted again that Adams makes more on paper of this penchant for feminine companionship than he did in actual life. His close association with young men like Hallett Phillips and "Bay" Lodge has been mentioned. One should recall, too, his frequent admonition to a departing guest, "Bring me men," and his perennial eagerness to find out what young men were thinking and what kind of new world they were consciously or unconsciously fashioning. "I have runners everywhere . . ." he wrote to a friend in January, 1899, "with orders to seize and bring in every likely young man they hear of." He added that young women were more plentiful.

In writing a preface to *Chartres* that seemed to restrict the book to the feminine reader, Adams probably knew that he was issuing a species of challenge to her male counterpart. Can a "nephew" turn aside long enough from his mechanical and monetary preoccupations to consider art, literature, and the more portentous problems of existence? Let him read *Chartres* and find out.

The first chapter contains an exposition on the history, physical site, and architecture of the abbey church of Mont-Saint-Michel, planned in 1020 and completed in 1135. Adams's method of presentation, is, characteristically, not the dry one of the classroom pedant. He asks his companion, and so his reader, on approaching the church to slough off the nineteenth or twentieth century and become a contemporary with William the Conqueror, Harold the Saxon, Taillefer the minstrel, and others whose personalities are suggested by the surroundings.

We are in the eleventh century—tenants of the Duke or of the Church or of small feudal lords who take their names from the neighborhood. . . . For the moment, we are helping to quarry granite for the Abbey Church, and to haul it to the Mount, or load it on our boat. We never fail to make our annual pilgrimage to the Mount on the Archangel's Day, October 16. We expect to be called out for a new campaign which Duke William threatens against Brittany, and we hear stories that Harold the Saxon, the powerful Earl of Wessex in England, is a guest, or, as some say, a prisoner or a hostage, at the Duke's Court, and will go with us on the campaign. The year is 1058.

Then follows a chapter devoted mainly to the *Chanson de Roland,* brief sections of which Adams translates from medieval French. "The poem and the church are akin; they go together and explain each other," both of them symbols of the masculine, military character and energy of the eleventh-century Normans. William and Harold may have come to the Mount and heard Taillefer sing the *Chanson* as they "dined or supped in the old refectory, which is where we have lain in wait for them."

Adams pays only a passing nod to the objection that "critics doubt the story, as they very properly doubt everything," because the *Chanson* may belong to a slightly later date. Typically, he is interested here and throughout the book not so much in offering a painstaking chronology of exact historical data as in recapturing the vital, unified spirit of a lost age and in enabling the reader to feel it. This is not to question the value of the book as scholarship: Adams almost always derives his facts from research, not from romance, and when for reasons of art he becomes cavalier with history he says so and thus no reader need be misled. At the same time, his dominating intention is that of the imaginative artist, not that of the simple recorder.

Thanks to later writers like Proust and Pirandello, contemporary readers have become accustomed to the literary treatment of time as a mere fiction, manipulated to serve the purposes of the craftsman. With attention to these and other passages that might be cited from *Chartres,* one may say that Adams was something of a pioneer with this technique. He had no wish to employ it consistently, however, for to have done so would have been to obliterate the constantly implied contrast between medieval and modern times that is part of his over-all aim. He asks readers, in effect, to become inhabitants of the eleventh or twelfth century and at the same time remember that they belong to the nineteenth or twentieth. Repeatedly Adams brings the two periods into a curiously ironic juxtaposition within the same sentence. Elaborating, for example, on his belief that an examination of the Middle Ages leads to the conclusion that "one knew life once and has never so fully known it since," he exclaims: "For we of the eleventh century, hard-headed, close-fisted, grasping, shrewd, as we were, and as Normans are still said to be, stood more fully in the centre of the world's movement than our English descendants ever did."

Later, in the fourteenth chapter of *Chartres,* recreating with artistic freedom the famous verbal duel at the University of Paris between Pierre Abélard and William of Champeaux, Adams has William remark rather incredibly: "Certainly you are free, in logic, to argue that Socrates and Plato are mere names—that men and matter are phantoms and dreams. No one ever has proved or ever can prove the contrary. Infallibly, a great philosophical school will some day be founded on that assumption." In writing such portions of *Chartres,* Adams obviously enjoyed himself. Much of the wistful charm apparent on almost every page derives from a recognition that the author has entered an area of time that he feels to be his own, if any is, and that there he may adopt an attitude of particular ease and may view other areas, especially ours, with gentle contempt. One can hardly dwell, even tentatively, in the twelfth century without repudiating most of the values of the twentieth. One of the functions possible to literature is that of emphasizing the mortality of human pretensions while winning for them simultaneously an extension in time. The reader of *Chartres* moves through an extension of the Middle Ages.

As the book goes forward, the reader accompanies Adams across part of France and through the revivified decades in scrutinizing various aspects of medieval art and thought. From Mont-Saint-Michel one proceeds to Paris, touching at Coutances, Bayeux, Caen, Rouen, and Mantes, and thence to Chartres. As the church on the Mount is the statement in stone of eleventh-century military energy and restlessness, so Chartres Cathedral avers twelfth-century faith and repose. Above all other architectual works, it is the court of the Queen of Heaven. It has already been noted how in characterizing her Adams pays his supreme tribute to the delicacy, the capriciousness, and the solacing beauty of woman, employing phrasing that may have been evoked by memories of Marian Hooper Adams. To Adams the cult of Mary dominated and unified the humanity of twelfth-century France, and the pages he devotes to her are especially significant as part of the basic framework of his dynamic theory of history, presently to be examined. Her force in the Middle Ages is to be compared and contrasted to that exerted today by the dynamo, and the centrality she accomplished, in focusing the emotions and the inner, "spiritual" energies of her adorers, has disintegrated over seven centuries into the near-chaos of modern society.

In successive chapters of *Chartres* Adams sets up his hypothesis of medieval unity not only in terms of the cathedral architecture, with its evidence of the complete adoration of a divine womanly symbol, but also in terms of the light literature, mysticism, and scholarship of the period—all within the same mental and emotional frame of reference. The twelfth chapter, with its disquisition on the *chante-fable* of *Aucassins et Nicolette* is one of the most appealing, partly because here again Adams offers his own sympathetic translation of the French lines. He tends always to reveal some diffidence in doing so; at the same time he is free enough with the phrasing to produce verse in English testifying to his own latent poetic feeling and skill. Take, as instance, part of Aucassins' soliloquy, sung while he spends the night in the forest:

Estoilete, je te voi,	I can see you, little star,
Que la lune trait a soi.	That the moon draws through the air.
Nicolete est aveuc toi,	Nicolette is where you are,
M'amiete o le blond poil.	My own love with the blonde hair.
Je quid que dix le veut avoir	I think God must want her near
Por la lumiere de soir	To shine down upon us here
Que par li plus clere soit.	That the evening be more clear.
Vien, amie, je te proie!	Come down, dearest, to my prayer,
Ou monter vauroie droit. . . .	Or I climb up where you are!

Here and elsewhere in the book one of the most learned scholars of his time proves that he carried within his complexity a vein of utter simplicity.

It is a vein revealed again in the fifteenth chapter, devoted in large part to delineating the character and attitudes of St. Francis. One of the most vivid human portraits in the book, accomplished in about ten pages, it is remarkable not just for the artistic skill displayed in the composition but for the almost startling sympathy shown by the writer with his subject. Adams pays high tribute to the ability and force of various men in the Middle Ages—William the Conqueror, Abélard, Bernard of Clairvaux, St. Thomas Aquinas—but he reserves his most intense warmth of admiration, and perhaps a strong nostalgic envy, for St. Francis; not only for the conventionally known saint preaching with Christlike gentleness to the birds, but for the passionate leader fierily denouncing five thousand of his assembled clerical brethren who wanted to adopt the rule of Benedict or Augustine or Bernard: " 'God told me, with his own words, that he meant me to be a beggar and a great fool, and would not have us on any other terms; and as for your science, I trust in God's devils who will beat you out of it, as you deserve.' " Whether if Adams had lived in the Middle Ages he would have attached himself to a figure like Francis rather than Thomas Aquinas—who sought to prove the existence of God by logic, inferring from universal motion a Universal Motor—becomes idle speculation; because Adams never lets one forget that the faith and logic of that time did not survive: "When both lines had been carried, after such fashion as might be, to their utmost results, and five hundred years had been devoted to the effort, society declared both to be failures."

Not impossibly, society may yet revive the contrasting approaches to universal interpretation of the mystics and the schoolmen, "For the two paths seem to be the only roads that can exist, if man starts by taking for granted that there is an object to be reached at the end of his journey." The "if" is supremely important. In *The Education,* even more than in *Chartres,* Adams was finally to show that the pathos of the contemporary mind is its incapacity to believe—an incapacity not detached, however, from an emotionally based compulsion to find life other than meaningless.

For a full understanding of the place occupied by *Chartres* in the development of Adams's thinking, one does well to observe something of how the book came into being.

After Mrs. Adams died, in December, 1885, Adams took

a trip to Japan with his artist friend John La Farge. When he returned he compelled himself to finish his *History,* and thereafter he temporarily withdrew from conventional scholarly activity. His journey to the South Seas in 1890–1891, again with La Farge, was evidently a deliberate attempt to forget the recent past, to medicate a badly frayed nervous system, and presumably rest his mind. But the mind of Henry Adams could never completely rest. (One night after the pair had had a friendly argument, La Farge suffered a nightmare in which he was convinced that Adams's mind was rattling around the room: it turned out to be a rat.) In places like Samoa, Tahiti, the Fiji Islands, and Ceylon, Adams must have meditated even more profoundly than his letters show on the contrasts between Eastern and Western cultures. The two literary works that resulted from this long journeying—the book *Tahiti* and the poem "Buddha and Brahma"—furnish only hints as to the direction of his thought.

According to his own account in *The Education,* he lay in January, 1892, in a London hospital (probably for a routine checkup) pondering on the growing complexity of European and American life and was sufficiently appalled to wish for nothing more than to go back to the East, "if it were only to sleep forever in the trade-winds under the southern stars, wandering over the dark purple ocean, with its purple sense of solitude and void." Western civilization was filled with unpleasant and uncreative tensions. La Farge had asked him one day whether there might not still be room for something simple in art, and Adams had shaken his head. The world was no longer simple, and one whose tastes belonged to an earlier age might understandably toy with a wish to escape.

He was Henry Adams, however, not Rimbaud or Gauguin, and he was soon back again in Western life, ensconced in the house on Lafayette Square that he and his wife had planned, and ruminating on past and present with his neighbor John Hay, who was marking time until he should become Secretary of State. It seems, incidentally, an inescapable conclusion that, at this point as earlier, Adams would have been glad to serve the American people in some diplomatic capacity. "There never was a day," he later wrote in the twenty-first chapter of *The Education,* "when he would have refused to perform any duty that the Government imposed on him. . . ." Without wishing to excuse Adams's adoption of his family's almost eccentric reserve in never offering their services, and without ignoring the remark attributed to Justice Holmes by Owen Wister that "Adams wanted it handed to him on a silver plate," one can still lament this instance of how the official Washington mind has chronically refused since the Civil War to avail itself of intellect and integrity. Yet if Adams had not been thus pettily ignored by those in power, he might not have been able to keep his mind at the level, safely above that of the dingy warfare of politics and diplomacy, where it produced *Chartres* and *The Education.*

In July, 1893, Henry Adams was called back to Quincy from Switzerland by a telegram from his brother Brooks announcing the famous financial panic of that year. Awaiting the turn of events that would prove whether or not they had become paupers, the brothers mulled over the then partially written manuscript of Brooks's *Law of Civilization and Decay.* The historical thesis of this work, according to its author, was that

the economic centre of the world determined the social equilibrium, and . . . this international centre of exchanges was an ambulatory spot on the earth's surface which seldom remained fixed for any considerable period of time, but which vibrated back and forth according as discoveries in applied science and geography changed avenues of communication, and caused trade routes to reconverge. Thus Babylon had given way to Rome, Rome to Constantinople, Constantinople to Venice, Venice to

Antwerp, and finally, about 1810, London became the undisputed capital of the world. Each migration represented a change in equilibrium, and, therefore, caused a social revolution.

The panic of 1893 was a sign, and not the first, that a shift was taking place from London to New York. Brooks had amassed an astounding sum of historical data from which he was able to conclude, thus, that many of mankind's wars are a predictable result of economic tension. His introduction to *The Degradation of the Democratic Dogma,* published in 1919, the year following Henry's death, contains the simple assertion that the catastrophe indicated by conditions in 1893 came in 1914, though Brooks had originally guessed 1930. It also contains what hindsight seems to reveal as a prophecy of World War II. The first World War, wrote Brooks, was economic. "But an economic war is the fiercest and most pitiless of all wars, since to make a lasting peace in competition implies either the extermination or enslavement of the vanquished. If the vanquished is to be conciliated, that is to say, restored to a position in which he can act as a freeman, he must be granted rights which will enable him to compete on equal terms with the victors, and the old conditions will be automatically revived. That is to say there must be still more bitter struggle within a generation,—at furthest."

In 1893, of course, Brooks Adams's thinking was still tentative. What impressed Henry was that it seemed to point to what he himself had conceived of as he had written his *History:* a science, or at least a philosophy, of history—a philosophy that in the present instance indicated anarchism and not collectivism as the logical outcome. *The Education* records: "Henry made note of it for study." Presumably, partly to check on his brother's results, and partly to give rein to his own intellectual curiosities, he turned once more to devising a scientific historical theory of his own.

His mind shifted into high gear when he visited the Chicago

World's Fair in the latter part of 1893. What he found there drew his intellectual attention much more strongly than did the monetary panic which, during the same year, was convulsing the nation. The mechanical exhibits, especially those featuring the dynamo, convinced him that the American people now had virtually unlimited force at their disposal, but they did not know where they were driving it or, more accurately, where it was driving them. Back again in Washington, Adams worked with long columns of statistics, seeking to define the goal of man's activities, but he could reach no conclusion. Of only one national development could he feel sure: the adoption of the gold standard indicated the final acquiescence of American society to a capitalistic, centralizing, mechanical way of life, and the repudiation of older values that had been symbolized for Adams in "his eighteenth century, his Constitution of 1789, his George Washington, his Harvard College, his Quincy, and his Plymouth Pilgrims. . . ." The early democratic dream, whose failure he had recorded in his *History*, was now irrevocably laid away, and the hope for a worthy American society would have to emerge, if at all, in some very different guise. He detested bankers and corporations but had to acknowledge that, during the future he could foresee, they would control the country; and surveying his own background and his present status he purported to feel particularly useless, a superannuated pedagogue. He was fifty-six years old.

Readers know, as he could not, that the most energetic and brilliant phase of his career was barely under way. In 1894 he was, through no particular desire of his own, president of the American Historical Association. Had he attended the annual meeting in December, he would have had to deliver a presidential address. Probably in part for the purpose of avoiding the conspicuousness this duty would have involved, he left Washington at the end of November for a jaunt with his young friend Chandler Hale into Central America and the Caribbean. In lieu of the presidential address, he sent a letter to the Association from Guadalajara, Mexico. This communication—published in the *Annual Report* of the Association for 1894 under the title of "The Tendency of History" and eventually reprinted in *The Degradation of the Democratic Dogma,* edited by Brooks Adams in 1919 [1]—points to the strong possibility that history might soon become a science. Should it do so, historians would find themselves facing a serious crisis; for conflicting interests like those of "the church and the state, property and communism, capital and poverty, science and religion, trade and art" could not all be happy at being told that human society must by mathematical certainty follow a defined path. The reaction of the historians in their meeting is not recorded. One can summon up, however, a vision of their bewilderment at being thus blandly put on their guard against a situation that most of them had no conception of at all, and being invited by their retiring president "to consider the matter in a spirit that will enable us, should the crisis arise, to deal with it in a kindly temper. . . ."

Henry later told Brooks that the letter to the Association was meant to prepare the members' minds for the impact of the latter's *Civilization and Decay,* then still being written. With all its brilliance and thoroughness, it was to disappoint the older brother by its lack of a "scientific summary," which the younger freely confessed presented a task beyond his powers to furnish. If it were to be done by an Adams, Henry would have to do it. As events proved, he was not disinclined to try.

In a mood of heightened curiosity and expectation (granted

[1] Rather confusingly, *The Tendency of History* was used as the title of a volume of Henry Adams's writings published by The Macmillan Company in 1928. The volume contains *A Letter to American Teachers of History* (privately printed by Adams in 1910) and "The Rule of Phase Applied to History" (written in 1908) but not the 1894 letter, "The Tendency of History."

that the dejection, which he records in *The Education,* over society's evident plight was probably real enough), he went to France with the Lodges in the summer of 1895 and experienced, according to his own narrative, a sudden artistic excitement as he stood in the presence of medieval art at Caen, Coutances, and Mont-Saint-Michel. Characteristically he pays tribute to a woman, in this instance Mrs. Henry Cabot Lodge—whom he ranked as a human being far above her Senator husband—for rescuing him from ennui and providing him with new intellectual and emotional attachments. Plainly, however, his study of the Middle Ages with its salient emphasis on features contrasting to those of the present century came to him at this time as a perfectly logical development. It is probably enough to give Mrs. Lodge credit for organizing the particular excursion that brought Adams into the physical presence of Norman medieval architecture. Several years later, in November of 1899, he paid a visit with John La Farge to Chartres Cathedral, where Adams awakened as never before to beauty and worship in glass and stone. By the turn of the century he had essentially formulated his dynamic theory of history, which required first of all the establishing of two points of historical reference—one in the medieval past, the other in the twentieth-century present. *Mont-Saint-Michel and Chartres* was the first important literary consequence of this theory, and *The Education* was to be the second.

Again, what impressed Adams most of all in his new study of the Middle Ages was the evidence of the unifying power exerted by the Virgin over the spirit and deeds of men. Repeatedly one encounters passages in *Chartres* where he seems to reveal his own embarrassment at being caught up so unmistakably by emotions and sensations closely similar to those that medieval men and women must have known. Chartres

Cathedral, he asserts in his eighth chapter, "was made what
it is, not by the artist, but by the Virgin":

> If this imperial presence is stamped on the architecture and
> the sculpture with an energy not to be mistaken, it radiates through
> the glass with a light and color that actually blind the true servant
> of Mary. One becomes, sometimes, a little incoherent in talking
> about it; one is ashamed to be as extravagant as one wants to be;
> one has no business to labour painfully to explain and prove to
> one's self what is as clear as the sun in the sky; one loses temper
> in reasoning about what can only be felt, and what ought to be
> felt instantly, as it was in the twelfth century, even by the *truie
> qui file* and the *ane qui veille.*

Not more than one in a hundred or a thousand can share
this medieval feeling, "for we have lost many senses." In fact,
remarks Adams with typical vividness, "the feebleness of our
fancy is now congenital, organic, beyond stimulant or strych-
nine, and we shrink like sensitive-plants from the touch of a
vision or spirit. . . ."

One need not be obnoxiously moralistic to feel that this
intermittent chiding of the twentieth-century reader is one
of the strong positive elements in *Chartres,* for it is precept
directly attached to example. It is well for a generation swimming in a diluted Freudianism to be compelled, through
Adams's discussion of the Virgin, to realize that love may be
treated as a principle, and not simply as an anatomical routine
learned best from a textbook and destined for inclusion in a
statistical report. It is well for it to realize, too, that the world
has not necessarily gained by surrendering, in the name of
cynicism or "science," its capacity to dream, so that it is by
now unable to rise by imagination to even a tentative concept
of divinity beyond that of a dead and anthropomorphic being.
The artist and the saint know better than most psychologists
that men and women are prone to behave like animals, but
they go on to insist, as the psychologists seldom presume to

184

or dare, that the animality can be qualified by an ideal.

Chartres is the record of a specific ideal now virtually dead, though one of the fascinations of the book for the student of Adams is that of observing how close he comes to giving that ideal a renewed, personal validity. It is difficult, for example, not to attribute autobiographical import to his observation in the seventh chapter: "Many a young person, and now and then one who is not in first youth, witnessing the sight in the religious atmosphere of such a church as this, without a suspicion of susceptibility, has suddenly seen what Paul saw on the road to Damascus, and has fallen on his face with the crowd, grovelling at the foot of the cross, which, for the first time in his life, he feels." Or there may be a veiled allusion here to James Russell Lowell's poem "The Cathedral." Written in 1869, it chronicles the poet's own visit to Chartres, and the nostalgia it prompted in him for that earlier time when ritual was a reality and not, as for Lowell and others of a later date, a curiously impressive but half-empty routine. There would seem to be small doubt that this poem influenced Adams, though its feeling is too shallow and its thought too confused to give it rank as more than a vague suggestion of *Mont-Saint-Michel and Chartres*.

Whatever the depths of Adams's sympathy, however, with medieval religious emotion, he never was able to make it completely his own. It was the pathos of his predicament that the scholar in him intruded on the believer and qualified emotion with analysis. "When we philosophers at last arrive," he wrote in May, 1909, to his former pupil, Charles F. Thwing, "—when we learn to know our God,—we roll on the ground and pray; but we don't publish books."

Referring to the multitude of legends concerning Mary, legends showing her partiality for criminals, sinners, and sundry social outcasts, and her frequent displeasure with men of rank or money, Adams concludes in *Chartres* that she represented something extralegal. She was an emblem of men's rebellion against the status quo championed by the feudal lords and the priests, and out of her pity and womanly caprice she did not hesitate to set aside state and church; and she also set aside, or absorbed, the Trinity. "The rudest ruffian of the Middle Ages, when he looked at [the] Last Judgment laughed; for what was the Last Judgment to her! . . . On her imperial heart the flames of hell showed only the opaline colours of heaven. Christ the Trinity might judge as much as He pleased, but Christ the Mother would rescue; and her servants could look boldly into the flames."

Such a view is, of course, anything but orthodox. An earnestly devout Roman Catholic can be annoyed if not enraged at this skeptical descendant of New England Puritans, so serene in his conclusion that the people of the Middle Ages effectually took the problem of eternity into their own hands and, when they chose, ignored the clergy.[2] Probably Adams would respond, if at all, that his observations on the Virgin were not adduced to please or displease any particular sect but only to serve as a historian's explanation of the amazing prevalence of her cult. She symbolized, he was convinced, the wondrous coercion of the eternal womanly and was thus an emphasized instance of the same phenomenon seen in the deference paid to various women of the medieval age, whether

[2] For a passionate and readable, though only thinly scholarly, expression of orthodox chagrin with Henry Adams see the Reverend H. F. Blunt, "The Maleducation of Henry Adams," *Catholic World*, CXLIV (April, 1937), 46–52. A more moderate view is voiced by the editors, pp. 110 f., commenting on the article: "Those who see in *Mont-Saint-Michel and Chartres* a prose poem and therefore allow its author a certain poetic license, will be inclined to dispute Dr. Blunt's conclusions. There are some who may find cause for wonder, that a New England Yankee could have so far progressed away from his original Puritanism as to appropriate even as much as Mr. Adams did of Catholicism." See also Frances Quinlivan, "Irregularities of the Mental Mirror," *Catholic World*, CLXIII (April, 1946), 58–65.

fictitious or real—Nicolette, the beloved of Aucassins; Eleanor of Guienne; Mary of Champagne; and Blanche of Castile. She recalled the ancient adoration of Venus and so was, as an emblem, less religious than sexual. Working as a sensitive scholar, Adams compiled enough evidence to make his interpretation of the Virgin impressive as historical hypothesis, however much it might pique past and present theologians.

Such was the strength of Mary's hold on the emotions of twelfth-century men and women that, as Adams has already been observed to say, she in effect directed every step in the construction of Chartres Cathedral. He quotes at length the eloquent letter of Archbishop Hugo of Rouen, descriptive of the process:

Who has ever seen!—Who has ever heard tell, in times past, that powerful princes of the world, that men brought up in honour and in wealth, that nobles, men and women, have bent their proud and haughty necks to the harness of carts, and that, like beasts of burden, they have dragged to the abode of Christ these waggons, loaded with wines, grains, oil, stone, wood, and all that is necessary for the wants of life, or for the construction of the church? But while they draw these burdens, there is one thing admirable to observe; it is that often when a thousand persons and more are attached to the chariots—so great is the difficulty—yet they march in such silence that not a murmur is heard, and truly if one did not see the thing with one's eyes, one might believe that among such a multitude there was hardly a person present. When they halt on the road, nothing is heard but the confession of sins, and pure and suppliant prayer to God to obtain pardon. At the voice of the priests who exhort their hearts to peace, they forget all hatred, discord is thrown far aside, debts are remitted, the unity of hearts is established.

Whether such a scene as this can be taken as showing the almost miraculous social unity of the men and women not only in the community of Chartres but also throughout medieval Europe must naturally be doubted. Adams elsewhere refers to many of the discords apparent in the church itself —the conflict, for example, between Abélard and Bernard— and notes the sundry economic and political tensions that produced, as in any age, both crime and warfare. Adams's dynamic theory of history was to be at once an artistic and a pragmatic achievement, successful if it defined in workable terms the manifest tendencies within human society. Placed against the order and unity of a previous age, the chaos of modern times becomes more monstrous and appalling but also more comprehensible, and artistically it matters little whether the unity of that previous age be real or partly mythical.

This question of Henry Adams's own religious beliefs is closely pertinent to an understanding of his dynamic theory of history and of most of his comments in *Chartres* and elsewhere on life and the universe. He came, of course, from a family traditionally Puritan and Calvinistic which by his own day had decided with most New Englanders to adhere to the liberal tenets of Unitarianism. In *The Education* he makes clear, however, that as a mature man he found himself unable to endorse any churchly principles: "Even the mild discipline of the Unitarian Church was so irksome that they [Henry Adams and his brothers and sisters] threw it off at the first possible moment, and never afterwards entered a church. The religious instinct had vanished, and could not be revived, although one made in later life many efforts to recover it." As usual, Adams in this passage is being unnecessarily self-depreciative. No man so strongly drawn, as he shows himself to be in *Chartres,* to the character of St. Francis of Assisi, and so filled with admiration for the writings of St. Augustine and of St. Thomas Aquinas, could entirely have lost the "religious instinct." It seems true, nevertheless, that except perhaps for brief moments, as hinted at in the passage quoted above about the Virgin, he never achieved faith. His feeling for the Virgin as a symbol enabled him to write his remarkable poetic "Prayer" to her; but it did not lead him to or even near the Church. In saying this one must, it is true, repudiate the conclusion reached by Mabel Hooper La Farge that her Uncle Henry Adams, in composing the "Prayer to the Virgin of Chartres" "leaves no shadow of a doubt that he himself perceived 'that was the true light.' "

Not that he failed to be remarkably tolerant of revelation. One possible result of *The Law of Civilization and Decay,* he wrote to his brother Brooks in 1894, was that "it might help man to know himself and hark back to God. For after all man knows mighty little, and may some day learn enough of his own ignorance to fall down again and pray. Not that I care. Only, if such is God's will, and Fate and Evolution— let there be God!" Yet if this be tolerance, indeed seeming to verge on faith, it is not positive faith. Adams seemed to place the burden of proof on the Almighty to show himself.

He was much interested in churchly religion as a "working energy." In a letter to his niece, written May 23, 1917, he asked that she send him a prayer book, but there is no evidence that he ever seriously considered becoming a convert; indeed, such evidence as that embodied in his remarks, already quoted in the first chapter, about his friend Father Fay, points entirely the other way. The most nearly workable moral adjustment, as he wrote Henry Osborn Taylor in 1915, was the Stoic attitude. In the last of his letters (to Gaskell, February 19, 1918) to be printed, he praises Marcus Aurelius. He had much admiration for Augustine's *Confessions* as a work of art and, presumably, as an expression of sincere faith; but if he ever accepted the God addressed therein, he must have done so in a literary way—by undergoing that famous suspension of disbelief whereby many a reader accepts the ghost in *Hamlet* or the burning bush in Exodus. As historian, Adams examined both the intuitive and logical bases of religion. Both had once been firm, but both had finally crumbled; and though it was conceivable, he knew, that either might eventually be rebuilt, he for one could only be a nostalgic witness of the failure.

To a mind as delicate and intrinsically doubting as his, any interpretation of life could seem to be little more than one version of man's perpetual illusion in a violent, disunified, and therefore godless world. Religion, he was later to assert in his essay, "The Rule of Phase Applied to History," can be regarded as "the self-projection of mind into nature in one direction, as science is the projection of mind into nature in another. . . . In neither case does—or can—the mind reach anything but a different reflection of its own features. . . ." Thus in his own terms he agreed with St. Francis that reality can never be directly apprehended and that the indirect picture studied by man must always be subject to the irregularities of the mental mirror.

It does not follow, however, that illusions—whether of religion or of science—should be entirely disdained. Illusions carefully erected may well be honored for their convenience though not for their assured objective truth; and, plainly, Adams had much admiration for interpretations of the universe as various as those of Plato, Aristotle, Francis of Assisi, Thomas Aquinas, and Lord Kelvin. With particular attention to the conflict in the Middle Ages between mystics and schoolmen, he observes in *Chartres:*

This period between 1140 and 1200 was that of transition architecture and art. . . . The Transition is the equilibrium between the love of God—which is faith—and the logic of God—which is reason; between the round arch and the pointed. One may not be sure which pleases most, but one need not be harsh toward people who think that the moment of balance is exquisite. The last and highest moment is seen at Chartres, where, in 1200, the charm depends on the constant doubt whether emotion or science is uppermost.

190

In this passage and others like it one discerns the remarkable blending of tolerance and doubt that characterized Adams's thinking. He is drawn here simultaneously to the rational and irrational attitudes but fully accepts neither. Nor does he accept "the moment of balance," at least in an intellectual sense. He finds it exquisite and charming, as an artist can, but he does not endorse it as an indubitable statement of universal reality.

What, then, was the "force" embodied in the Virgin, or—seven centuries later—in the dynamo? What is matter? What is mind? What is the universe? No human being speculating as Adams did could avoid these basic questions. One might say, indeed, that *Chartres* was written out of their insistence; and let any reader so naïvely uncharitable as to complain that *Chartres* does not contain their final answer, achieve his own revelation and announce, if he can, the solution to life's stubborn mystery. The intellectual humility of Adams prevented him from asserting anything beyond what he could confidently discern: that existence is fulfilled and moved by an energy infinitely superior to man, and whether man confronts it in the religious sanctuary or in the scientific laboratory, he must acknowledge himself stricken with frustrated wonder. A brief passage in the sixteenth chapter of *Chartres* is pertinent: "Schoolmen as well as mystics would not believe that matter was what it seemed—if, indeed, it existed;—unsubstantial, shifty, shadowy; changing with incredible swiftness into dust, gas, flame; vanishing in mysterious lines of force into space beyond hope of recovery; whirled about in eternity and infinity by that mind, form, energy, or thought which guides and rules and tyrannizes and is the universe."

Such words imply a kind of religion, though it does not induce ritual and prayer, and though it could bring no comfort to its writer except knowing that he had honestly done his best and achieved a certain triumph over confusion and mystery by confessing them. The sadness that pervades the later writings of Henry Adams is the sadness of a mind and spirit in desperate quest of certainty but finding only tentative illusion; cognizant of man's penchant for self-deception and deeply aware of the solace and beauty that self-deception can bring but compelled at last in the name of honesty to repudiate it. It is a human and perhaps latter-day sadness, not absent from the writings of a mathematician and mystic like Blaise Pascal, of an artist like Feodor Dostoevsky, or a scientist like Sigmund Freud. It lifts Henry Adams from the realm of mere provincial importance into that of universal greatness.

Thus if in *The Education,* next to be examined, Adams seems concerned with an attempt only to describe the workings of force, rather than to explain its essence, this is because he has already faced the problem of that explanation in *Chartres,* saying there what had to be said. The utmost achievement of the reasoning logician—that of Thomas Aquinas in his *Summa Theologica*—is equated with the utmost achievement of the intuitive artist—that of the architect of Chartres —and so the cathedral becomes at last a symbol of the precariousness of man in his universe:

The peril of the heavy tower, of the restless vault, of the vagrant buttress; the uncertainty of logic, the inequalities of the syllogism, the irregularities of the mental mirror—all these haunting nightmares of the Church are expressed as strongly by the Gothic cathedral as though it had been the cry of human suffering, and as no emotion had ever been expressed before or is likely to find expression again. The delight of its aspirations is flung up to the sky. The pathos of its self-distrust and anguish of doubt is buried in the earth as its last secret. You can read out of it whatever else pleases your youth and confidence; to me, this is all.

And for one who comes later, there can perhaps be little more. Yet one may take the cue from Adams and believe that

if civilized life is to be possible, a workable faith must somehow reassert itself and, whether born of logic or love, must
temper man's immemorial fear of death and persuade him of
a strength within himself coeval with the stars.

Help me to bear; not my own baby load,
But yours; who bore the failure of the light,
The strength, the knowledge and the thought of God,—
The futile folly of the Infinite!

—Prayer to the Virgin of Chartres

VII

The Folly of the Infinite

THE EDUCATION of Henry Adams, which has attained standing as one of the near-classics of modern literature, seems never to have satisfied its author. The many acquaintances to whom he gave privately printed copies were asked to criticize it for him, but most of them never did, probably because they could not understand the precise nature of his effort.

Though the popular edition, issued in 1918 after Adams's death, bore the subtitle of *An Autobiography,* Adams himself had designated *The Education* as "a study of twentieth-century multiplicity," logically supplementing *Mont-Saint-Michel and Chartres,* "a study of thirteenth-century unity." In his preface to *The Education* he ostensibly denies that it is autobiography at all. Citing Jean Jacques Rousseau as one who unwittingly erected a monument of warning against the ego, Adams avers that in his own instance the ego has become only "a manikin on which the toilet of education is to be draped in order to show the fit or misfit of the clothes. The object of study is the garment, not the figure." With customary ambivalence, however, he adds that the manikin must be "treated as though it had life. Who knows? Possibly it had!"

Even without such a caveat from the author, any reader would probably notice at once certain features of *The Educa-*

tion that set it off from typical autobiography. Most men writing of themselves do not, for example, exclusively employ the third-person pronoun. Nor do they deliberately allow a twenty-year gap in the chronology, as Adams does between his twentieth and twenty-first chapters, and devote much of the final third of the book to speculations on the quality of reality and the manifestations of universal energy. The reader soon discovers, in short, that Adams is primarily concerned not to offer a garrulous disclosure of his own predilections but to establish himself as a point in time, to be utilized as a convenience in the attempted working out of a historical hypothesis.

At the same time it must be urged that in many ways *The Education* is, inevitably, an intensely personal book. Granting that Adams meant to achieve a strategic impersonality through the third-person technique, one can hardly believe him to have been unaware of the special egoistic emphasis that also resulted from this usage. When Julius Caesar, to cite a famous instance, wrote his *Commentaries* out in the field for consumption back home, he evidently knew well that he continually called attention to himself by avoiding the first person. The reader is not permitted to forget that it was Caesar in Gaul; and so, not dissimilarly, the reader is constantly reminded that it was Adams in America. Also, the twenty-year omission in the narrative does more than convince the alert reader that by the end of a certain chapter Adams had established his "point" and felt no need, in terms of his fundamental intention, to bear down on it: such an omission becomes, through the implications of silence, a tribute to Marian Hooper Adams. Even in the final chapters, most directly concerned with giving exposition to the dynamic theory of history, few passages do not demand careful examination for the further insight they can provide regarding the author's mind and character.

196

Henry Adams perhaps revealed more of his essential self through nuance and implication than if he had avowedly followed the naïve romantic formula of Rousseau and tried to disclose himself as frankly as possible. True, the reader must be on his guard against inferring something different from what is actually implied; and he must be wary of erecting too convenient a theory to explain the human mystery glimpsed behind the treatment and style. Writing in *The American Scholar* (Winter, 1945–1946), Mr. Max Baym contends that *The Education* is the product of an essentially romantic ego, gloomily pleased to regard itself as misunderstood or ignored in a crude, unfriendly, and ultimately disastrous world. Pursuing this critical hypothesis, Baym notes the parallels that Adams seems to draw between his own case and that of Hamlet, one of the more notable examples of the "failure as hero," and, whether directly or by implication, that of other fictitious or real men who have found their times tragically out of joint. Thus, Adams's repeated assertions of failure—as student, journalist, teacher, historian, and social theorist— were merely part of a deliberately cultivated stylistic pattern. By reading correctly, one can infer from Adams's various avowals and disavowals the actuality as stated by Brooks Adams in his introduction to *The Degradation of the Democratic Dogma:* "He poses, more or less throughout his book, as having been a failure and a disappointed man. He was neither the one nor the other, as he knew well." Baym suggests that Adams's theory of history, "his conception of the catastrophic march of experience, with man's intermittent awareness of it," is an exemplification of his romanticism.

Such analysis is stimulating, but in its comprehensiveness it has only a precarious validity. By a simple critical formula it seems to account for the personality and thought of a man too complicated to be caught in any single, convenient formula whatever. Many elements in the character of Henry Adams can be rightly called romantic, and a kind of analogy concerning emotional origins might be drawn between, say, Adams's dynamic theory of history and Lord Byron's self-conscious pageant of his bleeding heart; but the personal and intellectual contrasts between Adams and Byron are so compelling that one must be on guard against the analogy and in the end call it specious. The tendency to regard man as a lonely, picturesque figure, at once doomed and morally defiant in a universe beyond his comprehension, is not, after all, the peculiar property of the romantics. One remembers that Alexander Pope, prime exemplar of eighteenth-century neoclassicism, could write of man as one,

> Placed on this isthmus of a middle state
> A being darkly wise, and rudely great. . . .
> Created half to rise and half to fall;
> Great lord of all things, yet a prey to all;
> Sole judge of truth, in endless error hurled:
> The glory, jest, and riddle of the world!

In such lines Pope was expressing no more than what the thoughtful, sensitive person in each generation becomes aware of without espousing any one school or attitude. It is difficult if not impossible to decide that Adams should be identified with a particular writer or group of writers, for his interest and respect were solicited by figures as widely separated in time and thought as Marcus Aurelius, St. Augustine, Blaise Pascal, Jean Jacques Rousseau, Auguste Comte, Matthew Arnold, and Lord Kelvin—to name only a salient few. He regarded himself as a product of the eighteenth century but also called himself a child of the twelfth. Emotionally he seemed to be aligned at varying moments with the Roman Stoics, the medieval Mariolatrists, and the oriental devotees of Kwannon. How place such a man? He probably was not just indulging in cavalier phrasing when at one point in *The Education* he wrote the passage from which the title of this book has been drawn, referring to himself as "the runaway star Groombridge, 1838, commonly known as Henry Adams." Though one can agree that when he applied the term failure to his worldly activities, he held his tongue in his cheek, or at least used the term in a way not falling within ordinary usage, one must hesitate to appraise his thought and theorizing as those of a deliberate or unconscious romanticist controlled by a specifically labeled ego. Evidently prone to pessimism, as so many sensitive observers seem to be, he was, nevertheless, not organically impelled to abide by attitudes and conclusions other than those he reached as a disciplined scholar and artist.

A further problem for one who reads *The Education* to discover its author is that it shows not only omissions but also some factual distortions. Adams himself, of course, indicated often enough that he had scant respect for facts strictly as such; he may have foreseen and answered criticism on this point by the assertion in his preface that "the tailor adapts the manikin as well as the clothes to his patron's wants." If the patron or reader, however, insists that his wants are different from those conceived for him by the tailor or author, dissatisfaction must ensue. An insistence of this kind seems in part to have prompted the writing of Mr. Ernest Samuels's admirably careful study, *The Young Henry Adams,* wherein are cited, for example, inaccuracies in Adams's account of his Harvard student days. Not only does Adams complain of never hearing a teacher mention, during those years from 1854 to 1858, the title of Karl Marx's *Capital*—a work that did not begin to appear in print until 1867—but he protests excessively that the whole curriculum was, in effect, intellectually thin and emotionally empty: "Four years of Harvard College, if successful, resulted in an autobiographical blank, a mind on which only a water-mark had been stamped." Yet, as

Samuels emphasizes, most of the teachers were men of noticeable force and were, in many instances, scholars of rank who
imparted copious information and rigorous mental discipline.
They included, after all, such figures as Louis Agassiz, Asa
Gray, Jeffrys Wyman, Josiah Cooke, Joseph Lovering, Francis
Bowen, Henry W. Torrey, and James Russell Lowell. As
noted, the senior-class oration of Henry Adams survives to
show that his outlook at graduation was marked by considerable youthful idealism, rather than the premature cynicism
so strongly imputed to it in retrospect by the older man;
and undoubtedly his teachers must receive credit for having
prized and fostered in their students a sense of positive duty
toward mankind.

After noting such distortions, however, one must again observe rather paradoxically that the summary offered in *The
Education* has an over-all validity. From the standpoint of
the older man—and it is he, to repeat, who draws most interest
—the training received at Harvard was in numerous respects
less than satisfactory. Hopeful in tone, and surely stamping
on the maturing brain something more legible than a water-
mark, it was on the whole illiberal, tending to reinforce a
young New Englander's inherited conservatisms. Samuels
makes the point, for example, that Louis Agassiz was a devout
anti-Darwinian, and his power of downright rhetoric seems
to have impressed young Adams more than did the gentle,
forward-looking tolerance of Asa Gray. In history, Professor
Torrey was especially devoted to Guizot, whose interpretation
of past human events was not likely to challenge the principle
of government by an elite which Adams, through family influence, was easily disposed to endorse, though American
society was even then repudiating it. In literature, Lowell provided gracious discursiveness rather than vigorous analysis.
Book lists still preserved show that young Adams's outside

reading was immense, but, for the most part, conventional. Such aspects as these of his Harvard education the older man may have had lurking in his mind, when, more than forty years later, he formally belittled the reward of his college years. One may say with justice that if the young man did not learn everything he might have, the fault was not all Harvard's; but in saying this, one does not impair the main fact, and it is that which holds ultimate attention, so that explanations and contradictory details become subsidiary.

Speaking more broadly to this point, one feels justified in urging again that whatever may be revealed by the work of present and subsequent scholars concerning the life and career of Henry Adams, *The Education* will remain the indispensable book to anyone seeking to understand him. It is a book that grows with each perusal and brings one at last to the conviction that in its own terms it is a triumph of indirect self-accounting. Here, for one resolute in the task of discovery, are the pattern and meaning of its author's life as he came to conceive them, not defined by a close itemization of the sundry influences—men, places, and books—that touched him, but by an artistic revelation of that which wrought from within him. One begins to believe that the fifteen-year-old who knew frenzy in his brain at the sight of Court Square packed with bayonets was also the octogenarian who watched with ill-repressed excitement as Western society was torn to pieces and trampled underfoot. One finally discerns, more significantly, that whatever this man had in his long background that should have made him always decorously rational and passive, he actually became daringly irrational at last and prodded the universe ironically into various successive shapes, trying to decide which one displeased him least, and so implied the persuasive hypothesis, at once ancient and startling, that reality is of one's own life and one's own thought.

The prose style of Henry Adams, particularly as it appears in *The Education,* is worth more extended study than it can be given here. With its carefully wrought sentences, its sedulously chosen vocabulary, and its consistent tone of ambivalent irony, it is much of the time intensely intellectual; and since one is perhaps wont to feel that the intellectual manner is less American than European, certain critics have shown themselves embarrassed in trying to classify, as they seem to feel they must, such a style. In his *Outlook for American Prose,* Joseph Warren Beach writes:

In the manner of Henry Adams it is impossible to catch the accent of the American, certainly for us who pitch our tents beside the Mississippi. The communication is dated from Washington, but it really hails from somewhere in the stars equidistant from London, Rome, Boston and Mont Saint Michel. It is beautiful, it is strong, it is as simple as it could possibly be under the circumstances. It is in the best tradition of English international prose, from Irving to Havelock Ellis. But since Mr. Mencken wrote *The American Language,* we have grown jealous of the word American. We have grown jealous, and proud, and modest; and it is our modesty and our pride together which forbid us to claim Henry Adams as they forbid us to claim George Santayana.

This statement was made in 1926, and much has happened since then to temper Americans' convictions of their isolation, literary as well as political. Probably their modesty and even their pride are still intact, but they may be less inclined to presume that to be American one must write mainly in Middle Western colloquialisms—Professor Beach cites Sherwood Anderson—and avoid academic polish. They may be less inclined, in other words, to deny the obvious: that their culture, so eclectic in its genesis, has produced nothing if not variety and can tolerate extremes. Both Adams and Sherwood Anderson wrote American prose, though separate subheadings are required to classify them. Such a term as "English international prose," not unreasonable in certain respects, carries misleading and even disturbing implications. If one thrusts beyond the boundaries of our literature all writings by Americans in America showing discipline and subtlety owed in part to European associations, the result might well be resented. One might thus disinherit together, for example, writers as disparate and as American as Thomas Jefferson and Ernest Hemingway, because both came directly under French influence.

The question is probably too strictly one of definition to merit extended discussion. It is not fatal to a dignified national pride to concede that Henry Adams wrote prose probably acceptable to a cultivated Englishman; but one must insist still more that he wrote for a cultivated American—in short, of and for his own. Further, unless by some critical legerdemain the Adams family can be defined as not American, one must add that the author of *The Education* had a literary background more nearly native than that of many less disciplined craftsmen. Behind him were three literary generations, and at an early age he had become steeped in the writings of them all. If their styles, and his own, were formed with perceptible reference to the classics and to the best of English literature, one can gladly enough accept such evidence of an educated tradition which all can share. Indeed, if America is to have an intellectual and artistic heritage of which her sons and daughters may avail themselves without apology, it must bear proof that the time-tested modes of expression have not been too arduous for native talents; that literary excellence, without loss of the individual accent, has been achieved within an international tradition in this country as well as in England; and that experimentalists of today and hereafter have a recognizable point of departure. As prose, *The Education* and Adams's other more important books can furnish such a point.

Any attempt to define his idiom in terms of his reading must be cautiously undertaken, for he read almost everything. Richard P. Blackmur remarks that certain annotations by Adams in his maturity show "the tenacity with which Henry hung on to his classical reading. There are specific references to Juvenal, Josephus, Martial, Pliny, Tacitus, Varro, Suetonius, Dio Cassius, Propertius, Petronius, Horace, and Lucian." It has been seen that he knew and used both French and German. Though he says in *The Education* that he could never appreciate the majesty said to be present in French verse, one finds inescapably in *Chartres* that he read "La Chanson de Roland" and other selections in the original with remarkable sympathy; and toward the close of his life he especially delighted in old French songs. To German, he perhaps reacted somewhat unfavorably; in *The Life of George Cabot Lodge* he observes that a knowledge of that language might well be more damaging than helpful to one trying to achieve good English style. In English literature, he indicates partiality for the eighteenth century, and one may safely infer some innate congeniality with the neoclassical mode. As a boy, he says in *The Education,* he read the eighteenth-century historians "because his father's library was full of them. . . . So too, he read shelves of eighteenth-century poetry, but when his father offered his own set of Wordsworth as a gift on condition of reading it through, he declined. Pope and Gray called for no mental effort; they were easy reading; but the boy was thirty years old before his education reached Wordsworth." In June, 1875, he wrote to Henry Cabot Lodge: "I feel a little awkward about literary judgment. Everyone snubs the last century and I see that Stephen considers Scott to be poor stuff. I confess I do think Pope a poet, and Gray, too, and Cowper, and Goldsmith." But he read all or most of the leading writers of the nineteenth century, too, and "thought Matthew Arnold the best form of expression of his time." Nor did he neglect the Americans, among whom he seemed to show preference for such figures as Jefferson, Irving, Hawthorne, Lincoln, Whitman, James, and Mark Twain.

His own style is best understood, by reference to Buffon's famous dictum, as a distinct echo of his own personality. From his thought and emotion come the dignity and tension of the paragraphs in *The Education* and his other works; and from the same source comes the often double-barbed irony. He was disposed to invoke irony not to convey, as in Swift's *Modest Proposal,* say, the opposite of the asserted meaning but to achieve compromise between the extremes. He was fond, both as conversationalist and writer, of saying something and yet at the same time not saying it. Some readers have probably made a greater puzzle than they need to of this sophisticated usage. To take a simple instance, Adams remarks in the twenty-first chapter of *The Education* that "he had enjoyed his life amazingly, and would not have exchanged it for any other that came in his way; he was, or thought he was, perfectly satisfied with it." Is he fully in earnest? In one sense, of course, he is. It is established easily enough that he seldom lacked zest for the incidents of daily experience, that he prized the companionship of friends, and that in many ways he relished his activity as a scholar, such as that of collecting materials for the *History.* Undoubtedly he had lived life with considerable fullness, and he could well say that he had enjoyed it. At the same time, his words refer to the period which saw the desolation of his inherited political ideals and, later, the suicide of his wife. It is thus virtually impossible to take his remark at full face value. The final conclusion is the obvious one of compromise.

Even in particular sentences, chosen almost at random, the

Janus-faced quality is present, so that their full impact depends on one's constant awareness of it. Such observations as the following are typically Adams:

From the old world point of view, the American had no mind; he had an economic thinking machine which could work only on a fixed line. The American mind exasperated the European as a buzz-saw might exasperate a pine forest.

No one means all he says, and yet very few say all they mean, for words are slippery and thought is viscous. . . .

The progress of evolution from President Washington to President Grant, was alone evidence enough to upset Darwin.

All opinion founded on fact must be error, because the facts can never be complete, and their relations must be always infinite.

Perhaps Henry Adams was not worth educating. . . .

An understanding of the writing manner of *The Education* leads, however, to more than a comprehension of particular remarks. Adams's whole attitude toward his time and his place in it partakes of ironic ambivalence. Thus does he frequently complain that his formal education was antiquated and faulty, since it did not prepare him to fit into nineteenth- and twentieth-century society and be successful there. The object of education, he avers, should be to teach a capable mind "how to react with vigor and economy. . . . Education should try to lessen the obstacles, diminish the friction, invigorate the energy, and should train minds to react, not at haphazard, but by choice, on the lines of force that attract their world." As a Harvard teacher, he remarks in his twentieth chapter, "he wanted to help boys to a career." He was convinced that he was not doing this, though he observes with dry semisatisfaction that the students themselves did not complain: "They thought they gained something. Perhaps they did, for even in America and in the twentieth century, life could not be wholly industrial."

What should one make of the last-quoted remark? Taken literally it seems to be almost an apology from a scholarly intellectual for his inability to give his pupils trade-school training, or at least some form of instruction that can have other than accidental pertinence in the practical, workaday world; and one may well be dismayed at hearing from Henry Adams the banal, mammonistic criticism of higher education likely to emanate from business tycoons, vocational advisers, and the presidents of Rotary Clubs. But, as often, the context makes a literal interpretation untenable. In the same passage Adams asserts that if he had undertaken to institute reform at Harvard, he would have begun by placing in each classroom a second professor whose function would be strictly limited to expressing views opposing those of the first. Thus would the minds of both students and teachers be rescued in some degree from the inertia of settled opinions. Now this is definitely admirable, all the more so because it suggests the educational methods of Socrates and rests the emphasis where ideally it is due: on the exercise and cultivation of the human mind. But no reader even mildly intelligent, nor Adams himself, could suppose that such a performance would "help students to a career." The result would be to settle in them a chronic challenging of all ideas and values and to destroy that serene acceptance of pedestrian ethics that so assists the triumphant Babbitt toward his goals. Plainly, when Adams uses the term education to refer narrowly to that formal training that fits (or unfits) one for a prosperous career in one's own society, he is being characteristically ironic. By education he really means whatever he could learn, from first to last during his life, of himself, of the men and women he knew or observed, of mankind at large, and of the universe and its workings. Education thus conceived can never attain completion, though it reach its earthly cessation in death. It is the function of an ideal, one learns from Plato, to be unattainable.

Naturally one wishes to explain, if possible, how Adams's particular cast of mind and emotion, which gave rise to his irony, came to be fashioned. The irony, it has been indicated, operated as the vehicle of his customary refusal to assume the finality of any minute or imposing item of supposed truth. Yvor Winters, in *The Anatomy of Nonsense,* seems to feel that Adams's insistence on the tentative quality of almost all observations and judgments was the outgrowth of a Calvinistic confusion of mind, remotely fathered by William Ockham and unwisely fostered by Adams himself. This may perhaps be taken as a partial explanation, though the condemnatory element in it must be regarded somewhat askance as coming from a critic in whom the diffident mode of refraining from dogmatic attitudes has not always been prominent. Examining the problem further in terms of "influence," one must feel that Adams's chronic uncertainty, especially in his maturer years, was more distinctly the gift of modern science than of the Puritan background. To the extent that his attitudes were the product of science, they almost necessarily became steadily more tentative. The certainties of Newtonian physics (which conveniently reinforced, through their transmutation into philosophic metaphor, the personal and political forthrightness of Henry's great-grandfather, the second President) were dissipating. By the turn of the century many scientists were ready to confess that any acceptable description of matter eluded them; radium, discovered two years earlier by Madame Curie, was a "metaphysical bomb." In 1903 Karl Pearson remarked in his *Grammar of Science:* "Order and reason, beauty and benevolence, are characteristics and conceptions which we find solely associated with the mind of man." To which Adams applied his bland comment: "The assertion, as a broad truth, left one's mind in some doubt of its bearings. . . ." One's mind today is still in some doubt. Adams was in a sense "ahead of his time" in arriving at an intellectual attitude of uncertainty and uneasiness that might be inferred in recent decades from, for example, Einsteinian relativity.

But, again, such analysis of the state of Adams's mind and emotions reflected in his style, is probably more complicated than necessary. One does better to remember mostly the man himself and infer from him that an obsessive sense of ambiguity is the penalty for refinement and fullness, rather than obliquity, of vision. As a glance at the nearest politician is likely to reveal, assurance is often furthered by simplicity and ignorance. Henry Adams was neither simple nor ignorant: this book and others about him would not demand writing if he were. To a subtle and complicated sensibility he gradually added the knowledge and critical equipment of a lifelong scholar, and his particularly intricate version of the human experience resulted. Contrast *The Education* with the *Pilgrim's Progress*. The differences are astounding; yet each book issued from a man who was asking, in accents appropriate to his time and training, the age-old question: "What shall I do to be saved?"

Further effort may now be made to explain the genesis of Henry Adams's dynamic theory of history. Note first of all that the attempt to understand and guide society by reference to the "laws" of the universe of which it forms a part is probably as ancient as human sensibility. What is religion, indeed, but a hypothesized working description of reality, achieved through ordered observation or intuitive insight, and pointing to what man should do to conform to its implications? In most literature that one tends to label profound, this element of speculation is present. One discovers the same fundamental animation in works as various as the Sumerian epic of *Gilgamish*, the *Dialogues* of Plato, and the *Summa Theologica* of Aquinas.

In the modern age as in the ancient, no coherent body of knowledge can long remain isolated from the speculative thinker, who strives to apply it to a comprehension of men's general and specific problems. Sir Isaac Newton, to cite an obvious instance, stimulated not only other scientists but also poets, religionists, and statesmen. When Newton died in 1727, James Thomson memorialized in blank verse what the Age of the Enlightenment conceived to be the breadth of his accomplishment:

> The noiseless tide of time, all bearing down
> To vast eternity's unbounded sea,
> Where the green islands of the happy shine,
> He stemmed alone: and to the source (involved
> Deep in primeval gloom) ascending, raised
> His lights at equal distances, to guide
> Historian wildered on his darksome way.

To many of the contemporaries and successors of the great physicist, the Newtonian universe of balance and harmony seemed to furnish the pattern for human institutions and ensure an ordered, happy society if men would but utilize the faculty of reason to discern "Nature's Laws" (which had previously lain "hid in night") and apply them. Newton himself, as Basil Willey points out, had concluded his *Opticks* with a suggestion that by a fuller knowledge of the mechanical world, wherein the properties and actions of all things follow from two or three principles of motion, "the bounds of Moral Philosophy will also be enlarged." Acting on this and similar hints, David Hartley elaborated the principle of the association of ideas as a variety of "moral gravitation."

With more immediate pertinence to the present study, one should remember that some of the speeches in the American Constitutional Convention—that political manifestation of eighteenth-century enlightenment of which, unfortunately, there exists no verbatim record—evidently contained Newtonian echoes. When Benjamin Franklin objected to the proposed setting off of the two legislative houses against each other, by analogy to Newtonian particles, John Adams passionately quoted Newton. As Muriel Rukeyser observes, probably no one in America had a knowledge of Newton superior to that of Franklin; he had his own reasons for refusing to honor the analogy; yet it was John Adams who prevailed, both in the special instance and in the general policy which produced a government containing checks and balances.

Now and again an attempt to apply Newtonian science to politics can be found also in the writings of John Quincy Adams. In April, 1823, for example, he wrote to Hugh Nelson of the then apparent destiny of Cuba: "There are laws of political as well as physical gravitation; and if an apple severed by the tempest from its native tree cannot choose but fall to the ground, Cuba, forcibly disjoined from its own unnatural connection with Spain, and incapable of self-support, can gravitate only towards the North American Union, which by the same law of nature cannot cast her off from its bosom."

One wonders whether the learned plea for Cuban freedom from Spain, written in 1896 by Henry Adams for presentation before the Senate by Don Cameron, is to be understood partly by reference back to this passage in the letters of the grandfather. If so, the younger Adams would seem to have shared with the older one the error of supposing Cuba "incapable of self-support," at least to the extent that the Newtonian analogy required.[1]

[1] That Adams's feelings for Cuba were anything but those of a conventional imperialist can be gathered from a letter written to Brooks Adams, June 11,

In any event it is interesting that Henry Adams was apparently conforming to a family intellectual habit when, in *The Education,* he invoked the law of mass to account for the attraction exerted by the "body" of scientific knowledge on the human mind; and he conformed to that habit again in playing with Lord Kelvin's second law of thermodynamics as possible rationale for a supposed dwindling of man's vital energies.

Still considering the role of family influence, one can recognize that the thinking of his younger brother, Brooks Adams, undoubtedly provided Henry with a very significant stimulus. As already noted, late in the summer of 1893 Henry was called back from Europe by letters announcing the dire financial panic of that year. In Quincy the two brothers discussed the general state of affairs at length, with particular reference to Brooks's theory of history that civilization followed the exchanges—the theory he was to set forth in *The Law of Civilization and Decay.* "Among other general rules," *The Education* reports, "he laid down the paradox that, in the social disequilibrium between capital and labor, the logical outcome was not collectivism, but anarchism; and Henry made note of it for study." The older brother read the younger's manuscript and made numerous suggestions, none of them, however, serving to alter the fundamental conception. He advised Brooks against publishing such a work, because it would offend adherents to the gold standard and thus probably be fatal to his political ambitions, if any. One can easily detect the irony in such counsel addressed by one Adams to another, urging him to do what no member of the family had ever done: to honor expediency over conviction. As Henry must have foreseen, Brooks methodically went on with his

---

1898: "I want peace. I want it quick. . . . I want it to save Cuba from the sugar planters and syndicates whose cards McKinley will play, and who are worse than Spain."

work, and *The Law of Civilization and Decay* came out in its first edition in London, October, 1895. It still stands as a major pioneer monument in the attempt to formulate a science of history pointing to the disintegration of Western society. At the time of its printing, Oswald Spengler, whose more widely acclaimed *Decline of the West* (1918) was to be written in a similar spirit and embody some of the same contentions, was still a boy in his early teens.

Henry Adams's letter, "The Tendency of History" (1894) —which has already been cited as intended to smooth the way for Brooks's volume—was praised by Charles Beard in 1943 as standing "high among the most comprehensive, penetrating, and profound utterances ever made, at least in the United States, on the office of the historian and the nature of history. That it was and has been largely ignored by American historians is to their discredit and no derogation of the intellectual powers of Henry Adams. The terrible course of history since 1894 and the plight of historians in Europe seem to be, in many ways, illustrations of Henry Adams's discernment, pleas, and warnings, made manifest in his Letter."

In a further effort to understand how Adams arrived at the position established in "The Tendency of History," and how he came finally to write the concluding chapters of *The Education,* it is helpful though not decisive to note some of the influences of his education and reading. Ernest Samuels emphasizes his early acquaintance with the thought of men like Auguste Comte, Herbert Spencer, and Henry Buckle, "all of whom expected to reconstruct society according to rational and scientific principles." By a study of sequences Comte conceived of society as having passed through "theological" and "metaphysical" stages and arriving at the "positivist," wherein man was to utilize his highest intelligence in planning a social order bringing to each and all the blessings of industry and science. Comte is mentioned in *The Education* at least six times; at one point in the fifteenth chapter, dealing with the period 1867–1868, Adams avows that he did the "next best thing" to becoming a Marxist: "he became a Comteist, within the limits of evolution." Marx, also, one hardly needs reminding, formulated a theory of history whereby presumably events of the past, present, and future might be fitted into an understandable pattern of cause and effect.[2]

The parallelism between Adams's thinking, both in the *History* and later, and that of Herbert Spencer is most striking. In his *First Principles,* as Samuels points out, Spencer strove to "interpret the detailed phenomena of Life, and Mind, and Society, in terms of Matter, Motion, and Force" and equated physical with social force, arriving at the conclusion that society would ultimately reach extinction in the universal process of equilibrium. In 1857 Buckle had argued, in his *History of Civilization in England,* that a science of history should be erected because "there must be an intimate connexion between human actions and physical laws." Adams deferred to Buckle in "The Tendency of History" and again in *The Education.*

Grateful in this instance as in others for Mr. Samuels's scholarship, one must, nevertheless, avoid hypothesizing that Adams finally propounded his dynamic theory of history because it was suggested to him by earlier writers. The noting of "influence" can never be more than a partial aid in rationalizing the conclusions of a first-rate thinker. One must ask of Henry Adams, for example, why out of his wide knowledge of the literature of science he became partial to the implications of Lord Kelvin rather than to those of Darwin,

2 "Did you ever read Karl Marx? I think I never struck a book which taught me so much, and with which I disagreed so radically in conclusion" (Henry Adams to Charles Milnes Gaskell, June 18, 1894).

as, for example, Woodrow Wilson did. Why did Adams in effect repudiate the Baconian conviction that nature, of which man is a part, is improved rather than impaired by time, and thus return after his own fashion to the still older Galenist notion that the world is in its last, weary phase?

The answer must come again from one's understanding of Adams as a person and, also, from a realization of how much the dynamic theory of history is a mere carrier, rather than a causative agent of, his thought. One must concede in him the presence of what seems to be an innate inclination toward pessimism that made him wary of the gladsome hopes propounded by the popularizers of evolution; wary, finally, even of the optimism implicit in Comte. The general analogy to be drawn between his attitudes and those of Arnold, Ruskin, and other British writers increasingly disillusioned with the consequences of the industrial revolution is in a sense accidental; for his pessimism, like theirs, was steadily strengthened by observation of the course of events. Though forebodings sprinkle his letters written as a very young man, he found then little reason to assume other than that the world of his maturity would be one able and willing to make use of the best talents of his generation; it would be a world still far from perfect but would hold continuing promise. As *The Education* makes clear, disillusion fell upon him after the Civil War, but he could still write passages in the *History* and in *Democracy* showing his reluctance to abandon as working principles the ideals of the founding fathers. By the time he wrote *The Education,* however, he could discern only appalling confusion in human affairs and appalling incompetence in human beings. He sat down to describe and give tentative explanation to what he saw; to suggest how and why human affairs in America, and indeed in most of the Western world, seemed to be getting worse instead of better. Elaborating the hypothesis submitted in his *History*—that society can be treated as an entity, and that the historian's task is to observe the play of force upon force, rather than to record simply the supposedly independent conduct of human beings—he propounded the dynamic theory of history.

Whatever one's conclusion concerning the final validity of the dynamic theory, one can hardly deny it to be the product of an informed and daring mind. It has been seen how Adams laid the groundwork for it in his study of the century 1150–1250, set forth in *Mont-Saint-Michel and Chartres*. According to his appraisal, the most significant quality of this century was its unity. By contrast the most noticeable quality of our own century, as he characterizes it in *The Education*, is its disunity, if not imminent chaos. Prompted by intellectual curiosity and emotional need, Adams sought to give history a logical pattern by supposing that this later period in society's development, his own period and ours, can be explained as the lineal descendent of the earlier—in terms of force. If the Virgin can be said to symbolize the force which medieval man invoked to build cathedrals and give himself faith in life, then perhaps the dynamo may be said to symbolize the force invoked by modern man to produce those wonders by which, presumably, he undertakes to express and satisfy the cravings of his own mind and spirit. It may be that Adams originally hoped to discover that the dynamo could be a unifying force in the twentieth century, somewhat as the Virgin was in the twelfth. In any event, what he actually found was a verification of his general conviction that life is a hastening process of social disintegration and uncertainty, rather than its opposite.

Pursuing in *The Education* this audacious analogy, Adams hypothesizes in the terms of physics and argues that if the discovered forces of nature be conceived of as one energy or "mass," and the mind of man as another, then by the rule that a larger mass attracts a smaller it may be asserted that the forces of nature capture man, and not vice versa. Thus, the accumulation of mechanical powers, which has helped to make our time one of multiplicity and confusion, is an inevitable process over which man has no more control than over the operation of the presumed law of gravity. To make matters more troublesomely urgent, this process goes forward in obedience to a law of acceleration.

Supplementing his theory as offered in *The Education,* Adams invokes in his *Letter to American Teachers of History* (privately printed in 1910) Lord Kelvin's second law of thermodynamics. In somewhat technical terms, this law states that "the entropy of the universe tends to a maximum." Most laymen will be grateful for Adams's popular exposition of it, which asserts that beside the comforting law of the conservation of energy (according to which the amount of energy in the universe remains constant, since energy can neither be created nor destroyed) one must place the disturbing one of its dissipation or degradation. Kelvin averred, says Adams in his paraphrase, "that all nature's energies were slowly converting themselves into heat and vanishing into space, until, at the last, nothing could be left except a dead ocean of energy at its lowest possible level—say of heat at $1°$ Centigrade, or $-272°$ Centigrade below freezing point of water,—and incapable of doing any work whatever, since work could be done only by a fall of tension, as water does work by falling to sea-level." Man, of course, along with the rest of creation, is doomed eventually to reach this dead end. His reason and will, Adams hypothesized, show signs in our own time of dwindling in force and effectiveness.

Readers interested in this mode of theorizing will also wish to examine "The Rule of Phase Applied to History," an essay which Adams wrote in 1908, though it was not published until 1919. Here, taking a rule of physics propounded by

Willard Gibbs, Adams argues that society may be passing through successive "phases," roughly comparable, say, to the phases of matter seen in the transformation of a solid to a liquid and of that liquid to a gas. Again, in social transformations a law of acceleration seems to be discernible. Thus Adams suggests tentatively that man lived in a "Religious Phase" for about 90,000 years, ending at about the year 1600; then came a "Mechanical Phase," lasting 300 years, until 1900; following this would come, he thought, an "Electric Phase" of only seventeen years; thereafter, presumably, an "Ethereal Phase" of only four years. This would bring society to the year 1921. After that point Adams did not know whether one should expect a static, stationary period or a period characterized by a sort of unimaginable control by man "of cosmic forces on a cosmic scale." If Adams were alive today he might be inclined slightly to revise some of his dates, and he might well suggest that by dividing the atom man has begun to assert his control, if one can be optimistic enough to call it that, of cosmic forces on a cosmic scale.

Now if all this scientific theorizing about history is to be taken as a literal attempt to describe and explain human events in terms of physical formulas, even the most sympathetic reader will be inclined to accord Adams little more than a wry smile. Some years ago I presumed to examine the dynamic theory point by point, emphasizing the fundamental contrast between the kinds of "force" represented, respectively, by the Virgin and the dynamo.[3] A convincing common value for them—whether in terms of dynes and poundals, or in terms of mystical exaltation—simply eludes mathematical reason. This can be stated quite aside from the fact that the

[3] See "Henry Adams's Quest for Certainty," in Hardin Craig (ed.), *Stanford Studies in Language and Literature* (Stanford University Press, 1941), pp. 361-373.

twelfth century probably did not fully possess the near-miraculous unity, even within the church itself, that Adams attributes to it in *Chartres;* and that many of the scientific concepts employed by Adams—Newton's law of gravity and Gibbs's rule of phase, for example—have lately been seriously discountenanced.

Such criticisms undoubtedly have their pertinence. Adams would have liked, ideally, to set up a literal analogy between history and science, so that the future could be unfailingly plotted by reference to the past and present. He fully understood, however, the difficulties involved. "I am puzzled," he wrote in 1914 to his English friend Gaskell, "to convert our vital energy and thought into terms of physical energy."

Further, though Adams was scrupulous to invoke, to whatever extent he could, the precise techniques of the scientist and mathematician, he was working also as an artist; and to the extent he was so working, any analytical criticism of the technical validity of his terms widely misses the point. In his chapter on Adams in the *Literary History of the United States* Robert E. Spiller suggests that Adams's use of physical formulas, in a way that most physicists themselves could only be amazed by, is in some ways comparable to John Milton's use, in *Paradise Lost,* of Ptolemaic cosmogony. By Milton's time the Copernican theory, already two centuries old, was the only one scientifically acceptable to educated minds, including Milton's; but the poet sought verity rather than veracity and evidently was not perturbed at utilizing an outmoded hypothesis to gain artistic impressiveness and coherence. Various statements from Adams, some of them already noted, indicate that at least some of the time he considered the motive behind his dynamic historical theory to be, in a broad sense, allegorical: "One sought no absolute truth. One sought only a spool on which to wind the thread of history without breaking it. . . . Any schoolboy could work out the

problem if he were given the right to state it in his own terms."
He wrote to his younger brother, Brooks Adams, that "The
Rule of Phase Applied to History" was only a sort of jigsaw
puzzle, "put together in order to see whether the pieces could
be made to fit," and he complained that "the fools begin at
once to discuss whether the theory was true." It may be that
in using the term "fools" he was honoring the editors of the
American Historical Review, who rejected "Phase" as being
not entirely suitable to their readers. Certainly it does not
furnish the easy kind of exposition that historians were, and
are, accustomed to; yet it is difficult to believe that the more
alert among Adams's contemporaries would not have been
impressed by the brilliant suggestiveness of various passages.
Consider, for example, the following:

He [the physicist-historian] may assume, as his starting-point, that
Thought is a historical substance, analogous to an electric current,
which has obeyed the laws,—whatever they are,—of Phase. The
hypothesis is not extravagant. As a fact, we know only too well
that our historical Thought has obeyed, and still obeys, some law
of Inertia, since it has habitually and obstinately resisted deflec-
tion by new forces or motives; we know even that it acts as though
it felt friction from resistance, since it is constantly stopped by all
sorts of obstacles; we can apply to it, letter for letter, one of the
capital laws of physical chemistry, that, where an equilibrium is
subjected to conditions which tend to produce change, it reacts
internally in ways that tend to resist the external constraint, and
to preserve its established balance; often it is visibly set in motion
by sympathetic forces which act upon it as a magnet acts on soft
iron, by induction; the commonest school-history takes for granted
that it has shown periods of unquestioned acceleration. If, then,
society has in so many ways obeyed the ordinary laws of attraction
and inertia, nothing can be more natural than to inquire whether
it obeys them in all respects, and whether the rules that have been
applied to fluids and gases in general, also apply to society as a
current of thought. Such a speculative inquiry is the source of

almost all that is known of magnetism, electricity, and ether, and all other possible immaterial substances. . . .

He wrote, thus, not at all in the mood of confidence and dogmatism, but in the mood of "speculative inquiry." He was engaged in intellectual play, which is, however, of all forms of play the most serious.

Perhaps the clearest statement Adams ever made regarding the tentativeness of his scientific-historical theorizing was contained in a rough-draft preface to this "Rule of Phase" essay, which preface he sent to George Cabot Lodge sometime before March, 1909. In it Adams avers that the theory as expounded in *The Education,* in terms of astronomy, was meant merely as one possible illustration of the method. "The next step required an effort of thought on the reader's part, for it was clear that, if he knew a little of science, he would of his own accord go on to apply the same law in the terms of other branches of study than astronomy, not to prove its truth, but to prove its convenience. The statement in one set of terms implies that it can be made equally well in all." He goes on to suggest how the professor of history might lecture to students of chemistry:

The human mind . . . can be conveniently treated as a group of electric ions, each charged on a mathematical corpuscle, and obeying the law of electric mass. Viewed thus, as an electric charge, distributed on particles of gas in a vacuum tube traversed by an electric current, the acceleration will be as the volume of the current, increasing to infinity by the usual law of squares, according to the curve given in any recent text book. History then becomes an application of logarithms.

In the thirty-fourth chapter of *The Education* Adams submits that the ratio of increase in the volume of coal power might serve as a dynamometer, indicating the direction and rapidity of society's "progress." In the form of utilized power, the coal output of the world roughly doubled every ten years between 1840 and 1900. An ocean steamer at about the time of Adams's birth (1838) utilized something like 234 steam-horsepower; at the time he was writing *The Education,* around 1906, the much larger vessel then in vogue utilized about 30,000. Adams would not have been astonished to learn that thirty years later the figure for the "Queen Mary"—deriving its power from oil—was to be almost seven times as large. He probably would have pointed out, further, that in practical terms something close to a maximum would seem thus to have been reached.

Undoubtedly what interested and alarmed Adams about each of these somewhat varied scientific-historical speculations was that they seemed to verify his hypothesis about the growing complexity and danger of the present-day world. Whether one equated intellectual and social "forces" with the forces involved in Newton's theory of gravitation, in Kelvin's second law of thermodynamics, in Gibbs's rule of phase, in electrical science, or in the utilization of coal for steam power—the findings brought one to much the same conclusion: society was destined very soon to achieve an absolutely unprecedented massing of forces, which the mind of man would either succumb to in tragic bewilderment or, more luckily, would somehow synthesize to fashion a new life on earth. Adams himself put matters more bluntly in a letter to his brother Brooks, May 7, 1901:

All we can say is that, at the rate of increase of speed and momentum, as calculated on the last fifty years, the present society must break its damn neck in a definite, but remote, time, not exceeding fifty years more. This is an arithmetical calculation from given data, as, for example, from explosives, or electrical energy, or control of cosmic power. Either our society must stop or bust. . . . I do not myself care which it does. That is the affair of those who are to run it.

He cared deeply, nevertheless, for in a state of tormented anxiety he persisted in his speculations.

There are moments when one envies the dead. Any reader who takes Adams literally and notes that the limit set for modern society is 1951, may well feel such envy while pondering the passage quoted above, or may feel at least as Macbeth did when he saw Birnam Wood marching. It is possibly a comfort to reflect, however, that Adams, despite the dogmatism frequently present in his letters, never took his own conclusions as final. *The Education* was "avowedly incomplete" because its author suggested only several paths of procedure and did not explore the perhaps dozen or so possible others that a comprehensive acquaintance with modern science would disclose. It is characteristic of Adams that he seems to blame himself, rather than the inevitable limitations of any one person's strength and time, for the fragmentary quality of his performance.

He knew, surely, what any competent scientist is aware of: that no one method or set of experiments can be regarded as final. The scientist works not in terms of certain, ultimate cause (though in the name of human dignity he holds this forever before him as an ideal), but in terms of probability. Probability arises from the findings in one experiment. If the findings in a second experiment are at least roughly equivalent, the probability then becomes stronger. It becomes still stronger with similar findings in a third experiment, and so on. If the findings in repeated and continual experiments all point to the same end, the scientist gains confidence in his original hypothesis and eventually may cease to regard it as a mere hypothesis but as something so strongly impregnated with probability that it can be adopted for convenience as a workable fact. But the scientist, if he be worthy of his name, will never quite lose sight of the lurking latency of error. He will be sufficiently a philosopher to feel the force of David

Hume's contention that causation is never established in a manner answerable to logic. To invoke the humdrum instance, although the sun has punctually risen on a hundred thousand successive days, it may not rise tomorrow.

Both science and religion, asserts Adams in a remarkable passage already referred to, in "The Rule of Phase Applied to History," are in a sense illusions. Religion can be regarded as "the self-projection of mind into nature in one direction, as science is the projection of mind into nature in another. . . . In neither case does—or can—the mind reach anything but a different reflection of its own features. . . ."

When he was in a mood to be content with nothing less than certainty, Adams knew how inadequate his methods had been to achieve it. "I don't give a damn what happened," he burst out one day in 1911, when he was conversing in Paris with Waldo G. Leland, "what I want to know is why it happened—never could find out—stopped writing history." In March, 1913, he wrote to Gaskell: "There is no such thing —I am confident,—as real consequence in history. The generations are actually separate and unconnected."

He thus was not one to assert glibly that his efforts had met with success. It is noteworthy, however, that he seems not to have fully relinquished the attempt to equate history with science. As late as February, 1914, again in a letter to Gaskell, he was commenting in terms of Kelvin's second law of thermodynamics on society's condition. Whatever he might conclude "rationally" and scientifically, he would continue "irrationally" and artistically to impose some kind of pattern on the chaos of experience. Indeed, he did not have to go to the world of art to find precedent for his attitude. When the great French mathematician Jules Henri Poincaré found the validity of Euclid challenged, he replied that whether true or not it is convenient.

It perhaps hardly needs saying that the present attempt at

exposition would have drawn Adams's contempt for its obviousness. It is set forth here because too many would-be critics, among whom is the present writer, have captiously accused Adams of not realizing from first to last the tentativeness of his procedure; have accused him, indeed, of lacking a first-rate mind. The truth is that much of the difficulty has arisen because of the very brilliance and complexity of Adams's mind. If he had been only a historian, or a scientist, or an artist, or a mystic, the problem of understanding and explaining him would be simplified; but it was at least his impulse to be all of these at once; and certainly his mind was in no literal way compartmentalized. As historian he was fascinated by the human past and wanted to record it and appraise its possible bearing on mankind's present and future. As scientist he insisted simultaneously on as comprehensible an account of the "facts" as the human mind, with the aid of precise procedures and instruments, could give them. As artist he wanted his thought and writing to satisfy the artistic demands of unity and balance. As mystic he aspired toward a moment, eternal in its implications, of revelation and vision —when by a flash of insight the mysteries of life and the stellar universe would be resolved into certainty, and the human spirit could for once find rest, elsewhere than in death. For death, which brings termination, does not indubitably bring solution.

One can still be instructed and startled by some of Adams's guesses, which were more than guesses since they derived from the minute examination of social, political, and economic trends that his historical theorizing involved. Recall, for example, John Bigelow's report in his diary of a conversation with Adams in February, 1899:

I spent yesterday afternoon . . . with Henry Adams. He is an inspired prophet or crazy. He says Russia and Germany must be regarded as one in casting the horoscope of the future. That all the Latin States, France included, are going out with the tide. . . . The only first class powers that will long survive as such are Russia including Germany and the United States. England too he says will be living on her accumulated fat in 10 years. . . . Adams thinks apparently, in fact he said, that the time approached when the world [would] belong to Russia and the United States.

Less than a decade later, Adams wrote in *The Education* that by 1903 he had decided that "the wall of Russian inertia that barred Europe across the Baltic, would bar America across the Pacific; and Hay's policy of the open door would infallibly fail."

As a general description, to be invoked for its convenience as well as for its artistic merits, the dynamic theory of history still stands. The state of men's affairs indeed shows stupendous energies substantially out of control. With this century half gone, the nations flounder in an uneasy torpor of intellectual and moral debility. Two world wars and the threat of a third have scarcely proved to be sources of renewed faith and strength.

Yet, ironically, there is no fundamental cause for greater despair in our own time than one hundred or one thousand years ago. The human brain still throws out its perplexing questions and its tentative answers, and the human heart still beats. The earth, though men have abused her, does not forsake them. At night the stars still shine. The sun, as Qoheleth and Ernest Hemingway have observed, also rises. These are naïve observations to advance in a sophisticated and pessimistic decade. It is seasonable, nevertheless, to advance some.

Symptomatic, perhaps, of the fractured morale of our time is that some of its most alert spirits seem able to survive only by consciously setting up a dualistic concept of existence, whether conventional or esoteric. The late William Butler Yeats devoted much of his maturity to the scrutiny of spiritism and the occult, arriving thus at a coherent though irrational system of symbols that he imposed, as a literary artist, on the facts of everyday experience. T. S. Eliot, appalled at the spiritual barrenness that he explored in *The Wasteland,* has turned to the traditional solace of Anglo-Catholicism—not with the involuntary joyousness of the medieval mystic, one is forced to say, but with a sometimes chill and arduous employment of the will, born of the conviction that an un-Christian morality is not possible. Aldous Huxley, having depicted a morally bankrupt society in *Point Counter Point* and others of his earlier volumes, now devotes part of his talent to expounding the "perennial philosophy" which, as a means whereby the individual human being may intuitively identify himself with a perhaps divine universal oneness, has always intrigued him.

As already suggested, Henry Adams certainly respected and even invoked this irrational or suprarational mode of escape from the sensitive individual's plight in today's world. His study of the Middle Ages, with emphasis on the cult of the Virgin, was prompted in part by needs aside from reason, and in Adams's poem "Buddha and Brahma" the old man counsels the younger:

> All wise men
> Have one sole purpose which we never lose:
> . . . A perfect union with the Single Spirit . . .
> But we, who cannot fly the world, must seek
> To live two separate lives; one in the world
> Which we must ever seem to treat as real;
> The other in ourselves, behind a veil
> Not to be raised without disturbing both.

The extent to which Adams entertained in his private life the oriental-occidental ambivalence here recognized is not easy to gauge; mystical moments rarely survive as literary record. But it may be repeated for emphasis that he was the

227

intuitive artist as well as the logical scholar. It may be that, living within himself, he consummated "a perfect union with the single Spirit," though his letters lack that luminous confidence in life that might be expected to result. It is probably futile, if not presumptuous, to seek a final answer to this somewhat personal question.

One is on surer ground in asserting that, whatever Adams's dependence on intuition, he never repudiated the mind. His ironic sense of mundane reality was too strong ever to be shunted away. Living and thinking in his own time, he held almost automatically to the eighteenth-century conviction that the end of life is life, and that paradise is to be sought on an earth peopled by walking, breathing men, and not just in a beatific world of the spirit problematically situated in space and time. True, he tempered and at times even effaced eighteenth-century optimism with twentieth-century skepticism. Still, a golden age had once existed, in the twelfth century, and one might now and again look back to it wistfully, marking the contradictions between it and his own. The result of such a study could not be utter hopelessness: if human life had once been good, it might eventually be so again—whatever the disasters and chaos of the specific moment. The final assertion of *The Education*—that perhaps some day the author and his friends might be allowed to return to earth together "to see the mistakes of their own lives made clear in the light of the mistakes of their successors"—carries a stronger belief in the continuity of the human process than the irony of the phrasing at first permits the reader to discover.

Once more, then, Henry Adams was not an unalloyed pessimist. He himself has made it too easy for readers to infer only a despairing conclusion from his writings. Employing unflinchingly those peculiarly human attributes, the mind

228

and the will, in a study of past, present, and future, he was
compelled to discern the frightening circumstance of contemporary society. The picture he has left for later students is
a dark one, but it is touched by a ray of indomitable intelligence. He never gave up. "As long as he could whisper,"
to use his own words in *The Education,* "he would go on as
he had begun, bluntly refusing to meet his creator with the
admission that the creation had taught him nothing except
that the square of the hypothenuse of a right-angled triangle
might for convenience be taken as equal to something else."
Mankind is habituated to discovering heroism on the battle-
field, in the theatrical image of the plumed knight who kills
or is killed by other men. Let it pay belated tribute to the
aging scholar in his study who quietly faces the universe.

For Henry Adams, with all his typically human limitations
and his unheroic idiosyncrasies, had an unmistakable Socratic
greatness. Too many of the troubles of mankind can be traced
to people who decide prematurely that they *know,* such people being, unfortunately, depressingly numerous and difficult
to elude, whether they happen to be one's next-door neighbors or a gang of European fascists. Human salvation, if possible at all, must come ultimately through those rare spirits
who are perpetually humble, perpetually inquiring. Blessed
are the meek, it has been written, for they shall inherit the
earth. No personal egotism, no sense of loneliness and forlorn-
ness, could move Adams at last to assert as valid for others
anything beyond what his reason revealed to him; no matter
that this, as he had to admit, was far less than sufficient to
answer that yearning for certainty that was so much more
imperious in him than in most men.

It is too early to despair that in any particular generation
the deftest minds fail to untie the knotted question of human
destiny; what is essential is that the effort shall not lapse.
Perhaps in our own disordered time more atomic bombs will

fall and appallingly produce individual and collective tragedy. One can, nevertheless, believe that when the worst has been done, there will stand upon the affronted earth a few human beings not disposed to submit, not fearing to oppose still the recurrent challenge of time with the imperfect yet phenomenal weapons of intuition and reason. In their modest and simple valor, they will be the heirs of Henry Adams and guardians of the millennial hope.

VIII

Conclusion

NOW THAT Henry Adams has been dead for three decades, his sardonic ghost may smile at the bewildered world whose literary scholars, with wonted belatedness, are paying him the tribute of intense study.

One result of this freshening scrutiny has been the lifting of Adams from the rank of a somewhat esoteric curiosity to that of an undoubted major figure in letters. In 1921 *The Cambridge History of American Literature* granted him, as part of the discussion of "Later Historians," not quite two pages. In 1948 the *Literary History of the United States* allotted him an impressive chapter of more than twenty pages and added five of bibliography. The reason becomes obvious the moment one calls, in accents of the present day, the roll of his more important works. His collected letters are probably the best this country can show; his *History* remains a near-triumph of scholarship and literary form; his *Gallatin*, though a flavor of pedantry too strong for popular taste may deprive it of unchallenged supereminence, holds its place as a definitive biography. One may classify *Chartres* and *The Education* as one will: they stand unique as an increasingly significant attempt to show articulation between past and present and to define the mystery of existence. Placed beside such solidity of achievement, in the shadow of its comment on man's deepest dilemma, the accomplishments of certain one-time greats—Irving, Cooper, Bryant, Whittier, Longfellow, Lowell, Holmes—become almost frivolous.

It should be emphasized, moreover, that solidity is but one of the impressive qualities in Adams's writings. Interfused with the wisdom of his later books, especially, and inseparable from it, is an ironic lightness, a tongue-in-cheek aptness for contrast and paradox, that marks the consummate humorist in the truest sense. It is a quality at once intellectual and humane which, for the most part, the reader must apprehend for himself: it cannot be neatly illustrated in a few quoted passages, and many critics have missed it. Though on such a point heated disagreement is almost certain, one who appreciates the persistent, subtle drollery of Adams is likely to conclude that Mark Twain and others of his tradition are usually mere fumblers in slapstick.

Always it is Henry Adams himself, disclosed only in part by his works, who challenges most. Though his complicated sensibility cannot be lightly summarized, one may suggest in conclusion that it operated on three levels of subject matter. This is not the same as saying that the sensibility itself had three levels; it had none or, if one prefers, a thousand; but necessarily it addressed itself first and most obviously to the everyday world of objects and events; secondly, to the problem of reconciling, if possible, those objects and events with universal reality; and finally, to the weighing of any solutions adduced.

The first level, thus arbitrarily defined, is, of course, the common one of eating, sleeping, loving, conversing, and working; and through the multiplication of the individual into the group, it is that of politics, economics, religion, social mores, and war. It is the only level that most human beings, who live the unexamined life that Socrates said was not worth living, ever experience. One must not conclude, to be sure, that it can be, or should be, ignored by the more sensitive. With probable correctness, democracy predicates its essentiality.

Much of the part played by Henry Adams in life as a habitual diurnal activity is necessarily lost from mind and can never be recalled. On the other hand, one finds some of it memorialized, by express record or implication, in his letters and in *The Education*. One discerns that the impact of his individuality on those among whom he moved was vigorous and often startling. Prone to melancholy, he was seldom without a droll or tender remark to temper the sting of experience. Outwardly quiet, at times even suggesting indolence, he had an energy that carried him over eighty mentally active years and rendered him, to the final instant, keenly sentient and critical of his surroundings. Perfectly mannered, and sometimes respectful enough of forms and authority,[1] he could be contemptuous of prelates and presidents, of governments and societies, and of the entire human race. In his presence life could have been dull only to the dull, and he did not encourage their company.

Along with numerous critics one may adroitly suppose that had he been born fifty years earlier, into a world not brusquely dishonoring most of his talents and his education, he would have been less isolated. Taking a hint from his forebears, one can guess that he would have spent much more of his strength than he did in a semisuccessful striving to make an imperfect system better. It is hard to believe, however, that

---

[1] In his preface to *Henry Adams and His Friends*, Harold Dean Cater offers the following anecdote: "One evening, just after the United States entered the war, Henry Cabot Lodge came to dinner with his daughter Constance and Sir Cecil Spring-Rice and his wife. Lodge's language about President Wilson had always been full of personal dislike, but this evening he was particularly violent in his attacks. Suddenly Mr. Adams interrupted the tirade. He brought his fist down on the table and said sharply: 'Cabot.' There was a moment's silence. 'I've never allowed treasonable conversation at this table and I don't propose to allow it now.' The dinner was finished in icy silence."

he would not have shown in his nature, even more than did his grandfather in his, the Socratic gadfly element: that perennial intransigence which, planted as though by sport in a small number of human beings, renders existence for the majority often perplexing but rescues it from utter stagnation and occasionally from disaster. It is the irrepressible protest of the self-realized sensibility against the imitative. In a realm of activity more commonplace than that which usually drew the attention of Henry Adams, it is what makes men hang juries, disrupt school boards, and write indignant letters to the papers. More significantly, it becomes the sublimation of Clerk Maxwell's devil, upsetting scientific, political, and moral axioms and foregone conclusions. The fat-hearted and mentally legacied hate it, for it threatens what they most cherish: the status quo. Not that they always recognize their enemy and savior, for it tends to complicate itself in an intelligence nimbler than their own. They are constantly bracing their defenses, however, with stubborn codes, and when they discern rebellion in a man they sometimes find a way of disposing of him temporarily. They discipline Galileo and banish Voltaire; they call Shelley a romantic crackpot; they denounce Darwin as blasphemous; they accuse Freud of being ribald and Joyce of being meaningless; and they smile, until the bomb drops, at Einstein as a long-haired Jewish professor. Yet the portentous, disrespectful imp will not quite down. He reappears within each generation, bewildering with his grim or playful insistence that the man-made world is not completely right. He is most baffling when he shows almost every sign of respectability, perpetrating few outward grossnesses beyond being artist, scholar, and thinker, and writes with a quiet and splendid madness within his sanity. In this sense no rebel of our era is more elusive, or perhaps less escapable at last, than Henry Adams. Few books can be named that so politely and thoroughly take twentieth-century man apart as do *Chartres* and *The Education*. It remains to be seen how much longer twentieth-century man can remain jovially unaware of his disassembly, though there are signs that recognition is being forced upon him.

As for the second level of experience to which Adams addressed his sensibility, it has been noted how with the passing years he became increasingly obsessed with the need of giving coherent description to that multiverse in which collective and individual man, for a moment inconceivably brief, finds himself. It is a rare experience to read the complete works of Henry Adams in their order and observe how his mind steadily broadened in an attempt to define, first, the destiny of his country, then that of all mankind, and, finally, that of the cosmos. He was at last dedicated to that ancient longing and quest for over-all unity which certain intense spirits in every age find compulsive. Even our prototype in the Garden of Eden, *The Education* avers, found himself "between God who was unity, and Satan who was complexity, with no means of deciding which was truth," yet unable to avoid making a choice.

Within the pattern of Western life, perhaps only the church, Adams observed, has ever affirmed unity with full conviction; though one remembers the Gothic buttress hiding in the earth the last secret of self-distrust and doubt. Specifically, St. Francis affirmed the divine oneness of all things and believed his affirmation instantly, without the necessity even of thought; indeed, to St. Francis thought was impiety, so utterly did he believe. Reference has already been made to Adams's envy. "That's the way to do it!" he seems to say—"if only one can." There is nothing to indicate that he did not regard the experience of St. Francis as valid. If one have the special sensitivity which detects a universal Entity residing beyond (or beneath) sight, sound, smell, taste, and touch, and have also a mind that does not skeptically survey and challenge the results of that sensitivity—then one has achieved salvation. Adams could not quite so achieve it, at least more than temporarily, though he was tolerant of one who could, and he was ready to concede that the religious experience might occur with full force again in the future as it had in the past. "For after all man knows mighty little," goes the passage written to his brother Brooks, "and may some day learn enough of his own ignorance to fall down again and pray. Not that I care. Only, if such is God's will, and Fate and Evolution—let there be God!" And what could be more revealing of the modern plight than this half-ironic reversal of the roles in Genesis?

St. Thomas enjoyed the same advantage as St. Francis, that of initial belief. As long as one automatically accepted God first of all (John Henry Newman did it six centuries later), regarded unity as certain, it became only a fascinating intellectual exercise to devise a system whereby the energy of man's mind could be explained as an emanation from the central divine motor. Whether the system of Aquinas hung together or not, and it hung together amazingly, did perhaps not finally matter; for probably to him the unity was there, whatever the success of man's efforts at elucidation. Even in the early part of the modern age, the philosophers of the eighteenth-century Enlightenment, grappling in their own idiom with the same fundamental problem, enjoyed to some extent this medieval advantage. There is basis to suppose, for example, that when Alexander Pope composed his *Essay on Man*—with its varied rationalistic echoes of Aquinas, Spinoza, Leibniz, Shaftesbury, King, and Bolingbroke—he was setting up a mere argumentative façade to dignify an emotional conviction previously established, though not to be held to by Pope without some intellectual embarrassment. The world of the enlightened philosophers was the best of all possible worlds in a sense that Voltaire, as he deals with it in *Candide*, seems not to have understood. As Arthur O. Lovejoy points out, it was the only world they could discern as metaphysically possible. The great chain of being depended from God, and God was the centripetal principle of security, order, and truth.

Henry Adams, however, had a distinctly contemporary mind and could not completely re-erect the collapsing metaphysical structure of the past, dwell in it contentedly, and assume God and unity. So his predicament and so his meaning. He could wish for unity and search for it and then, not finding it, strive to create it in terms congenial to the twentieth century. Engaged in such a trial, he was approximating within his own space-time concepts what men before him had done. His difficulties were as much greater than theirs as the complications of modern life and thought surpass those of previous ages; and the requirements of courage were certainly no less.

Too wise and audacious merely to wait for death, he spent his old age invoking the aid of all the science he could muster and had to concede that science pointed not to unity but to complexity; and science suggested that total experience might be best described in terms of universal dissipating force, of which the vital energy of man is but one of the segments. By unleashing the forces of nature man is blindly hastening their dissipation, which will probably not occur, however, before he pulls down his own house upon him. Everything seems to show that his own force, the power of his mind and will, is approaching exhaustion—no longer sufficient to avert the cataclysm that his petty ingenuity has fashioned. Adams did not exult over the conclusion toward which his observations led him, nor was he resigned. His last comment on the unsolved puzzle of reality and man's share in it was an emotional outcry of appalled but undefeated anger, to which long thoughtfulness and discipline imparted an idiom disarmingly intellectual. He recognized that his theorizing was all a deliberate fiction, impressive and quasi-believable because it seemed to work, because it wrenched a kind of orderly, grisly meaning from chaos. There were imperfections in it, as he well knew, and he hints repeatedly that anyone who cannot surmount them had best devise a system of his own: "Everyone must bear his own universe." Any description of the cosmos, and any definition of the part in it played by man, has to be fiction; for it comes from man, whose inquiries can be directed only toward that illusion of reality provided by his own senses and his own thought; and the utmost effort of the mind unveils not absolute truth but the mind's wavering reflection. This, then, is the third level on which one discovers the sensibility of Henry Adams: that whereon it turns challengingly back upon itself, recognizes the inescapable faultiness of its own workings, and yet does not surrender.

He had long known what the end would be, for he had written in "Buddha and Brahma":

> Thought
> Travelling in constant circles, round and round
> Must ever pass through endless contradictions,
> Returning on itself at last, till lost
> In silence.

Yet there remains a glint of self-realization in the limitless dark of compulsion, the defiant intellect from which thought first emerged and from which it may emerge again.

So Henry Adams becomes at last an instance of the foredoomed effort to understand the universal mystery, of endurance beyond defeat, and of the only kind of triumph in which one can now readily believe: that of the affirmed invincibility of the human spirit in the face of what must overwhelm it. It is something to have had in our land and time a symbol of the tragic valor possible to man as he fronts infinity and finds it void of all certain promise but his own.

APPENDIX

Prayer to the Virgin of Chartres

By Henry Adams

Gracious Lady:—
Simple as when I asked your aid before;
Humble as when I prayed for grace in vain
Seven hundred years ago; weak, weary, sore
In heart and hope, I ask your help again.

You, who remember all, remember me;
An English scholar of a Norman name,
I was a thousand who then crossed the sea
To wrangle in the Paris schools for fame.

When your Byzantine portal was still young
I prayed there with my master Abailard;
When Ave Maris Stella was first sung,
I helped to sing it here with Saint Bernard.

When Blanche set up your gorgeous Rose of France
I stood among the servants of the Queen;
And when Saint Louis made his penitence,
I followed barefoot where the King had been.

For centuries I brought you all my cares,
And vexed you with the murmurs of a child;
You heard the tedious burden of my prayers;
You could not grant them, but at least you smiled.

If then I left you, it was not my crime,
Or if a crime, it was not mine alone.
All children wander with the truant Time.
Pardon me too! You pardoned once your Son!

For He said to you:—"Wist ye not that I
Must be about my Father's business?" So,
Seeking his Father he pursued his way
Straight to the Cross towards which we all must go.

So I too wandered off among the host
That racked the earth to find the father's clue.
I did not find the Father, but I lost
What now I value more, the Mother,—You!

I thought the fault was yours that foiled my search;
I turned and broke your image on its throne,
Cast down my idol, and resumed my march
To claim the father's empire for my own.

Crossing the hostile sea, our greedy band
Saw rising hills and forests in the blue;
Our father's kingdom in the promised land!
—We seized it, and dethroned the father too.

And now we are the Father, with our brood,
Ruling the Infinite, not Three but One;
We made our world and saw that it was good;
Ourselves we worship, and we have no Son.

Yet we have Gods, for even our strong nerve
Falters before the Energy we own.

Which shall be master? Which of us shall serve?
Which wears the fetters? Which shall bear the crown?

Brave though we be, we dread to face the Sphinx,
Or answer the old riddle she still asks.
Strong as we are, our reckless courage shrinks
To look beyond the piece-work of our tasks.

But when we must, we pray, as in the past
Before the Cross on which your Son was nailed.
Listen, dear lady! You shall hear the last
Of the strange prayers Humanity has wailed.

PRAYER TO THE DYNAMO

Mysterious Power! Gentle Friend!
Despotic Master! Tireless Force!
You and We are near the End.
Either You or We must bend
To bear the martyrs' Cross.

We know ourselves, what we can bear
As men; our strength and weakness too;
Down to the fraction of a hair;
And know that we, with all our care
And knowledge, know not you.

You come in silence, Primal Force,
We know not whence, or when, or why;
You stay a moment in your course
To play; and, lo! you leap across
To Alpha Centauri!

We know not whether you are kind,
Or cruel in your fiercer mood;
But be you Matter, be you Mind,
We think we know that you are blind,
And we alone are good.

241

We know that prayer is thrown away,
For you are only force and light;
A shifting current; night and day;
We know this well, and yet we pray,
For prayer is infinite,

Like you! Within the finite sphere
That bounds the impotence of thought,
We search an outlet everywhere
But only find that we are here
And that you are—are not!

What are we then? the lords of space?
The master-mind whose tasks you do?
Jockey who rides you in the race?
Or are we atoms whirled apace,
Shaped and controlled by you?

Still silence! Still no end in sight!
No sound in answer to our cry!
Then, by the God we now hold tight,
Though we destroy soul, life and light,
Answer you shall—or die!

We are no beggars! What care we
For hopes or terrors, love or hate?
What for the universe? We see
Only our certain destiny
And the last word of Fate.

Seize, then, the Atom! rack his joints!
Tear out of him his secret spring!
Grind him to nothing!—though he points
To us, and his life-blood anoints
Me—the dead Atom-King!

A curious prayer, dear lady! is it not?
Strangely unlike the prayers I prayed to you!

Stranger because you find me at this spot,
Here, at your feet, asking your help anew.

Strangest of all, that I have ceased to strive,
Ceased even care what new coin fate shall strike.
In truth it does not matter. Fate will give
Some answer; and all answers are alike.

So, while we slowly rack and torture death
And wait for what the final void will show,
Waiting I feel the energy of faith
Not in the future science, but in you!

The man who solves the Infinite, and needs
The force of solar systems for his play,
Will not need me, nor greatly care what deeds
Made me illustrious in the dawn of day.

He will send me, dethroned, to claim my rights,
Fossil survival of an age of stone,
Among the cave-men and the troglodytes
Who carved the mammoth on the mammoth's bone.

He will forget my thought, my acts, my fame,
As we forget the shadows of the dusk,
Or catalogue the echo of a name
As we the scratches on the mammoth's tusk.

But when, like me, he too has trod the track
Which leads him up to power above control,
He too will have no choice but wander back
And sink in helpless hopelessness of soul,

Before your majesty of grace and love,
The purity, the beauty and the faith;
The depth of tenderness beneath; above,
The glory of the life and of the death.

When your Byzantine portal still was young,
I came here with my master Abailard;
When Ave Maris Stella was first sung,
I joined to sing it here with Saint Bernard.

When Blanche set up your glorious Rose of France,
In scholar's robes I waited on the Queen;
When good Saint Louis did his penitence,
My prayer was deep like his: my faith as keen.

What loftier prize seven hundred years shall bring,
What deadlier struggles for a larger air,
What immortality our strength shall wring
From Time and Space, we may—or may not—care;

But years, or ages, or eternity,
Will find me still in thought before your throne,
Pondering the mystery of Maternity,
Soul within Soul,—Mother and Child in One!

Help me to see! not with my mimic sight—
With yours! which carried radiance, like the sun,
Giving the rays you saw with—light in light—
Tying all suns and stars and worlds in one.

Help me to know! not with my mocking art—
With you, who knew yourself unbound by laws;
Gave God your strength, your life, your sight, your heart,
And took from him the Thought that Is—the Cause.

Help me to feel! not with my insect sense,—
With yours that felt all life alive in you;
Infinite heart beating at your expense;
Infinite passion breathing the breath you drew!

Help me to bear! not my own baby load,
But yours; who bore the failure of the light,
The strength, the knowledge and the thought of God,—
The futile folly of the Infinite!

Bibliography

I. Writings by Henry Adams Cited in This Volume

"American Finance, 1865–1869," *Edinburgh Review,* CXXIX (April, 1869), 504–533.

"The Anglo-Saxon Courts of Law," in Henry Adams, ed., *Essays in Anglo-Saxon Law* (Boston: Little, Brown and Co., 1876), pp. 1–54.

"British Finance in 1816," *North American Review,* CIV (April, 1867), 354–386.

"Buddha and Brahma" (poem: with a letter to John Hay, April 26, 1895), *Yale Review,* V (n.s.; October, 1915), 82–89.

"Captain John Smith," *North American Review,* CIV (Jan., 1867), 1–30. Reprinted in *Historical Essays* (New York: Chas. Scribner's Sons, 1891), pp. 42–79.

Chapters of Erie, and Other Essays. Boston: James R. Osgood and Co., 1871. In collaboration with Charles Francis Adams, Jr. Reprinted, 1886.

"Charles Lyell's Principles of Geology" (review), *North American Review,* CVII (Oct., 1868), 465–501.

"Civil Service Reform," *North American Review,* CIX (Oct., 1869), 443–476. Reprinted as *Civil Service Reform, by Henry Brooks Adams* (pamphlet) (Boston: Fields, Osgood and Co., 1869).

"Class Day Oration," Friday, June 25, 1858. Unpublished.

"College Politics," *Harvard Magazine,* III (May, 1857), 141–148.

"Diary of a Visit to Manchester," Boston *Daily Courier,* Dec. 16, 1861. Reprinted by Arthur W. Silver, ed., *American Historical Review,* LI (1945), 74–89.

The Degradation of the Democratic Dogma, with an Introduction by Brooks Adams. New York: Macmillan Co., 1919. Republished, 1920. Also, New York: Peter Smith, 1949.

Democracy: An American Novel (published anonymously). New York: Henry Holt and Co., 1880. Republished, 1882, 1885, 1902, 1908, 1925. Also, London: Macmillan and Co., 1882. Also, London: Ward, Lock and Co., 1882. Also, Leipzig: B. Tauchnitz, 1882. Also, as *Democratie, roman Americain,* Paris: Plon et Cie, 1883.

Documents Relating to New England Federalism, 1800–1815, Henry Adams, ed. Boston: Little, Brown and Co., 1877. Reprinted, 1905.

The Education of Henry Adams. Washington: privately printed (40 copies), 1907. Also, as *The Education of Henry Adams: An Autobiography,* Boston: Massachusetts Historical Society (ed. for members, 250 copies), 1918. Also, Boston: Houghton Mifflin Co., 1918, 1927, 1928, and 1935 (popular ed.). Also, London: Constable and Co., Ltd., 1928. Also, Boston: Houghton Mifflin Co., 1930 (Riverside Library ed.). Also, with Preface by James Truslow Adams, New York: Modern Library, 1931. Also, as *Mon Education,* trad. par Régis Michaud et Franck L. Schoell, Paris: Doivin et Cie, 1931. Also, with 12 etchings by Samuel Chamberlain and Introduction by Henry S. Canby, New York: Limited Editions, Merrymount Press, 1942.

Essays in Anglo-Saxon Law, Henry Adams, ed. Boston: Little, Brown and Co., 1876. Reprinted, 1905.

Esther: A Novel (under the pseudonym of Frances Snow Compton). New York: Henry Holt and Co., 1884. Also, London: Richard Bentley and Son, Ltd., 1885. Also, with Introduction by Robert E. Spiller, New York: Scholars' Facsimiles and Reprints, 1938.

Formative Years. See *History of the United States of America.* . . .

"Freeman's Historical Essays" (review), *North American Review,* CXIV (Jan., 1872), 193–196.

"Freeman's History of the Norman Conquest" (review), *North American Review,* CXVIII (Jan., 1874), 176–181.

"Green's Short History of the English People" (review), *North American Review,* CXXI (July, 1875), 216–224.

"Harvard College," *North American Review*, CXIV (Jan., 1872), 110–147. Reprinted in *Historical Essays* (New York: Chas. Scribner's Sons, 1891), pp. 80–121.

Henry Adams and His Friends: A Collection of His Unpublished Letters, Harold Dean Cater, ed. Boston: Houghton Mifflin Co., 1947.

Historical Essays, New York: Chas. Scribner's Sons, 1891.

History of the United States of America during the Administrations of Jefferson and Madison. 9 vols. New York: Chas. Scribner's Sons, 1889–1891. Republished, 1891–1898, 1891–1901, 1909–1911, 1921. Also, with an Introduction by Henry Steele Commager, 4 vols., New York: Albert and Chas. Boni, Inc., 1930. Also, condensed and edited with Introduction by Herbert Agar, as *Formative Years: A History of the United States during the Administrations of Jefferson and Madison*, 2 vols., Boston: Houghton Mifflin and Co., 1947.

"The Independents in the Canvass," *North American Review*, CXXIII (Oct., 1876), 426–467. With Charles Francis Adams, Jr.

John Randolph. Boston and New York: Houghton Mifflin Co., 1882. Republished, 1883, 1898, [1908?], [1917?].

"King," in *Clarence King Memoirs* (New York: G. P. Putnam's Sons, 1904), pp. 157–185.

"King's Mountaineering in the Sierra Nevada" (review), *North American Review*, CXIV (April, 1872), 445–448.

"The Legal Tender Act," *North American Review*, CX (April, 1870), 299–327. In collaboration with Francis A. Walker. Reprinted in *Historical Essays* (New York: Chas. Scribner's Sons, 1891), pp. 279–317.

A Letter to American Teachers of History. Baltimore: privately printed, J. H. Furst Co., 1910. Reprinted in *The Degradation of the Democratic Dogma* (New York: Macmillan Co., 1919), pp. 135–263. Also in *The Tendency of History* (New York: Macmillan Co., 1928), pp. 1–128, as "The Tendency of History."

Letters of Henry Adams, 1858–1918, Worthington C. Ford, ed. 2 vols. Boston and New York: Houghton Mifflin Co., 1930–1938.

Letters to the Boston *Daily Advertiser* (unsigned), Dec. 7, 1860–Feb. 11, 1861, *passim*. For itemized listing see Ernest Samuels,

The Young Henry Adams (Cambridge: Harvard University Press, 1948), pp. 314–315.

Letters to the Boston *Daily Courier* (signed "H. B. A."), April 30–July 13, 1860, *passim*. For itemized listing see Ernest Samuels, *The Young Henry Adams*, p. 314.

Letters to the New York *Times* (unsigned), June 7, 1861–Jan. 21, 1862, *passim*. For itemized listing see Ernest Samuels, *The Young Henry Adams*, pp. 315–316. The letter printed July 26, 1861, captioned "The American War," is attributed by Samuels to Henry Adams but was written from Natchez, Mississippi, by the London *Times* correspondent there. In the same issue a fragment entitled "Why Troops Were Sent to Canada" might have been written by Adams, but internal evidence strongly suggests some other author.

Letters to a Niece and Prayer to the Virgin of Chartres, by Henry Adams, with a Niece's Memories, Mabel La Farge, ed. Boston: Houghton Mifflin Co., 1920. (Also, see entries under "Prayer to the Virgin of Chartres.")

The Life of Albert Gallatin. Philadelphia: J. B. Lippincott, 1879. Also, New York: Peter Smith, 1943.

The Life of George Cabot Lodge. Boston and New York: Houghton Mifflin Co., 1911. Reprinted in Edmund Wilson, ed., *The Shock of Recognition* (Garden City: Doubleday, Doran and Co., 1943), pp. 747–852.

Memoirs of Marau Taaroa, Last Queen of Tahiti, Henry Adams, tr. and ed. No place named: privately printed, 1893. Republished, revised, and enlarged, under the title *Memoirs of Arii Taimai E*, Paris: privately printed, 1901. Also, under main title *Tahiti*, with Introduction by Robert E. Spiller, New York: Scholars' Facsimiles and Reprints, 1947.

Mont-Saint-Michel and Chartres. Washington: privately printed (150 copies), 1904. Revised and republished, Washington: privately printed, 1912. Also, "by authority of the American Institute of Architects," with Introduction by Ralph Adams Cram, Boston: Houghton Mifflin Co., 1913; reissued, 1936. Also, Boston: Massachusetts Historical Society, 1919.

"My Old Room," *Harvard Magazine*, II (Sept., 1856), 290–297.

"The New York Gold Conspiracy," *Westminster Review,* XXXVIII (Oct., 1870), 411–436. Reprinted in Henry Adams, *Historical Essays* (New York: Chas. Scribner's Sons, 1891), pp. 318–366. Also, in Richard Garnett *et al.,* eds., *The International Library of Famous Literature,* London: The Standard, 1900, XIX, 8886–8894. Also, in F. C. Hicks, ed., *High Finance in the Sixties,* New Haven: Yale Univ. Press, 1929, pp. 120–155. Also, republished as "Henry Adams Disposes of Fisk and Gould," in Mark Van Doren, ed., *An Autobiography of America,* New York: Albert and Chas. Boni, 1929, pp. 621–645.

"Palgrave's Poems" (review), *North American Review,* CXX (April, 1875), 438–444.

"Prayer to the Virgin of Chartres" (poem). See *Letters to a Niece.* . . . Also, in Lucy Lockwood Hazard, ed., *In Search of America* (New York: Thomas Y. Crowell Co., 1930), pp. 34–39. Also, in *American Federationist,* XXXVIII (Dec., 1931), 1483.

"Recognition of Cuban Independence," *Senate Report No. 1160 of the 54th Cong., 2d. Sess.* (Dec. 21, 1896), pp. 1–25. (Submitted to the Senate by Senator Don Cameron of Pennsylvania.)

"The Rule of Phase Applied to History," in Henry Adams, *The Degradation of the Democratic Dogma, with an Introduction by Brooks Adams* (New York: Macmillan Co., 1919), pp. 265–311. Also, in *The Tendency of History* (New York: Macmillan Co., 1928), pp. 129–175.

"The Session," *North American Review,* CVIII (April, 1869), 610–640.

"The Session, 1869–1870," *North American Review,* CXI (July, 1870), 29–62. Republished as a campaign document, under the title *The Administration—A Radical Indictment! Its Shortcomings, Its Weakness, Stolidity. Thorough Analysis of Grant's and Boutwell's Mental Calibre. No Policy. No Ability.* National Democratic Executive Resident Committee, 1872. Also, reprinted in *Historical Essays* (New York: Chas. Scribner's Sons, 1891), pp. 367–412.

Tahiti. See *Memoirs of Marau Taaroa, Last Queen of Tahiti.*

"The Tendency of History," American Historical Association *Annual Report* for the year 1894 (Washington, 1895), pp. 17–

23. Also (pamphlet), Washington: Government Printing Office, 1896. Also, reprinted in *The Degradation of the Democratic Dogma* (New York: Macmillan Co., 1919) pp. 122–133.

The Tendency of History. New York: Macmillan Co., 1928. See *A Letter to American Teachers of History.*

"A Visit to Manchester: Extracts from a Private Diary" (unsigned), Boston *Daily Courier,* Dec. 16, 1861. Also, reprinted in A. Silver, "Henry Adams's Diary of a Visit to Manchester: with Text," *American Historical Review,* LI (Oct., 1945), 74–89.

"Washington in 1861," *Proceedings of the Massachusetts Historical Society,* XLIII (1910), 656–689.

The Writings of Albert Gallatin, Henry Adams, ed. 3 vols. Philadelphia: J. B. Lippincott and Co., 1879.

II. Works Containing Letters of Henry Adams

Adams, James Truslow. *The Adams Family.* Boston: Little, Brown and Co., 1930.

Agassiz, Alexander. *Letters and Recollections of Alexander Agassiz.* Boston, 1913.

Alden, John E., "Henry Adams as Editor: A Group of Unpublished Letters Written to David A. Wells," *New England Quarterly,* XI (March, 1938), 146–152.

Belmont, Perry. *An American Democrat.* New York: Columbia University Press, 1940.

Bigelow, John, ed. *Letters and Literary Memorials of Samuel J. Tilden.* 2 vols. New York: Harper and Bros., 1908.

Bixler, Paul H., "A Note on Henry Adams," *Colophon,* V, Part 17, May, 1934, no pagination.

Cater, Harold Dean, ed. *Henry Adams and His Friends.* Boston: Houghton Mifflin Co., 1947.

——, "Henry Adams Reports on a German Gymnasium," *American Historical Review,* LIII (Oct., 1947), 59–74.

Cook, Albert S., ed., "Six Letters of Henry Adams," *Yale Review,* X (Oct., 1920), 131–140.

——, "Three Letters of Henry Adams," *Pacific Review,* II (Sept., 1921), 273–275.

Cortissoz, Royal. *John La Farge: A Memoir and a Study*. Boston: Houghton Mifflin Co., 1911.

——. *The Life of Whitelaw Reid*. 2 vols. New York: Chas. Scribner's Sons, 1921.

Davis, Edward H., ed., "Letters and Comment" (four letters of Henry Adams), *Yale Review*, XI (Oct., 1921), 218–221.

Ford, Worthington C., ed. *A Cycle of Adams Letters, 1861–1865*. 2 vols. Boston: Houghton Mifflin Co., 1920.

——. *Letters of Henry Adams, 1858–1918*. 2 vols. Boston: Houghton Mifflin Co., 1930–1938.

Gwynn, Stephen, ed. *The Letters and Friendships of Sir Cecil Spring-Rice*. Boston: Houghton Mifflin Co., 1929.

Hay, John. *Letters of John Hay and Extracts from Diary*, 3 vols. Washington: printed but not published, 1908. (Material selected by Henry Adams, edited with names deleted by Mrs. Hay. Keys at Illinois Historical Society, Springfield; University of Chicago Lincoln Library; Massachusetts Historical Society.)

Holt, Henry. *Garrulities of an Octogenarian Editor*. Boston: Houghton Mifflin Co., 1923.

Holt, W. Stull, "Henry Adams and the Johns Hopkins University," *New England Quarterly*, XI (Sept., 1938), 632–638.

James, Henry, *Letters of Henry James*. 2 vols. Boston: Atlantic Monthly Press, [c. 1920].

James, William. *Letters of William James*, 2 vols. Boston: Atlantic Monthly Press, [c. 1920].

Jameson, J. F., "Obituary," *American Historical Association Reports*, I (1918), 71–72.

La Farge, Mabel, ed. *Letters to a Niece and Prayer to the Virgin of Chartres, by Henry Adams, with a Niece's Memories*. Boston: Houghton Mifflin Co., 1920.

Laski, Harold J., ed., "Henry Adams: An Unpublished Letter," *Nation*, CLI (Aug. 3, 1940), 94–95.

Leslie, Shane, "Letters of Henry Adams," *Yale Review*, XXIV (Sept., 1934), 112–117.

Lodge, Henry Cabot. *Early Memories*. New York: Chas. Scribner's Sons, 1913.

Luquiens, Frederick Bliss, ed., "Seventeen Letters of Henry Adams," *Yale Review,* X (Oct., 1920), 111–140.

Munroe, James P. *Life of Francis Amasa Walker.* New York: Henry Holt and Co., 1923.

Nevins, Allan. *Abram S. Hewitt.* New York: Harper and Bros., 1935.

Ogden, Rollo. *Life and Letters of E. L. Godkin,* 2 vols. New York: Macmillan Co., 1907.

Perry, Bliss. *Life and Letters of Henry L. Higginson.* Boston: Atlantic Monthly Press, 1921.

Rhodes, James Ford, "Henry Adams, '58," *Harvard Graduates' Magazine,* XXIV, 1917–1918.

Taylor, Henry Osborn. *Human Values and Verities, Part I.* Privately printed, 1929.

III. *Writings about Henry Adams*

Academy of Arts and Letters, New York. *In Memoriam: A Book of Record concerning Former Members of the American Academy of Arts and Letters.* New York: The De Vinne Press, 1922. (Adams's portrait and record on pp. 65, 67. See also p. 219.)

Adams, Brooks, "The Heritage of Henry Adams," in Henry Adams, *The Degradation of the Democratic Dogma* (New York: Macmillan Co., 1919), pp. 1–122.

Adams, Charles Francis. *Charles Francis Adams, 1835–1915.* Boston: Houghton Mifflin Co., 1915.

Adams, James Truslow. *The Adams Family.* Boston: Little, Brown and Co., 1930.

——. *Henry Adams.* New York: Albert and Chas. Boni, Inc., 1933. (Bibliography of the writings of Henry Adams, pp. 213–229.)

——. Introduction to *The Education of Henry Adams* (New York: Modern Library, 1931), pp. v–x.

——. *The Tempo of Modern Life.* New York: Albert and Chas. Boni, Inc., 1931. (See especially pp. 171–186, 200–256.)

Agar, Herbert, Introduction to Henry Adams, *Formative Years: A History of the United States during the Administrations of Jefferson and Madison* (2 vols; Boston: Houghton Mifflin Co., 1947), I, ix–xxv.

Aiken, Conrad, "Letters from America: The Lucifer Brothers in Starlight," *Athenaeum*, 1920, I (Feb. 20, 1920), 243–244.

Anderson, Isabel (Mrs. Larz Anderson), ed., *Letters and Journals of General Nicholas Longworth Anderson: Harvard, Civil War, Washington: 1854–1892*. New York: F. H. Revell Co., 1942.

"At Mr. Adams's," *New Republic*, XV (May 25, 1918), 106–108.

"Autobiography of a Failure: The Education of Henry Adams," *Nation*, CVII (Oct. 12, 1918), 403.

Baldensperger, Fernand, "Les Scruples d'un americain attardé; 'L'éducation de Henry Adams, autobiographie,'" *Correspondant*, CCXLV (Dec. 25, 1920), 1040–1062.

Bassett, John Spencer, "Later Historians," in *Cambridge History of American Literature*, III (New York: Macmillan Co., 1921), 171–200. (For specific comment on Adams, see pp. 197–200.)

Basso, Hamilton, "Mind in the Making," *New Yorker*, XXIII (March 29, 1947), 103–106.

Baym, Max I., "The 1858 Catalogue of Henry Adams's Library," *Colophon*, No. 4, Autumn, 1938, pp. 483–489.

——, "Henry Adams and the Critics," *American Scholar*, XV (Winter, 1945–1946), 79–89.

——, "Henry Adams and Henry Vignaud," *New England Quarterly*, XVII (Sept., 1944), 442–449.

——, "William James and Henry Adams," *New England Quarterly*, X (Dec., 1937), 717–742.

Beach, Joseph Warren, "Henry Adams," in *The Outlook for American Prose* (Chicago: Univ. of Chicago Press, 1926), pp. 204–214.

Beard, Charles A., "Historians at Work, Brooks and Henry Adams," *Atlantic Monthly*, CLXXI (April, 1943), 87–93.

——, Introduction to Brooks Adams, *The Law of Civilization and Decay: An Essay on History* (New York: Alfred A. Knopf, 1943), pp. 3–53.

Becker, Carl L., "The Education of Henry Adams," *American Historical Review*, XXIV (April, 1919), 422–434. Reprinted in *Every Man His Own Historian* (New York: F. S. Crofts and Co., 1935), pp. 143–161.

——, "Henry Adams Once More," *Saturday Review of Literature*,

IX (April 8, 1933), 521–524. Reprinted in *Every Man His Own Historian,* pp. 162–168.

Bennett, Charles A. A., "Of Last Things, Modern Style," *Yale Review,* IX (July, 1920), 890–896.

Bixler, Paul H., "A Note on Henry Adams," *Colophon,* V, Part 17 (May, 1934), no pagination.

Blackmur, Richard P., "The Expense of Greatness: Three Emphases on Henry Adams," *Virginia Quarterly Review,* XII (July, 1936), 396–415. Reprinted in *The Expense of Greatness* (New York: Arrow Editions, 1940), pp. 253–276.

——, "Henry Adams: Three Late Moments," *Kenyon Review,* II (Winter, 1940), 7–29.

——, "Henry and Brooks Adams: Parallels to Two Generations," *Southern Review,* V (Autumn, 1939), 308–334.

——, "The Letters of Marian Adams, 1865–1883," *Virginia Quarterly Review,* XIII (April, 1937), 289–295. Reprinted in *The Expense of Greatness* (New York: Arrow Editions, 1940), pp. 245–252.

——, "The Novels of Henry Adams," *Sewanee Review,* LI (April, 1943), 281–304.

Blunt, H. F., "The Mal-education of Henry Adams," *Catholic World,* CXLIV (April, 1937), 46–52.

Bradford, Gamaliel, "Henry Adams," in *American Portraits, 1875–1900* (Boston: Houghton Mifflin Co., 1922), pp. 29–57.

Brooks, Van Wyck, "The Miseducation of Henry Adams," in *Sketches in Criticism* (New York: E. P. Dutton and Co., 1932), pp. 197–210.

——. *New England: Indian Summer, 1865–1915.* New York: E. P. Dutton and Co., 1940. (See especially pp. 250–275, 354–372, 474–490.)

Bruce, William C. *John Randolph of Roanoke.* New York: G. P. Putnam's Sons, 1922. (Introduction has criticism of Adams's *John Randolph.*)

Bullard, F. Lauriston, Prefatory Notes to *The Diary of a Public Man: An Intimate View of the National Administration, December 28, 1860, to March 15, 1861* (Chicago: privately printed, Abraham Lincoln Bookshop, 1945), pp. 1–24. A brief account of

Adams's editorship of the *North American Review* is given on pp. 12–13. As indicated in the text, chap. ii, it is possible to hypothesize that the anonymous *Diary of a Public Man* was written by Henry Adams, though this is not Bullard's suggestion.

Canby, Henry S., Introduction to *The Education of Henry Adams* (New York: Limited Editions, 1942).

Cargill, Oscar. *Intellectual America: Ideas on the March.* New York: Macmillan Co., 1941. (See pp. 551–569.)

——, Letter to the editors, *American Literature,* XVI (Nov., 1944), 226.

——, "The Medievalism of Henry Adams," in *Essays and Studies in Honor of Carleton Brown* (New York: New York University Press, 1940).

Cater, Harold Dean, Biographical Introduction to *Henry Adams and His Friends: A Collection of His Unpublished Letters* (Boston: Houghton Mifflin Co., 1947), pp. xv–cvii.

Chanler, Margaret. *Roman Spring.* Boston: Little, Brown and Co., 1934.

——, "Theodore Roosevelt's Washington," *Atlantic Monthly,* CLIV (Sept., 1934), 324–329.

Clark, J. A., "Henry Adams Sees His Shadow," *Commonweal,* XXIX (March 31, 1939), 627–629.

Clement, A. W., "Henry Adams and the Repudiation of Science," *Scientific Monthly,* LXIV (May, 1947), 451.

Coleman, Herbert T. J., "Henry Adams: A Study in Multiplicity," *Queen's Quarterly,* XXVIII (July–Sept., 1920), 1–14.

Commager, Henry Steele. *The American Mind: An Interpretation of American Thought and Character since the 1880's.* New Haven: Yale University Press, 1950. (See pp. 132–140.)

——, "Henry Adams," in *The Marcus W. Jernegan Essays in American Historiography* (Chicago: University of Chicago Press, 1937), pp. 191–206.

——, "Henry Adams," *South Atlantic Quarterly,* XXVI (July, 1927), 252–265.

——, "Henry Adams, Prophet of Our Disjointed World," New York *Times Magazine,* Feb. 20, 1938, pp. 11, 22.

Corwin, Edward S., review of *The Degradation of the Democratic Dogma, American Political Science Review,* XIV (Aug., 1920), 507–509.

Cournos, John, "Henry Adams—Another 'Failure,' " in *A Modern Plutarch* (Indianapolis: Bobbs-Merrill Co., c. 1928), pp. 275–284.

——, "Two Famous Failures," *Bookman,* LXVII (Aug., 1928), 690–691.

Cram, Ralph Adams, Introduction to *Mont-Saint-Michel and Chartres,* Boston: Houghton Mifflin Co., 1913.

Creek, Herbert L., "The Medievalism of Henry Adams," *South Atlantic Quarterly,* XXIV (Jan., 1925), 86–97.

Crothers, Samuel M., "Education in Pursuit of Henry Adams," *Yale Review,* VIII (n. s.; April, 1919), 580–595. Republished in *Dame School of Experience, and Other Papers* (Boston and New York: Houghton Mifflin Co., 1920), pp. 186–213.

Crowninshield, Benjamin W. *A Private Journal, 1856–1858* (Francis B. Crowninshield, ed.), Cambridge, privately printed, 1941.

——, "Private Journal Commenced at Hanover, October 20th, 1858." Unpublished manuscript owned by Francis B. Crowninshield.

Curti, Merle. *The Growth of American Thought.* New York: Harper and Bros., 1944.

Davis, Forrest. *The Atlantic System: The Story of Anglo-American Control of the Seas.* New York: Reynal and Hitchcock, 1941.

Delany, S. P., "A Man of Mystery," *North American Review,* CCXVI (Nov., 1922), 695–704.

[*Democracy,* Review of], *Edinburgh Review,* CLVI (July, 1882), 189–202.

Dennett, T., "Five of Hearts," *Scholastic* (H.S. teacher ed.), XXVIII (March 4, 1936), 6–7.

Dickason, David H., "Henry Adams and Clarence King: The Record of a Friendship," *New England Quarterly,* XVII (June, 1944), 229–254.

Dunning, William A., "Henry Adams on Things in General," *Political Science Quarterly,* XXVI (June, 1919), 305–311.

——, Review of *The Degradation of the Democratic Dogma, Political Science Quarterly*, XXXVI (March, 1921), 127–129.

Edwards, Herbert, "Henry Adams: Politician and Statesman," *New England Quarterly*, XXII (March, 1949), 49–60.

——, "The Prophetic Mind of Henry Adams," *College English*, III (May, 1942), 708–721.

Eliot, T. S., "A Sceptical Patrician," *Athenaeum* (London), May 23, 1919, pp. 361–362.

Elsey, George McKee, "The First Education of Henry Adams: with His Autobiographical Commencement Essay," *New England Quarterly*, XIV (Dec., 1941), 679–684.

Ford, Worthington C., "The Adams Family," *Quarterly Review*, CCXXXVII (April, 1922), 298–312.

——, "Henry Adams, Historian," *Nation*, CVI (June 8, 1918), 674–675.

Frewen, Moreton, "The Autobiography of Henry Adams," *Nineteenth Century*, LXXXV (May, 1919), 981–989.

Gabriel, Ralph H., "Frederick Jackson Turner vs. Henry Adams," in *The Course of American Democratic Thought* (New York, 1940), pp. 251–268.

Glicksberg, Charles I., "Henry Adams and the Civil War," *Americana*, XXXIII (Oct., 1939), 443–462.

——, "Henry Adams the Journalist," *New England Quarterly*, XXI (June, 1946), 232–236.

——, "Henry Adams and the Modern Spirit," *Dalhousie Review*, XXVII (Oct., 1947), 299–309.

——, ed., "Henry Adams Reports on a Trade Union Meeting," *New England Quarterly*, XV (Dec., 1942), 724–728.

"Great Failure," *Time*, XXXII (Sept. 12, 1938), 69.

Greenslet, Ferris, "Adams Interlude," in *Under the Bridge: An Autobiography* (New York: Literary Classics, Inc., 1943), pp. 144–152.

Hackett, Francis, "Henry Adams," *New Republic*, XVII (Dec. 7, 1918), 169–171. Reprinted in *The Invisible Censor* (New York: B. W. Huebsch, Inc., 1921), pp. 71–79.

Hicks, Granville. *The Great Tradition: An Interpretation of*

American Literature since the Civil War. New York: Macmillan Co., 1935. (For discussion of Adams, see pp. 131–139.)

Hind, Charles L., "Henry Adams," in *Authors and I* (New York and London: John Lane Co., 1921), pp. 13–18.

"Housatonic" (pseud.), "A Case of Hereditary Bias: Henry Adams as a Historian: Some Strictures on the 'History of the United States of America,' " New York *Tribune,* Sept. 10, Dec. 15, 1890. Privately reprinted in pamphlet form by the pseudonymous author (Washington, 1891).

Howe, M. A. D., "Elusive Henry Adams," *Saturday Review of Literature,* VII (Oct. 18, 1930), 237–239.

Hume, Robert A., "Henry Adams's Quest for Certainty," in Hardin Craig, ed., *Stanford Studies in Language and Literature* (Stanford, Calif.: Stanford University Press, 1941), pp. 361–373.

———, "Homage to Henry Adams," *Pacific Spectator,* II (Summer, 1948), 299–307.

———, "The Style and Literary Background of Henry Adams: With Attention to *The Education of Henry Adams*," *American Literature,* XVI (Jan., 1945), 296–315.

Irish, Marion D., "Henry Adams: The Modern American Scholar," *American Scholar,* I (March, 1932), 223–229.

Jameson, J. F., "Obituary," *American Historical Association Reports,* I (1918), 71–72.

———, Unpublished letter to George Lincoln Burr, Jan. 18, 1911. On file in the Cornell University Library.

Johnson, Allen, "Adams, Henry Brooks," *Dictionary of American Biography,* I (1928), 61–67.

Jordy, William H., "Henry Adams and Walt Whitman," *South Atlantic Quarterly,* XL (April, 1941), 132–145.

Kronenberger, Louis, "The Education of Henry Adams," *New Republic,* XCVIII (March 15, 1939), 155–158.

———, "The Epicurean Stoic," *New Republic,* XCVI (Oct. 12, 1938), 276–278.

La Farge, John. *An Artist's Letters from Japan.* New York: Century Co., 1897.

———. *Reminiscences of the South Seas.* Garden City: Doubleday, Page and Co., 1912.

La Farge, Mabel H., "Henry Adams," *Commonweal,* XVIII (May 19, 1933), 74–75.

——, "Henry Adams: A Niece's Memories," *Yale Review,* IX (Jan., 1920), 271–285. Reprinted in Mabel H. La Farge (ed.), *Letters to a Niece and Prayer to the Virgin of Chartres* (Boston: Houghton Mifflin Co., 1920), pp. 3–27.

Laughlin, J. Laurence, "Some Recollections of Henry Adams," *Scribner's Magazine,* LXIX (May, 1921), 576–581.

Le Clair, Robert C. *Three American Travellers in England: James Russell Lowell, Henry Adams, Henry James.* Philadelphia: privately printed, University of Pa., 1945.

Leslie, Shane, "The Education of Henry Adams," *Dublin Review,* CLXIV (April, 1919), 218–232.

Lewisohn, Ludwig. *Expression in America.* New York and London: Harper and Bros., 1932.

Lodge, Henry Cabot. *Early Memories.* New York: Chas. Scribner's Sons, 1913.

Loggins, Vernon, "Henry Adams," in *I Hear America . . . : Literature in the United States since 1900* (New York: Thos. Y. Crowell Co., 1937), pp. 38–45.

Lovett, Robert Morss, "The Betrayal of Henry Adams," *Dial,* LXV (Nov. 30, 1918), 468–472.

——, "Henry Adams' Letters," *New Republic,* LXIV (Oct. 22, 1930), 268–270.

Lydenberg, John, "Henry Adams and Lincoln Steffens," *South Atlantic Quarterly,* XLVIII (Jan., 1949), 42–64.

——, Review of Harold Dean Cater, ed., *Henry Adams and His Friends,* New York *Times,* Jan. 19, 1947, p. 3.

MacDonald, William, "Henry Adams," in John Macy, ed., *American Writers on American Literature* (New York: Horace Liveright, Inc., 1931), pp. 317–326.

Michaud, Régis, "Un Amateur de Decadence: 'L'Education' de Henry Adams," in *Autour d'Emerson* (Paris: Editions Bossard, 1924), pp. 201–215.

Miller, Richard F., "Henry Adams and the Influence of Woman," *American Literature,* XVIII (Jan., 1947), 291–298.

Mitchell, Stewart, "Henry Adams and Some of His Students,"

Proceedings of the Massachusetts Historical Society, LXVI (1942), 294–312.

———, "Letters of Henry Adams, 1858–1891," *New England Quarterly,* IV (July, 1931), 563–568.

Monaghan, Jay. *Diplomat in Carpet Slippers: Abraham Lincoln Deals with Foreign Affairs.* Indianapolis: Bobbs-Merrill Co., 1945.

Moran, Benjamin, Unpublished diaries. On file in the Manuscript Division of the Library of Congress, Washington, D.C.

More, Paul Elmer. *Commemorative Tribute to Henry Adams* (pamphlet). New York: American Academy of Arts and Letters, 1922.

———, "Henry Adams," in *A New England Group and Others: Shelburne Essays, Eleventh Series* (Boston and New York: Houghton Mifflin Co., 1921), pp. 115–140.

Morison, Samuel E., ed. *The Development of Harvard University.* Cambridge: Harvard University Press, 1930.

———. *Three Centuries of Harvard.* Cambridge: Harvard University Press, 1936.

Morse, John Torrey, Jr., "Albert Gallatin," *Atlantic Monthly,* XLIV (Oct., 1879), 513–521.

Mott, Frank Luther, "One Hundred and Twenty Years," *North American Review,* CCXL (June, 1935), 163–165.

Muller, Gustav, "Henry Adams: Ein Amerikanischer Geschichtsphilosoph," *Hochland,* XXVIII (1930–1931), 348–356.

Mumford, Lewis. *The Golden Day: A Study in American Experience and Culture.* New York: Boni and Liveright, 1926. (See pp. 217–225.)

Munson, Gorham B., "Prose for Autobiography: Henry Adams," in *Style and Form in American Prose* (New York: Doubleday, Doran and Co., 1929), pp. 263–269.

Neufield, Maurice F., "The Crisis in Prospect," *American Scholar,* IV (1935), 397–408.

Nevins, Allan. *Henry White: Thirty Years of American Diplomacy.* New York and London: Harper and Bros., 1930.

Nichols, Roy F., "The Dynamic Interpretation of History," *New England Quarterly,* VIII (June, 1935), 163–178.

Nuhn, Ferner, "Henry Adams and the Hand of the Fathers," in *The Wind Blew from the East* (New York: Harper and Bros., 1942), pp. 164–194.

Page, Evelyn, "The Diary and the Public Man," *New England Quarterly*, XXII (June, 1949), 147–172.

Parrington, Vernon Louis, "The Skepticism of the House of Adams," in *Main Currents in American Thought*, III (New York: Harcourt, Brace and Co., 1927), 212–236.

Perry, Bliss, "The Adamses," *Yale Review*, XX (Winter, 1931), 382–383.

Powell, John Walker, "Henry Adams and Democratic Education," *Standard*, XVIII (Feb., 1932), 172–178.

Pritchett, U. S., "Books in General," *New Statesman and Nation*, XXVIII (Nov. 4, 1944), 305.

Quinlivan, Frances, "Irregularities of the Mental Mirror," *Catholic World*, CLXIII (April, 1946), 58–65.

Randall, D. A., and J. T. Winterich, "One Hundred Good Novels. Henry Adams: *Democracy*," *Publishers' Weekly*, CXXXVI (July 15, 1939), 180–182.

Roelofs, Gerrit H., "Henry Adams: Pessimism and the Intelligent Use of Doom," *ELH: A Journal of Literary History*, XVII (Sept., 1950), 214–239.

Rukeyser, Muriel, "Tendencies in History," in *Willard Gibbs* (Garden City: Doubleday, Doran and Co., 1942), pp. 403–428.

Sabine, George H., "Henry Adams and the Writing of History," *University of California Chronicle*, XXVI (Jan., 1924), 31–46.

Samuels, Ernest. *The Young Henry Adams*. Cambridge: Harvard University Press, 1948.

Schlesinger, Arthur, Jr., "The Other Henry Adams," *Nation*, CLXVII (Dec. 25, 1948), 727.

Sedgwick, Henry Dwight, Review of *Letters to a Niece* and *A Cycle of Adams Letters, Yale Review*, X (n.s.; April, 1921), 643–650.

Shafer, Robert, "Henry Adams," *International Journal of Ethics*, XXX (Oct., 1919), 43–57.

——, *Progress and Science*. New Haven: Yale University Press, 1922. (See pp. 155–193.)

Sheldon, W. D., "Why Education Failed to Educate Henry Adams," *Sewanee Review,* XXVIII (Jan., 1920), 54–65.

Shepard, Odell, "The Ghost of Henry Adams," *Nation,* CXLVII (Oct. 22, 1938), 419.

Sherman, Stuart P., "Evolution in the Adams Family," *Nation,* CX (April 10, 1920), 473–477. Reprinted in *Americans* (New York: Chas. Scribner's Sons, 1922), pp. 288–315.

Shoemaker, Richard L., "The France of Henry Adams," *French Review,* XXI (Feb., 1948), 292–299.

Shumate, Roger Vernon, "The Political Philosophy of Henry Adams," *American Political Science Review,* XXVIII (Aug., 1934), 599–610.

Silver, A., "Henry Adams' 'Diary of a Visit to Manchester'; with Text," *American Historical Review,* LI (Oct., 1945), 74–89.

Simonds, Katherine, "Living in a Dead World," *Saturday Review of Literature,* XVIII (Sept. 10, 1938), 5.

——, "The Tragedy of Mrs. Henry Adams," *New England Quarterly,* IX (Dec., 1936), 564–582.

Smith, Bernard, "The Quest of Beauty in Idealism: Henry Adams," in *Forces in American Criticism: A Study in the History of American Literary Thought* (New York: Harcourt, Brace and Co., 1939), pp. 220–228.

Smith, Garnet, "Henry Adams," *Contemporary Review,* CXLI (May, 1932), 617–624.

Speare, Morris Edmund, "The Pioneer American Political Novel of Henry Adams," in *The Political Novel: Its Development in England and in America* (New York: Oxford Univ. Press, 1924), pp. 287–305.

Spiller, Robert E., "Henry Adams," in Robert E. Spiller *et al.,* eds., *Literary History of the United States,* II (New York: Macmillan Co., 1948), 1080–1103.

——, "Henry Adams and His Friends," *American Literature,* XIX (Jan., 1948), 368–370.

——, "Henry Adams: Man of Letters," *Saturday Review of Literature,* XXX (Feb. 22, 1947), 11–12, 33–34.

——, Introduction to Henry Adams, *Esther* (New York: Scholars' Facsimiles and Reprints, 1938), pp. iii–xxv.

——, Introduction to Henry Adams, *Tahiti* (New York: Scholars' Facsimiles and Reprints, 1947), iii–vii.

——, Review of *Letters of Henry Adams, 1892–1918, American Literature,* XI (Jan., 1940), 471–473.

Stone, James, "Henry Adams's Philosophy of History," *New England Quarterly,* XIV (1941), 538–548.

"A Study in Irony," *Spectator,* CXXII (Feb. 22, 1919), 231–233. Republished as "Henry Adams: A British Estimate," *Living Age,* CCC (March 29, 1919), 791–794.

S[ullivan], J. W. N., "The Power of Words," *Athenaeum,* I (May 21, 1920), 665.

Taylor, Henry Osborn, Review of *The Education of Henry Adams, Atlantic Monthly,* CXXII (Oct., 1918), 484–491.

Thayer, William Roscoe, "Henry Adams, Central in a Literary Discovery," Boston *Evening Transcript,* Aug. 10, 1918.

Thomason, J. W., "The Man Who Knew Everything," *American Mercury,* XLVI (Jan., 1939), 99–104.

Thoron, Ward, ed. *The Letters of Mrs. Henry Adams.* Boston: Little, Brown and Co., 1937.

Thurston, Henry W., "Madison and Commercial Restriction," *Dial,* XI (Feb., 1891), 307–309.

——, "The Statesmanship of Thomas Jefferson," *Dial,* XI (June, 1890), 33–35.

Thwing, Charles F., "Henry Adams," in *Guides, Philosophers, and Friends* (New York: Macmillan Co., 1927), pp. 223–236.

Townsend, H. G. *Philosophical Ideas in the United States.* New York: American Book Co., 1934.

Van Doren, Mark, "The Novels of Henry Adams," *New York Times Book Review,* Jan. 23, 1921, p. 8.

Wade, Mason, "The Angelic Porcupine," *Commonweal,* XLV (Feb. 21, 1947), 470–472.

Wecter, Dixon, "Harvard Exiles," *Virginia Quarterly Review,* X (April, 1934), 244–257.

Weiss, T., "The Nonsense of Winters' Anatomy (Part I: Henry Adams and Wallace Stevens)," *Quarterly Review of Literature,* I (Spring, 1944), 212–234.

Whipple, T. K., "Henry Adams," in *Spokesmen: Modern Writers and American Life* (New York: D. Appleton and Co., 1928), pp. 23–44.

——, "Henry Adams: First of the Moderns," *Nation,* CXII (April 14, 1926), 408–409.

White, William, "The Date of the Education of Henry Adams," *English Studies,* XX (Oct., 1938), 204–205.

Williams, Henry Horace, "The Education of Henry Adams," *Monist,* XXXI (Jan., 1921), 149–159.

Williams, Orlo, "Roosevelt and Henry Adams: Doer and Doubter," *National Review,* XCVI (Feb., 1931), 279–287.

Wilson, Edmund, "Novels of Henry Adams: *Democracy,*" *New Republic,* XLIV (Oct. 14, 1925), 203.

——, Prefatory remarks to Henry Adams, *The Life of George Cabot Lodge,* in Edmund Wilson, ed., *The Shock of Recognition* (Garden City: Doubleday, Doran and Co., 1943), pp. 742–746.

Winterich, J. T., *see* Randall, D. A.

Winters, Yvor, "Henry Adams, or the Creation of Confusion," in *The Anatomy of Nonsense* (Norfolk, Conn.: New Directions, 1943), pp. 23–87.

——, "Replies to Reviewers," *American Literature,* XVI (Nov., 1944), 221–222, 223–225.

Wish, Harvey. *Contemporary America: The National Scene since 1900.* New York: Harper and Bros., 1945.

Wister, Owen. *Roosevelt: The Story of a Friendship, 1880–1919.* New York: Macmillan Co., 1930.

Wright, Nathalia, "Henry Adams's Theory of History: A Puritan Defense," *New England Quarterly,* XVIII (June, 1945), 204–210.

Zukovsky, Louis, "Henry Adams: A Criticism in Autobiography," *Hound and Horn,* III (April–July, 1930), 338–357, 518–530; IV (Oct., 1930), 46–72.

IV. Dissertations

Cater, Harold Dean. "Henry Adams and His Friends: A Collection of His Unpublished Correspondence." Columbia University, 1947.

Hume, Robert A. *"The Education of Henry Adams:* A Critical Estimate." Cornell University, 1940.

Jordy, William Henry. "Science and Power in History: A Study in the Historical Temperament." Yale University, 1948.

Le Clair, Robert Charles. "Three American Travellers in England: James Russell Lowell, Henry James, and Henry Adams." University of Pennsylvania, 1944.

Meyer, Andrew Greer. "The Historical Theories of Henry Adams." New York University, 1947.

Miller, Richard F. "Henry Adams (1870–1890) as a Reformer, with an Adams Bibliography." University of Washington, 1947.

Samuels, Ernest. "The Early Career of Henry Adams." University of Chicago, 1942.

Suddath, Jennie. "Mark Twain and Henry Adams in Account with the Gilded Age." University of Missouri, 1942.

V. Bibliographical Compilations

Adams, James Truslow, "Bibliography of the Writings of Henry Adams" in *Henry Adams* (New York: Albert and Chas. Boni, Inc., 1933), pp. 213–229.

Johnson, Thomas H., "Henry Adams," in Robert E. Spiller *et al., Literary History of the United States,* III (New York: Macmillan Co., 1948), 373–377.

Leary, Lewis. *Articles on American Literature Appearing in Current Periodicals, 1920–1945.* Durham, N.C.: Duke University Press, 1947. (For listing of articles on Henry Adams, see pp. 121–123.)

Samuels, Ernest, "The Writings of Henry Adams, 1855–1877," in *The Young Henry Adams* (Cambridge: Harvard University Press, 1948), pp. 313–321; "Selected Bibliography," *ibid.,* pp. 353–362.

Winton, H. N. M. "A Bibliography of the Works by and about Henry Adams (1838–1918)." Stanford University, 1935. Unpublished typescript on file at the Stanford University Library.

Index

INDEX